NO MORE SECRETS

Sucked in *and* Spit Out

Judson Hoyt

Endorsements

"Judson Hoyt has written a memoir which amounts to a cautionary tale for anyone going into ministry. Wounds and struggles that haven't been dealt with are the fodder for secret sins that can dismantle a godly work, and this narrative is a true and tragic example. It's also a glimpse into an amazing time known as the Jesus Movement, and one of the many works that movement produced. Judson was there, and his story is pretty compelling."

— *Joe Dallas, Author and Speaker*

"In spite of the trials Judson has endured, his story gives insight into a journey revealing God's faithfulness while helping Judson find healing and wholeness in his life. No matter what we struggle with, there is hope in Christ! A wonderful read."

— *George Carneal, Author/Speaker, "From Queer to Christ"*

Judson Hoyt has written a courageous coming of age memoir as a same sex attracted teen during the Jesus movement of the 1970's. An amazingly honest and insightful account of a young man's struggle to conform his desires with a newfound faith. This book is for anyone who has ever felt like they aren't where they should be and feel lost about where they are going. In other words, for all of us.

— *William Jensen, William K Jensen Literary Agency*

"Judson Hoyt has written a thought-provoking account of his time as a key member of the fastest growing youth ministry in California during the 1970's, Shekinah Fellowship. Often, those in ministry remember only the good and only talk about God's will in order to avoid dealing with the loss of spending years of devotion to a church or pastor not worthy of it. Judson does that as well as hanging out the dirty laundry. We all agree not to talk about misbehavior as if doing so is a virtue. Silence is not always healing, but human beings are always complex. Hoyt risks telling his truth as the simple healing virtue. I would agree. I was there."

— *Elaine Suranie, Los Angeles County LBQ Women's Health Collaborative, Honoree of The Rainbow Key Award*

"This is a compelling witness of God's love, faithfulness and direction for a life through all the struggles, defeats and victories. Judson's experience in the Jesus Movement brought him to where he is today. This is a testimony to the fact that we "see through a glass darkly." Judson's life story is a journey that witnesses the orchestration God writes for all our lives in the symphonic path to a greater relationship with our Creator. Inspiring!"

— *Teddi Paul, CA, Entrepreneur*

"Through his own experiences, Judson takes us on his journey as he strives to find acceptance and fulfillment within the Ministry. Whilst the struggle with his own personal and social frailties are apparent, it is the rise of the celebrity, homosexuality and the hierarchal system along with grooming of individuals that is the ever-constant theme. The hypocrisy of some within the Ministry and those pulling their strings is abhorrent. A thought-provoking book and one which should be read by those considering entry to Ministerial office."

"Appearances are deceptive."

— *Lesley Norris, UK (retired nurse)*

"The story of Brant Baker and Shekinah Fellowship provides valuable lessons for ministers and believers of all generations. Shekinah grew rapidly, transformed many lives, and then just as suddenly disappeared. What really happened at Shekinah has been shrouded in secrecy. Until now. Judson Hoyt does an excellent job of revealing the whole story. I read this book with intense interest because I was intimately involved with Shekinah from 1974 to 1976. Yet, I had to read this book to finally understand Shekinah's story in its entirety. But this book isn't just about Brant and Shekinah. All believers can learn key principles about following Jesus in the highs and lows of ministry life. Thanks, Judson, for your diligent research and transparent sharing in the writing of No More Secrets: Lifted Up and Coming Out"

— *Joel Comiskey, Ph.D., Author/Speaker and founder of Joel Comiskey Group*

Authenticity and integrity are two things that the Church needs today. Judson Hoyt has written a book about his life and early involvement in a ministry that lacked both of these qualities. On the surface, the ministry appeared to be Godly. People were getting saved and becoming healed. With Saturday night services filling a huge theater and being broadcast live on Christian television, the ministry seemed to be a success. However, this was just a façade.

I know all of this not only because I read the book, but because I was a part of the ministry myself. For over a year, I was a member of staff as the pastor of a Sunday morning church that grew out of the Saturday night meetings. After we both left the ministry, I had the joy of marrying Judson to his wife, Kristy.

Churches are not perfect, but they need to be authentic and deal with bad leadership and immorality when it is present. This book will give you insights on how a ministry can get off track while most don't know it. When anyone tries to help and bring correction, the church brands them as disloyal. This book is an inside account of how things can go very wrong in a person's life and ministry. But it's also an account of grace, hope, and restoration.

— *Pastor Mike Bayer, Village Church of Laguna Woods CA*

Library of Congress Registration Number: TXu 2-147-927
Print ISBN: 978-1-54398-140-7
eBook ISBN: 978-1-54398-141-4

Acknowledgments

My life has been in the hands of my Lord, Jesus (Yeshua) Christ. I had a greater awakening in the times we live in and His word with this project. It seems I'm just now understanding about His grace and priceless gift of salvation that amazes me. It is a journey of ongoing life lessons until my time is done on this earth.

I want to thank my wife Kristy for her support and input during the writing of this book. As well, thank the rest of my family and friends for their encouraging words of support. A special thank you to Olivia and my daughter Jamie with the editing process.

Dedicated in memory of my older sister Meredith, my parents John and Frances (founder of Mariposa Woman & Family Center, Orange, Ca), my Uncle Eric, Aunt Nancy, my niece Arin. To past ministry friends: David Sloane (who sparked the seed with this project), Madge C, Arda H, Georgette A, Pam J, Sue O, Sister Edith, Loraine P, Mr. & Mrs. Adams, Trudi and others that have gone before me.

TABLE OF CONTENTS

FOREWORD

Judson Hoyt and I met in high school in Corona del Mar, California. My good friend Brad. introduced us. I was a bit jealous of Brad who seemed to take more of a liking to Jud than myself. One day after school, Jud invited us to come over to his house. None of us had a car yet, so we all walked the long trek from our high school across the open land of the dried up Back Bay to get there. I wasn't anticipating such a hike. My sexy Italian sandals were covered with dirt as we zigzagged to avoid large mud puddles of standing water left by the outgoing tide. I also wasn't expecting to find Jud living in such a modest house. He explained his parents had divorced and that he lived there with his father and his older sister. Jud brought us into his room, which was on the back porch, and I remember it being cold as the night drew on. The windows were hard to close. The draft that came through the window screens had a faint smell of the horse stalls outside his father rented out. Jud offered me a blanket to put around my shoulders. He put one on too. He had a kind paternal quality for someone his age. The adventure was a little scary and exciting at the same time, however, Jud appeared comfortable with his surroundings and that put me at ease. He was personable with an honest sense of fun. He could laugh at himself and was often the butt of his own humor, and of Brad's. He took it like a sport. There was definitely a closeness between them, (the extent of which I was not privy to at the time) yet they made sure I felt included.

There, occupying Jud's small living room was a baby grand piano. It seemed out of place in this, relatively speaking, small humble cottage on the outskirts of this affluent, developing Southern California community with its tennis and boating clubs. Here was where movie stars escaped from Hollywood to their second homes and parked their yachts, the likes of John Wayne and Natalie Wood. Seeing Jud's piano was reassuring to me, as my family had a piano too; my most joyous moments growing up were singing with my father while he played the piano.

As time went on, I spent several afternoons after school at Jud's house. I welcomed the adventure, leaving my "up and coming" bourgeois neighborhood of new, glassy split-level homes to visit this older section of town. More so, I welcomed the feeling of having friends. Jud's father seemed to have no objection to Jud having his friends over to the house. Having just awakened in the late afternoon to go to his graveyard shift security job, Jud's dad seemed preoccupied and weary. Jud would make him breakfast. Afterwards, Jud would ask his dad to play the piano for us and sometimes his dad would oblige him. He'd set his coffee cup down on the piano and Jud would pick out a song. He'd begin to play and sing. He was impressive but the impact was overshadowed by the weight of a burden I couldn't understand then. I was later to learn about and fully identify with-namely being in the grips of alcoholism. While visiting Jud, I was further comforted by Jud speaking fondly about his older sister, Meredith who lived there too. I rarely saw her, but Jud spoke adoringly about her. It also made me feel safe that Jud didn't make advances towards me. That said, while visiting Jud, I always felt like a voyeur in a bachelor pad.

Jud was very involved with nearby Calvary Chapel and he had invited me to attend. I had been looking for a church to join a few years earlier, so I was willing to give this a try. Jud was always praying, and he would ask us to pray with him. I felt slightly uncomfortable about this. No matter how hard I prayed, I didn't feel as connected with the Lord as Jud seemed to be. I thought maybe if I went to his church, I'd have a different experience. Once there, I became quite captivated by the beautifully performed folk music that we were encouraged to sing along with. Aside from the religious lyrics, the songs sounded like the folk music of the 60's which I'd play at home on my record player. I also was attracted to the warmth of the minister Chuck Smith. He seemed so approachable, like a Santa Claus. He wore casual clothes with his sleeves rolled up. He would often step away from behind the lectern and sit on the edge of the stage and speak with us. He was like a good father who put no barriers between us and him. This was different than the staid churches I'd visited in my community. I found myself returning to the church and purchasing tapes of the sermons I could listen to at home. I was most interested in the sermons on "intimate relationships." Naturally, I was, at that age, becoming more and more interested in sex. I also became fanatical about "spreading the word", urging my family, particularly my younger sister, to believe in Jesus as I did. I felt discouraged when they didn't seem interested at all. After much prodding, my best girlfriend acquiesced and agreed to come with me to Calvary Chapel. During a group song where we sang and swayed, she fainted! At first, I thought she was struck by the Holy Spirit. (I had heard about some healing sessions where people fell down after being struck with the Holy Spirit.) But no, she actually fainted due to lack of air. The church staff reacted appropriately. I was the confused one. Understandably, when I asked her to come back again to the church, she opted not to return.

Shortly thereafter, when I turned 16, I got my first job and found a boy-friend. Jud continued attending the church and later became involved with the Shekinah ministry, a nondenominational, evangelical group. I seemed to have no more need for the church at that point.

Although our paths separated upon graduation, if not before, I was grateful to Jud for connecting me with two seriously determined and extremely talented fellow students. They were a few years ahead of me in school. They wrote and produced their own original musical productions. Jud was as drawn to the theatre as I was. Fortunately for me, they cast me in their shows. Jud and I performed in one play together. Those two summers in high school spent performing original musical shows gave me the confidence to pursue theatre in college and I eventually performed professionally. Much like Jud, who gravitated to the performance opportunities and camaraderie in the Shekinah ministry, I too, was finding a way to express myself and feel at home in the theatre

Years later, with many chapters of life behind us, Jud and I connected on Facebook. Like most of us who have moved from our hometowns, I had lost touch with my high school friends. Despite the decades that had gone by, our reconnection brought forth that accepting warmth that is particular to those who shared such affecting years. When he asked me to read his book "No More Secrets", I soon learned, in reading it, that we had more in common than I had any conscious awareness of in high school.

"No More Secrets" captivated me instantly. So many of us growing up amid the tumult of the late 60's and early 70's in Southern California were searching for that second family that would provide us with a direction and a feeling of belonging. New Christian ministries sprung up as part of the youth counterculture. The Shekinah Ministry, with its charismatic leader Brant Baker, was one of these. What his followers didn't know was that Brant was leading a double life. Appointed to be Brant's personal assistant, Judson, a vulnerable teenager sensed a reflection of his own struggle to reconcile his new-found faith and his homosexual desires.

In reading his candid book, I couldn't help but note that Jud, who was raised in an alcoholic home, had become somewhat parentified, where the roles of parent and child are reversed. A parentified child tends to identify with the expectations of his parents early on at the expense of his own true talents and needs. Having cared for his father, Judson was the perfect choice to be Brant's assistant, as he could be hyper-vigilantly in tune with Brant's every need and whim. This was a dangerous assignment.

I found myself haunted by what I would call the power of control and manipulation imposed on the teenagers working for the Shekinah ministry. The oppression here resembled the alcoholic family system where the alcoholism is denied and children are given the message to keep it a secret, often referred to as the "no talk rule". They are taught to deny any feelings they may have about the drinker or otherwise, and to avoid discussing anything unpleasant at all. Upsetting situations are smoothed over with lies and everyone walks around on eggshells as the addict dictates the mood for the entire family. Children often blame themselves and feel ashamed about what they perceive they've caused. In the book, a similar dynamic happens with the ministry where a passive dependency is reinforced among the followers and autonomy is discouraged and perceived as a threat to the higher ups. Survival means accepting the dogma of the group.

It's ironic that in reading Jud's "coming of age" memoir, I discovered our commonalities some 40 years later. Perhaps, if we are teachable, we are continually coming of age? While my parents' marriage was over long before it legally ended, Jud, too, was trying to adjust to his parent's divorce. (Divorce seemed rare in the 70's and there was a stigma attached to it). Women, with no employment experience, were threatened by the poverty they faced pursuing this separation. Further, homosexuality was still considered pathological. What was one to do with all of the bisexual feelings that most of us have to one degree or another? Not to mention, the guilt of the exploration of it at puberty or earlier? Alcoholism was still considered morally weak as opposed to the disease concept which came later when Betty Ford, First Lady, bravely shared her own "secret" of alcohol addiction. My family had been dealt its own hand of that disease. The family dysfunction that it causes, and all the hidden trauma it leaves, had yet to be wholly identified and named by the psychiatric establishment or society at large.

During that period of time, others of us turned to cults, drugs, religious groups, or to transcendental Meditation (as the Beatles did). Some of us were lucky enough to find something we loved to do early on, having a strong sense of self and enough support to pursue it to avoid the chaos of the times. Some didn't make it out alive.

I was one of the lucky ones, so was Jud. We both started out drawn to the theatre. He pursued a number of careers while raising his own family. One of his dreams as a writer, while I ended up as a psychotherapist. After working as a professional actress in regional theatre, I eventually moved to New York to further pursue my acting career. I found that I couldn't take the rejection or the instability of it. I found myself drinking to cope with good feelings, bad feelings, and every feeling in-between. Three decades of sobriety later, I am forever humbled by the mystery of the multiple interventions that helped me climb out of despair. A new faith was born in me; not the emotionally ecstatic I sought in my youth. I began to realize I could help others, the way I had been helped. After becoming an alcoholism counselor, I went back to school and obtained a master's degree in social work and I became a psychotherapist. As time went on, I expanded my discipline, working with a variety of mental health issues.

Lastly, I must tell you my favorite story about Judson. It says a great deal about the chaos he was up against and how he endearingly tried to make everything right for his family and eventually, for the Shekinah ministry. It was in 1972 and I was going on my very first trip to Europe with my mother and sister. I had asked Jud if he would look after my grey pet mouse named "Luv". I was so pleased that Jud agreed to look after "Luv". When I returned 2 weeks later, I went over to Jud's house to pick him up. Jud sat me down in his bedroom off the porch and broke the bad news. He told me my mouse had died from the cold in his van while he was at a church service. He told me that he felt terrible about it. To make up for my loss, Jud had gone to the pet shop and purchased 3 (not 1) white mice with black spots on them to take Luv's place. When he went to give them too me, they had all gotten out of the cage. Jud said, "They must be here somewhere." So, we spent a good few hours hunting them down. Angry and frustrated, I took one of the mice home with me and left him with the other two. At the time, I was not amused, but eventually we all had a good laugh about it. Now, after reading his book, I can understand more clearly his desire to rectify the situation, to "make lemonade out of lemons" as they say.

In "No More Secrets", Judson does just that. He exposes the ministry for what it had become, or perhaps, had always been, unbeknownst to its followers. No longer the timid young man who first came to hear Brant Baker's embracing words, he has found his voice. Ironically, in the end, it is Judson who generously offers a healing hand of salvation to Brant. However, as with our families, there comes a time when we are forced to let go in order to save ourselves.

Margaret Humphreys, LCSW
Psychotherapist, NYC
margarethumphreys122@gmail.com

INTRODUCTION

It's the tail end of the Iraq war in the summer of 2010 in the Northern region of Kirkuk. The hot summer wind blows across the horizon with the smell of burning oil fields in the distance.

I'm halfway around the world from my home, experiencing a different culture and environment of extreme summer heat. I'm away from my wife, grown children, older siblings, and my eighty-seven-year-old mother who has Alzheimer's. She's lying in her bed in the last stages of life.

I have already started to write my memoirs in a journal and type the notes on my laptop. The stories I share are divided into a book series that follow me on my voyage in the stages of my life. For this first book I highlight my childhood through my turbulent years of being a teen into young adulthood. This will be the longest portion of this series. This book lays the foundation of the heart of this story that has brought me to this point and time. It is about events and the spiritual journey I've taken that shaped me over the course of my life, bringing me here to the present time.

There are devastating truths that few know about a charismatic leader from decades ago. A healing evangelist who both inspired me and reviled me. I know these truths, and I can no longer be silent. I know them because

I was his personal servant. I feel a strong need to tell the root of this story of my traumatic experience and my recovery from the trappings that hindered my thinking and left me spiritually raw.

This story would have made for controversy in the 1970's in a number of evangelical Christian circles. It would have been the kind of scandal that rocked the mega churches of the era and held spectators glued to their televisions during the nightly news. Yet it happened to me personally.

I haven't had the courage or compulsion to reveal this story until now. I believe it is time to share it, to learn from it and to reflect the reality of it to the reader. I want to connect to others who have gone through similar trauma from an organized religion or sect and perhaps help them be liberated from the damage.

In my teen years I was involved in an evangelical movement in Costa Mesa, California. This led me to be drawn into a Christian healing ministry in nearby Long Beach. The ministry grew rapidly, and it had great potential. It blew in like a tornado then died quickly, leaving the shattered dust of its remains.

Some of the main characters have died and left many others disheartened. It was not until over thirty years later that some of those relationships I formed back then could be reunited. Those of us in the organization found each other through a blog. We reflected on our nostalgic memories of that movement, and we posted some of our stories that stirred up mixed emotions for us.

I was happy that I connected with some of them, yet I felt angry that at those memories I had put aside. Flashes of those events returned to me again with a mix of guilt and embarrassment. I was sparked to write my story – the one you are reading now – but I had to experience those emotions all over again and find the courage to face them again. I think my experiences on the battlefield helped me do this – face past with courage and conviction and make sense of it all.

To research and ignite those memories of the Brant Baker ministry of Shekinah Fellowship, I dug out my memory box of letters, magazines, pictures, cassette tapes and videos. As I did, more stories started to appear with pictures and videos on the various websites and blogs. These helped recall my encounters and encouraged my further involvement.

I did not find any writings on the internet from the core founders discussing their involvement. It is as though they locked away the past and threw away the key, never to be divulged again. I lived with them at one time in a commune environment, and we worked together side by side. We were all passionate young adults, eager to share the message. Our ages ranged from our late teens to early twenties. Not one of us was over twenty-five.

A story like this can include a number of perspectives from those involved. From my position in the organization, my viewpoint was both from in front and behind the scenes.

In revealing my story, I focus on the events and characters who were in my circle as a teenager going into young adulthood. I talk about my perceptual thinking at the time.

I left the organization disenchanted. I got married and guarded my selected secret thoughts. I wondered just what happened to me. I was in a state of spiritual disillusion that left me empty and hungry for many years, even as I myself became an evangelical minister with the Assembly of God church.

I found my journey was not much different compared to others who experienced a similar trauma or addiction then recovered from evangelical churches and other organized religious sects. We all went through the same withdrawal, the same introspection and discovered very similar conclusions.

This journey really started before my birth – that's an easy concept for many to grasp. But I don't recall agreeing with my maker to have this gift to be in a human body. Did I really ask for these difficult events in my life, so my soul could grow? Did I agree to wrangle with them? I got the results of the mortal choices because I exercised free will.

With that in mind, I will lay the foundation for this story by high-lighting what I do recollect from my early life, going into my teen years. This leads up to the core of the story that centers around the evangelical ministry I was involved with. It continued to influence the thinking that followed me throughout my adult life. These thought patterns kept me stuck, unable to move on with my life, mired in self-perpetuating problems.

Through time I learned the lessons of life from the experience that shaped me on this voyage. Some people will disagree with conclusions I've come to over time because they are afraid, or they have conflicting traditions in their culture and upbringing. That is to be expected.

But this is my story, and the images I present here are of my early spiritual journey. The quest carried me through my adult life. It affected my decisions and part of the legacy I have left to my children and others. I hope you can relate the lessons I've learned to various areas in your life. I hope my experiences, for better or worse, will help to bring you knowledge and healing.

I have come out of this experience a stronger man, a more deeply spiritual man, with a greater understanding of what life is about. Though I don't recall asking for enlightenment, I believe I have touched the hem of it and come away with a blessing. Let me share this insight with you now.

CHAPTER 1:

THE JOURNEY BEGINS

Sheltered Early Life

I am the youngest of four siblings. Our ages span from my brother's birth in 1947 to mine in 1955. I grew up in an all-white neighborhood in Costa Mesa, California. I was never exposed to other ethnic groups until my late teens. The idea of other ethnic races in the world with different colors of skin was foreign to me when I was a young child. The thought made me curious and a little frightened.

Now, there are many stories to tell that are interwoven among my siblings while we were all growing up. Most of my memories are feelings of contentment in my early years. When I started to reach my early teens, a shift began in my personal identity as my body changed. I found myself more attracted to guys, even more than girls.

My parents reminded me of a romantic couple from an early black and white Hollywood movie in the 1940's. They lived in Los Angeles, California when they were first married in 1945. They found their way to Laguna Beach when they started to have children. By the time I was born, our family had moved from Laguna Beach to Costa Mesa. I lived there for less than a year when our family moved to a new suburban housing development named Halecrest in Costa Mesa.

We lived in an average three-bedroom rambler home. It was about 1,500 square feet once we added a family room. My father got the house for $15,000 on his GI bill with a mortgage payment that was one hundred dollars a month, maybe a little more. Eventually we added a built-in swimming pool – it was the first on our block.

The housing development was surrounded by wide open flat farmland with bean fields and fruit orchards of plums and oranges. From our home, you could also see rolling hills, the San Bernardino Mountains, Orange County Airport, and the El Toro Marine Corps Air Station.

There were no freeways. That soon would change when the surrounding farmland was rapidly engulfed by other housing developments, shopping centers and office buildings. The added freeways were considered a necessity, though they would block the wide-open view and soon be clogged with traffic jams.

As for me, I was a delightfully happy, sensitive, and creative child for the most part. My sisters adored me – well, at least most of the time. I started to develop a hearing problem when I was around four. I would often get severe earaches in my left ear. They made me cry, and they seemed to last a long time. My middle sister would try to cheer me up and make me laugh.

I developed a hearing loss from these ear infections and ended up having surgery to remove my adenoids. This stopped the earaches over time, and my hearing returned. However, this episode left me with a slight speech impediment. Eventually I grew out of it.

As a student I struggled from my elementary years through high school, especially when it came to core subjects like reading and comprehension, writing and arithmetic. I had to work hard to keep up to make average grades. If I 'd known I had Attention Deficit Disorder, maybe it would have been different.

Little was known about ADD then, and neither my teachers nor my parents picked up on the reason for the difficulties I faced. Since this syndrome ran in our family, it was especially hard for my parents to detect it. The comments in my report cards were never really negative since I seemed to be a delight to most of the teachers, even though I would struggle. My father wrote in my report card once. "Judson would do better if he cleaned out his ears that grew watermelons and potatoes."

One of my more eventful moments as a child was when I blew up the kitchen oven. It was an accident when I warmed up a can of compressed artificial snow. I was working on a school Christmas project when I made a slight error in judgment.

I remember it so clearly – something like this is hard to forget! It was very cold that morning. The instructions on the snow can said it would not work if the temperature was below 68 degrees. I put the can of snow in the oven to heat it up. While I waited, I went to brush my teeth, and I heard a pop explosion coming from the kitchen.

The oven door had blown out and the can had completely flattened in the oven. Glass was everywhere, shards from the window in the oven door. The force of the explosion spread glass all over the kitchen and even embedded it in the cupboard doors. If I had been in the kitchen when this happened, I would have had a serious problem.

My parents were still in bed, and I was surprised and frightened that they did not hear the noise. My father worked at night into the early morning as a newspaper carrier. They both had slept through the noise. I timidly went into my parent's room to say goodbye to my mother and break the news. "Mom I broke the oven."

My mother was half awake and simply said, "Okay, bye." She was horrified once she discovered what I'd done and relieved I was not harmed. She was also relieved the homeowner's insurance paid for the damage. I was not punished by my parents. In fact, they were overjoyed that I was not harmed after they saw the extent of the damage.

First Brushes With the Holy Spirit

Our family regularly attended a Presbyterian church on Sundays. I was in several Christmas pageants, playing a shepherd one time and one of the three kings another time.

Attending church gave me several moments in the spotlight onstage. I played Jesus in a Sunday school play when I was nine, acting out the story of how Jesus calmed the waters. When Jesus was in a boat and there was a storm, he spoke the word for the storm to be calm. When it came time to say my line speaking to the storm, "Peace, be still," I was so nervous my legs where shaking. I felt myself holding back the urge to pee while asking the disciples in the boat, "Why were you afraid?" How ironic that I was the one who was so afraid!

I felt proud when my father served as my personal Sunday school teacher. I wanted to know more about the Bible, and my father would read parts of the Old Testament to me. He told me these were stories handed down by word-of-mouth, and they changed through the years by the time they were written down.

When I was ten, our family just stop going to church. My father never said why. However, my mother started to attend a Unitarian church without him.

I recall watching several Christian ministers on television on Sundays from time to time. One was Rex Humbard, a television evangelist. I also watched Oral Roberts, who had a healing ministry based out of Tulsa, Oklahoma. There was Kathryn Kuhlman, who was a well-known eccentric redheaded healing minister at the time.

They all seemed bigger than life and had something special that was extraordinary to me. Kathryn Kuhlman was really strange and fascinating in a mystical way. I felt drawn to her. I did not realize she would play a bigger part in my life a number of years later.

Our Creative Family

My father was a creative, independent spirit involved in a number of career fields. He worked as an actor, writer, and publisher of a newspaper. He also worked as a newspaper carrier, advertiser, and salesman.

Most of my dad's early acting work was in small film parts and on stage before I was born. He was loyal and worked hard to provide for his family. He was a great storyteller and often told us tales at night before we went to bed. Some of the stories he told were short stories he was working on for submission to magazines. Sometimes he put his stories in letter form to read to us, involving us personally in these tales.

Apparently, my father used to be in a jazz band in the early 1940's, and he played the piano. We had an old upright piano and later got a baby grand. He always played the same few favorites. The only time we would hear him play was when he was waiting for my mother to get dressed to go out. He also played during the Christmas holidays.

My mother supported my father's many efforts to make a living and remained busy behind the scenes of various community plays my father was in. When I was five, my father played the role of Big Daddy in *Cat on A Hot Tin Roof*. The play was a family affair, with my sisters and me having small walk on parts, while my mother and brother worked backstage running the lights, props and scene changes.

During one of my performances, I became distracted when I saw my grandma Edith in the audience and fell off the stage. The audience gasped at seeing a little boy falling off stage, but just as quickly as I fell off, I jumped back on and continued with my role. Oh, the excitement of live theater!

Being the youngest, I spent most of my time with my mother as I was growing up. She was forever rearranging the furniture, looking at model homes, window shopping furniture and clothes stores. When she bought a new outfit, she would make her grand entrance, sometimes wearing one of her Elizabeth Tyler wigs. She would parade through the house to get my father's attention, and he'd smile with a drink in his hand. He'd put it down and applaud her, then he'd play a few bars on the piano.

I viewed my mother not as the June Cleaver type from *Leave It to Beaver*, but more independent in an expressive, flamboyant Elizabeth Taylor style. It must have been the way she wore her hair.

My mother was often animated when she expressed herself, using hand gestures to express her thoughts that would accompany a smile and a hardy laugh. When she'd had a few drinks, she became even more flamboyant and her voice became louder.

I thought she was a classy dresser. She always seemed to parade her new outfits and was ready to pose for a picture. I think she got that trait from a number of her relatives who were involved in theater and the Hollywood movie industry as actors, writers and directors.

As a kid, one often fantasizes and dreams about escaping their present world to become or do something important in life. For me, I would fantasize about being a Hollywood star myself someday. I thought I was chosen to become some kind of a star because of my celebrity relatives. My mother's younger brother, my uncle Eric Freiwald was in the Hollywood scene as a script writer for a few movies and television. He was the head writer for the film *The Long Ranger and the Lost City of Gold*. He was most known for the 188 episodes of *Lassie* with his co-partner Bob Schaefer. Eric also wrote for the daytime soap opera with his writing partner, my cousin, Linda (his daughter) *The Young and The Restless* for over twenty-five years.

My grandmother Edith was the oldest of the three Loughton siblings. She was reserved – very English – while her siblings went into show biz. One of them was my great uncle, the actor Eddie Laughton; I resembled him quite a bit when I was younger. His birth name was Edgar Hugh Loughton. He started out in vaudeville and enjoyed a long movie career in over 200 films. Many of them were short films with the Three Stooges.

My great aunt Frances Loughton was a stage actress. She married Hal K. Dawson. He was a stage actor who later appeared in over 260 films and television productions. He was a lifelong friend of Clark Gable.

My great aunt Phyllis Loughton became the first woman stage manager on Broadway. At some point Phyllis moved to Hollywood and worked with Paramount studios as a voice coach. She married George Seaton, who became a well-known film director of the time.

Since my great aunt Phyllis had connections in Hollywood, it was she who gave her husband George the push he needed to get his career going. He was well known for his film, *Miracle on 34th Street.* George wrote the screenplay and directed the movie.

Together George and Phyllis became a successful professional couple who lived in Beverly Hills. After her children grew up, Phyllis became the first woman mayor of Beverly Hills in the early 1970's. I do recall going to their home in Beverly Hills several times and to their home in Malibu for a family reunion.

Their Beverly Hills home was not a mansion, but it was a good-sized home, a world apart when compared to our simple suburban house in Costa Mesa. Their home had a large yard with a view across the hills. It had a pool and a small cottage they used as a guest house. Having these relatives catered to my imaginations of prominence. Little did I know the real work involved, prices to pay, and heart aches in the entertainment industry.

From the time I was eleven until I was fifteen, my father was building a successful career for himself as a stockbroker. It seemed to me that either he was changing, or I was just growing up. During this time, I became more aware of my parents as humans than the superheroes I loved as I believed they were in my early years.

Life Upgraded

I recall a couple early sexual experiences having erections. I was around ten and eleven, when I lived in our Costa Mesa house next door to a Catholic family with seven boys. I mainly played with the younger boys, and two of them where about my age. A few times we all ended up in my closet in my room, pulling our pants down, showing off our penises. I don't know who started it first, but it was a reaction and we all just pulled our pants down at once, giggling. Some of us would get an erection and were curious about this new discovery. We wanted to know what this was all about. We ended up touching each other's erect penises, exploring this wonder that was taking place and how it worked.

When I was around eleven, our whole family flew to Michigan for my grandparents' golden wedding anniversary. We were there for a week. I stayed at my uncle Earl's house, while the rest of my family stayed with other cousins. He had two older boys and an older girl.

My cousin Tim was a couple years older than I. He was taller, cute, more mature and stronger than me. I slept in the room he shared with his older brother Michael, who was no longer living at home. Michael was nineteen or twenty at the time.

A couple times we were alone in Tim's room. He wanted to wrestle with me in fun, and he kept trying to pull my underwear off. He wouldn't let up until I screamed and laughed. Then my Aunt Jenny would yell from downstairs for us to stop, and she'd tell Tim he needed to leave for school.

I loved my cousin, and I admired his strength and good looks. Yet this made me feel strange inside and self-conscious. I found myself trying to avoid him. The same year I went to stay with my cousins back to Michigan for a month. When Tim and I got together, he kept wanting to wrestle with me, teasing me by poking at me and putting his hands around my stomach, and putting his legs and thighs on me in fun.

I found out later that year, after our trip to Michigan, Michael was a homosexual. My dad told me. He'd learned it through a letter from his brother Earl. I did not understand what a homosexual really was and did not ask. From his hushed tone of voice and expression, I knew it was something not good. It seemed to be a whispered topic. It would be another year or so I knew the definition of the word *homosexual*. I soon discovered the meaning of other sexual words, adding to my vocabulary and awareness.

Within that year, my father got word my Aunt Jenny had died from a freak bicycle accident. I thought my aunt's accident had to do with her finding out her son Michael was gay.

It would be years later when I found out my cousin Tim was also gay. When I found this out, I recalled when Tim and I were wrestling and put the pieces together. I believed he was going through his own sexual discovery, working out his own identity.

I loved and admired my cousins Michael and Tim from the memories I had of them. I felt sad that we did not spend more time together and felt sorry for them about what they must have been going through. It would be many years later my cousin Tim died of AIDS.

By the time I was twelve, we moved from our simple home in Costa Mesa and upgraded to a larger house on the border of Newport Beach. The new place was double in size and had a pool. That summer I invited the Catholic boys I knew at the other house to go swimming.

After we went swimming, we'd go in my bedroom to change. Again, we'd all pull our pants down wagging our penises in fun until we got a boner.

During the year our family moved, my brother had been drafted into the Army and was getting ready to do a tour of duty in Vietnam. My older sister had moved out of the house, and she was working and going to school part time. It appeared things where financially secure for my parents, since they could afford to have a pool service, a gardener and part time housekeeper.

This ideal middle-class fantasy world would soon come crashing down around me since it lasted a few years then vanished, along with my innocence.

In time I made a few male friends – Alan, Brad and Tom. I ended up becoming good friends with Brad. I tried to be accepted in his group of girlfriends he had. Since we had a swimming pool, I was able to use that as an excuse to invite him over. We also liked the same television shows, such as *I Love Lucy*, and the old 1950's reruns.

I also started to watch a daytime soap opera *Dark Shadows,* which centered around a vampire and the family. I soon became addicted to the daily series. This show furthered my interest in the occult and the mystery of it. Sometimes Brad would come over and watch the show with me. We became fans, and I bought the album, collected the trading cards, and saw the movies when they came out.

As Brad and I further developed our friendship, we would talk about our awareness of sexual changes taking place with our bodies. We came up with our own theories and understanding of our sexuality. We didn't know much about it except for rumors and jokes in the locker room. We had to draw our own conclusions and were ill informed.

I felt very anxious about sex. My parents sat me down privately and gave me "the talk" over the breakfast table after my sister became pregnant at fifteen and a half. I was still clueless about sex and how it all worked. I told my parents, "don't you have to be married before you get pregnant?"

My father explained to me about sex while he drew a diagram on a paper napkin. He showed me what the penis does when it gets aroused. It still did not really make any sense to me, and I was somewhat frightened by it.

My mother just looked at me and said nothing. The next day she gave me a couple books about how our body works since she thought I should know more about sex. I must have been slow, but I still did not understand the connection on how it all worked.

Private Encounters

Brad and I continued with our long conversations about sex and about our bodies after my mother gave me the books. I shared them with Brad. This eventually led into mutual experimentation and masturbation with each other. Brad often prompted these interactions, but we both were consenting, and I was okay with it.

I thought our house was unusual since it had its own small underground fallout shelter in our backyard. The previous owner was a builder, and he constructed it during the height of the Cold War. There was a hatch you had to lift to gain access, then climb down a steep later that opened into the room below.

My parents let me turn the shelter into my own clubhouse. It was a safe place to retreat and spend time alone. In one corner of the shelter, Playboy centerfolds lined the walls from floor to ceiling. They came from stacks of magazines my brother got from my Uncle Eric. Looking back, I'm surprised my parents didn't seem to mind when I showed them how we decorated the bomb shelter.

One time when my parents were not home, Brad and I dressed up as women in my mother's clothes and wigs. We did it just to be funny. We paraded around the pool area, when my middle sister saw us, and we all laughed together.

My "sessions" with Brad mainly consisted of giving each other massages and sometimes masturbating each other. We often slept over at each other's places. We would end up sleeping naked, masturbating, then going to sleep. I felt comfortable with him and we grew attached to each other. We did not engage in any oral or anal sex. We didn't really know what that was until later. When I was a freshman in high school, I saw some porn pictures of men and women my brother shared with me. I showed them to Brad, and we were both mesmerized by the erotic photos, especially the naked men. We kept the pictures a secret to ourselves.

By the time I was in high school, my parents were experiencing turbulence in their marriage. My father's involvement with alcohol and gambling was starting to surface, sabotaging his career as a successful stockbroker. It seemed my mother was drinking more as well.

I was not aware of my parent's alcoholism, though it was contributing to the demise of their marriage. Alcohol seemed to be the norm in our house for my parents and their friends. They appeared always to be happy and lighthearted when they drank.

I knew something was going on when we no longer had a housekeeper, gardener and pool service. I ended up taking over the workload. It wasn't long after this period my life changed forever in ways I never could have predicted. I was about to discover a very different world, far beyond the superficial trappings of our suburban existence.

CHAPTER 2:
BORN AGAIN

During my freshman year in high school, from 1969 through 1970, I realized the world was rapidly changing around me. It wasn't just that I was growing up. I knew I was living in a time unlike any other in history. I was also feeling insecure and started getting depressed about what was taking place in my family. My parents had both given over to alcoholism, and our financial picture had changed rapidly as they parted ways.

My middle sister was attending a small independent Christian church called Calvary Chapel, located on the border between Santa Ana and Costa Mesa. It was nicknamed "The Hippie Church" because it broke away from the conventional Christian tradition. It was led by a middle-aged minister named Chuck Smith, who was part of the Foursquare denomination.

The church grew from a small home Bible Study group, which mushroomed very quickly. The congregation grew, moved to a new chapel, and kept expanding. It seemed the vogue place to attend at the time. It was popular with teens and young adults in the area who wanted to experience something more spiritually real than what Southern California's middle-class culture was offering at the time.

About the same time, my brother returned from Vietnam. He settled down and soon married. He and my sister-in-law ended up going to Calvary Chapel where they got married.

It was through my brother I learned the term "born again" that meant a follower of Jesus Christ. My middle sister told me how Jesus was helping her become a new person and work through her struggles.

One-time my middle sister talked to me while we were in our family room, watching a Billy Graham crusade on television. It was the close of the service, and the traditional alter call music was playing "Just As I Am." I felt powerfully moved, and I started to cry. She said it was the Holy Spirit talking to me. The only time I remember feeling something like that before was when I was watching Oral Roberts on TV, witnessing the healing of a little boy. I also felt that way once when I watched the Kathryn Kuhlman show. Something stirred deep inside me.

It was this conversion to Christianity by my middle sister and brother that got my attention towards the end of my freshman year. I ended up attending Calvary Chapel as well, and I accepted Jesus Christ into my heart as I understood Him at the time.

In fact, I was so excited about wanting to accept Jesus, I told my sister and brother I couldn't wait to go to church. I even told my friends from high school – Brad, Cindy and Sue – about going to church to accept Jesus. They looked at me strangely and did not say anything.

I thought I accepted Jesus once when I was around nine or ten, attending a Christian children's evangelist exhibit at our local Orange County Fair. I saw the exhibit and saw children going into a playhouse and being told a story. Afterward they would get a button that said, "I accept Jesus into my heart."

I was curious and went in to listen to the story, and someone prayed with me to accept Jesus. I remember feeling happy about that, and I got a button. When I went home that day, I showed my mother the button and told her what I had done. She did not seem to be interested. She just smiled and went on with her business. The joy I felt from that experience was short lived.

I met Chuck Smith when I went to my brother's wedding. He was a handsome forty-something leader. He was a happy person with receding curly black hair and a great confident smile.

When I decided to attend Calvary Chapel, this time I knew it was going to be different for me. I felt it. I went to Calvary Chapel during a weekday. Chuck Smith gave the invitation to come forward and accept Jesus into my heart, and I was never quite the same. It is hard to explain what happened to me, other than I felt something I'd never experienced before. It felt like a weight had been lifted from me, and I had a sense of joy and purpose.

We went into a back room, and Chuck Smith came in with a big smile. He said, "You have taken the most important step in your life and this is the beginning of a new journey for you." He briefly summarized what it meant to be born again, to be born of the spirit according to the explanation that was given in the Bible from John 3. I knew about Jesus from my other experiences and from the stories of my Presbyterian Sunday school, yet I did not really understand this "born again" concept or learned how to develop a relationship with the simple teachings of Jesus. This was a whole new beginning for me.

Early Times At the Calvary Chapel

To my wonder I ran into my childhood friend Melissa during my freshman year at school. I was pleasantly surprised to find out her family had moved around the corner from our house. Once again, we were neighbors. We spent time at each other's homes, just as we had a few years earlier.

Her ability to play the piano had really taken off. I admired that about her and went to a couple of her recitals. Her brother Frank still played the horn, and her father was a music teacher by then. I remember him substituting for my high-school music class once.

It was at this time Melissa came to Calvary Chapel. Her older sister had moved out of the house, and she attended for a short while. Later she decided to attend the Baptist church her mother was going to, so she stopped attending my family's church.

Melissa remained very studious with her music and school. We had serious discussions about our Christian faith at times, and we shared the same interest in the arts such as music and theater. We would sometimes go to these events. It was always good to talk to her, and we often reminisced about some of our childhood experiences together. Some were funny, and others were more serious. We continued to be good friends throughout high school, though we drifted apart as life pulled us in different directions.

The beginning of my freshman year was a confusing time in my life because of the new social surroundings. Besides this, I felt my body changing and I was becoming even more aware of my sexual identity. I knew I was different and felt self-conscious about it. I was feeling the peer and social pressure to have a girlfriend and engage in sex. Seeing teenage boys and girls necking in the hallways between classes, at lunch and at school events made me feel even more awkward. I often wondered, *why do I have to connect with girls this way? Why do we have to make out and not just be friends?*

It was frightening to think that making out might lead to sex. Getting a girl pregnant was terrifying to me since I had already seen my siblings' example of what can happen if you're not careful. It was more familiar and safer to me at the time to continue exploring sexual pleasure with Brad, indulging in our mutual masturbation to release any sexual tension and satisfy my curiosity.

In this period of discovery coming into my teen years, I thought about becoming a bodybuilder. I associated that with masculinity and being male. My father got me a set of barbells, and I started to work out with weights.

I bought a home course of the old Charles Atlas exercise and muscle development program that was advertised in comic books. The ads showed a skinny guy on the beach getting sand kicked in his face by a bully while he was talking to a girl. The humiliation motivated him to become a bodybuilder. Then it showed his transformation from a skinny guy into a confident muscle man. He punches the bully in the face, and he's admired by all the women.

I worked out regularly, following the instructions in Charles Atlas's course. I started to experience some development over the course of time. I greatly admired bodybuilders, and I saw them as something akin to superheroes with amazing strength. I never quite achieved that level of development, though I did see good results in the course of time.

I met Cindy and Sue E, girls I befriended in my freshman year, and I introduced them to Brad. At first, I dated Sue, and Brad was with Cindy. Later we ended up changing partners. Sue lived on Balboa Island, and Cindy lived in Corona del Mar. We would often go to each other's houses after school.

At first our friendships seemed safe and went only as far as holding hands. We seemed to be safe from any sexual foreplay. My brother had already briefed me on the ways of seduction, but I was just not ready to explore it yet. I was not ready to make the daring leap to go any further since I was afraid what it would lead to.

Brad was more aggressive than I was and engaged in long sessions of making out, first with Cindy, then with Susan. Between Susan and Cindy, I just had long talking sessions and we laughed a lot. I do remember our conversations sometimes would turn to God – what we thought at the time about who and what God was.

I had become very zealous in my newfound faith. I was constantly reading my Bible, even though I was a slow reader. I would go to church every chance I could to get away from the growing problems at home. I had been struggling as a student, and by constantly reading the Bible, it actually started to help my reading.

I changed my core circle of friends because of my born-again experience. I had become too zealous for some of the kids in my childhood circle, and I gained a new set of friends within that year. I am sure I pushed my old friends away because all I would talk about was God and Jesus. My old friends of Brad, Cindy and Sue joined my new-found life for awhile, and we all went to church events together. I discovered later that Chuck Smith lived close to my house, and it was comforting to know that. It was like having one of the apostles living near you.

I learned about it from my friend Susan O. I'd known her since junior high-school, and I got to know her better towards my junior year in high school. She lived a couple houses down from Chuck Smith. When I went to her house to visit, I would exchange greetings with Chuck whenever I saw him out front of his house.

I was soaking up all the Bible studies, music and worship services I could get from the different teachers at Calvary Chapel. I got a good foundation of the Bible and the culture of the Calvary Chapel from 1970 through 1972. I owed it to my brother and middle sister for getting many rides to church in those years before I could drive. The teachers at Calvary Chapel were my mentors at the time, and they had a profound influence on me.

These were the early years of the foundation of Calvary Chapel and what became known as part of "The Jesus Movement." One of the more prominent, dynamic personalities involved was a leader named Lonnie Frisbee. He was a young hippie, and he looked like one of those pictures of Jesus with long hair. The gifts of healing flowed through him, and you could feel his energy source as the presence of the Holy Spirit when he taught and prayed for people.

Speaking In Tongues

A week after I was born-again in 1970, I experienced a supernatural experience – what is called in the charismatic faith, 'the Baptism of the Holy Spirit.' I had already heard about the Holy Spirit but not the expression the "Baptism of the Holy Spirit." My brother was explaining this experience to me, and he encouraged me to go through with the Baptism of the Holy Spirit.

After one of the evening church services, I went into a small Sunday school room off the main chapel that was very crowded while my brother and sister in-law waited outside. I remember thinking I wanted this experience to be real for me. I was hopeful and deeply engaged. The fact that so many others filled the room brought a kind of validation to the experience I hoped to have. There were other believers as well who were awaiting the Baptism of the Holy Spirit. I took my place next to them and waited.

Lonnie Frisbee entered the room, and his charismatic presence filled the space. A hushed murmur went through the crowd. I felt like I was standing in the presence of anointed greatness, and I was filled with expectation. He gave a simple explanation of the Baptism of the Holy Spirit, both for me and for the others present, and I solemnly listened. He said it was like water from heaven coming down in a water glass that was turned upside down. Once the water glass was turned right side up, the water could fill the glass and continue until it overflowed.

As Lonnie finished his explanation, he came towards me and prayed for me, laying hands on my forehead. I felt an electric current as waves of energy went through my body, and I could barely talk. He continued with his hands on my forehead, and another bolt of electricity went through me. My head was leaning back as though something was pushing me into that position, and I felt a lump in my throat.

He said, "This brother is starting to speak in tongues." I didn't know what he was talking about, yet I felt like I had to say something. Lonnie started to speak in a language foreign to my ear, and other people also started to speak in different languages. I realized this had to be speaking in tongues. I started to speak myself, but it came out like grunting or chanting sounds. All the while I kept feeling this lump in my throat. I felt paralyzed, like I could not move as this energy current continued circulating through me. I wasn't scared but I felt overwhelmed by this sensation I had never experienced before.

Lonnie stayed with me a little longer, encouraging me to keep speaking the language, then he would speak in tongues again. He said, "It will keep coming to you."

Then he went to the person beside me, and a similar thing happened to that disciple. My eyes were open, and I was aware of what was going on. I could not move, nor did I want to move, because I wanted to continue to feel this way. I looked around the room and several people were looking at me, smiling and praying and speaking in tongues.

The noise level in the room was getting louder as more people spoke in tongues, and some were singing in a foreign language as well. It seemed like it came to a climax, as though all the voices came in harmony then the volume leveled off and stopped. Lonnie said something I could not quite make out, and he left the room.

We all started to leave the room, some of us stumbling as though we were drunk. As I explained to my brother and sister in-law what had happened, I started to hyperventilate, breathing heavily, and it was hard to talk.

The feeling stayed with me as I got into my brothers' van and we drove home. Each time I tried to explain what happened, the feeling came back. My sister-in-law was laughing happily for me about what was taking place as I was experiencing these emotions. They said I was glowing when I came out of the room. The feeling lasted for several hours, though I had great difficulty speaking. Whenever I opened my mouth to speak, the words I wanted to say would not come.

When Barry dropped me off at home, my mother was in the living room drinking some wine. She asked what was going on, since I looked so excited. I sat down with Barry and sister-in-law and started to explain, but as I talked, I began breathing heavily again and it was hard to talk.

My mother told me to calm down and talk slower. I managed to get a few more words out, but she did not respond much and seemed more concerned. brother, sister-in-law and I went to my bedroom, and my middle sister came in. Going over my story with them in my room, I managed to get through it this time. My brother told me my spiritual eyes will start to open more now. I think he did not know what else to say. He simply tried to be supportive.

Lonnie became part of my regular Wednesday night diet. He was there during various Bible Study events that Calvary Chapel held with its water baptisms, and we would go "street witnessing" to share our faith at different locations around Newport and Laguna Beach.

When Lonnie ministered in those early years, it was an overwhelming spiritual experience to be part of his exciting services. When he ministered, there was often a strong supernatural presence of energy and the Holy Spirit. People were healed at our events, and waves of emotion, joy and laughter would take over the people who gathered together with us.

It was the first time I had observed the gift of healing taking place in front of me. Lonnie would pray for people to be healed, and he would call out different people, naming what was wrong with them. He would then pray for them, and people would fall over backward on the carpeted chapel floor. They would arise healed.

Lonnie was the big buzz among the movement that was taking hold in those early years of Calvary Chapel. He was one of the main characters, the driving force that God was using to launch this movement.

The chapel was always packed with people hanging around outside to experience the excitement and the holy healing energy. It was like one of the early Bible stories of Jesus when the crowds would gather around to witness Him healing the people. It was electrifying, and I was thrilled to be part of it. These events changed the course of my young life and caused me to thirst for even more of the things of God.

During the early part of summer, Calvary Chapel held a water baptism at Corona del Mar beach near Pirates Cove. This is when I was baptized by Chuck Smith. There were hundreds who showed up on the beach, standing on the cliff side, watching Chuck and Lonnie baptize people and singing worship songs.

They held the baptisms every few weeks during the summer months, and the crowds got larger each time. There were often several ministers on hand to help with baptizing, since there were so many desiring to be baptized. They would have a barbecue in the afternoon followed by a small Bible Study, then everyone would hike over the rocks and cliffs by the cove to get ready for the baptism. The cove was always packed, and all the people lining the cliffs would sing new contemporary worship songs. The hymns would soon spread to several churches, and the performances in the cove made for a very uplifting experience to watch.

The "Jesus People" Movement Takes Hold

The popularity of Calvary Chapel was increasing and getting media attention, while the congregation experienced rapid growth. The Jesus People movement was spilling over throughout the Southern California area with music groups, concerts, coffee shops, Bible studies, and evangelist meetings. The energy of the movement was phenomenal to behold, and I felt blessed to be part of it. I was at the core of the movement, witnessing it from within.

Chuck Smith was making plans to do a television program on what was taking place at Calvary Chapel. However, when he got a call from Kathryn Kuhlman, his plans got an unexpected boost. She wanted the Jesus People of Calvary Chapel and other key figures in the movement to be on her weekly show "I Believe in Miracles." She wanted them to share what God was doing through this youth movement.

I went to CBS studios twice where four shows were taped each time. My friends Brad, Meg, and Ginger went for each taping. Each time we went to the studio, it took most of the day to do the tapings. I was starstruck to finally meet THE Kathryn Kuhlman, the celebrity I had seen so many times on my television set. I tried to remain calm.

At the time Calvary Chapel went into the studio, we did not know we would be on the Kathryn Kuhlman show. All that we were told was that some person paid for Calvary Chapel to be taped and we were going to CBS Television Studios in Los Angeles.

My friends and I sat together in the studio audience, then a slender redhead entered the studio door. She walked across the *All in the Family* set, holding her hand up, pointing in the air, shaking her long finger. "I am one of you, I am one of you!"

Everyone in the audience was awestruck for a moment. In unison, we all said, "It's Kathryn Kuhlman!" We were immediately mesmerized by her presence and fell in love with her. She chatted with us a little and gave us instructions about what we were going to do.

We all went into the next studio across the hall, and everyone was moved into place on the floor and the bleachers. Kathryn Kuhlman introduced her musicians with clear articulation.

"Ladies and Gentlemen, Dino at the piano!" He was a young good-looking Greek fellow who played like a professional Las Vegas showman. He was a flamboyant piano player, like Liberace. She also had a baritone vocal soloist, a good-looking man named Jimmy McDonald. She had an excellent rapport with her musicians. It showed in the passion they brought while playing for her.

In between tapings, we moved around to different seats in the bleachers to give the appearance of a new television audience. One of those times, I sat directly under Kathryn Kuhlman on the studio set. I was looking right up the roof of her mouth and could see all her gold fillings. Her voice is still clear in my head, and I will never forget those long fingers she had.

In between tapings, I went to the restroom where I heard someone in one of the stalls sounding strange and asking me for a light. He kept prompting me to come over to the stall. This frightened me, and I realized he was propositioning me. I'd heard somewhere that asking for a light was a code phrase for wanting sex. I left the restroom right away. I went back to the area where I was sitting and said nothing about the incident to anyone since it was so strange.

After the tapings, I went up to Miss Kuhlman and asked her to sign my Bible. She said, "Bless you. Of course, honey." I must have started something because soon after that, there was a crowd of people surrounding her who wanting their Bibles signed too.

I didn't know that years later I would see clips of myself from those tapings in a Lonnie Frisbee documentary film and on the internet. We were on the forefront of a movement.

Brad, Meg, Ginger and some others went to a couple of the Kathryn Kuhlman youth rallies at the Hollywood Palladium. Lonnie was there along with other "Jesus People" personalities. We waited for several hours out front, until finally the doors opened and the whole group sang our Calvary Chapel songs. When the doors opened, and we flooded into the auditorium to take our seats, Kathryn Kuhlman was wearing one of her famous chiffon dresses with puffy sleeves and a soft pink spotlight that illuminated her presence. She looked radiant.

Towards the end of the service, I remember Kathryn Kuhlman praying for me when she called the youth to the stage. The wave of the anointing electrical current going through my body was powerful, and I kept falling back. I attended several healing services at the Shrine Auditorium after that. We were squeezed in the crowd waiting out front. It would get intense. Then we were herded like cattle when the doors opened, sitting up in the rafters of the balcony, anticipating the service that would last for several hours.

The large choir sang, ushering us into the anticipation of Kathryn Kuhlman, taking the stage as we all began to sing "He Touched Me." She entered and seemed to dance a waltz, as though she was floating across that large stage in her white puffy sleeved chiffon dress. The auditorium was in rapture, floating on the energy that was surging through the place. Waves of love flowed throughout the auditorium as we continued to sing in the hall.

Once we stopped singing, Kathryn made a brief introduction and went right into introducing her piano player Dino, followed by Jimmy McDonald, the baritone soloist. Afterwards, she started preaching, and at some dramatic point, she would make a transition to start calling out healings that were taking place.

People came to the platform area up front to testify their experiences. Kathryn would pray for them, and the person would fall backward while someone caught them. Those services were a taste of heaven that kept me wanting to experience more. I saw them as a sign of things to come in my life. I felt deeply moved by these healings, time and again. It was a special and rich experience, and I was privileged to be part of it.

I discovered one of the Kathryn Kuhlman offices was on Fashion Island, the same building where my father had his private office in Corona del Mar at the time. Her gated community condo was next to the same country club where my father played golf. My middle sister worked as a waitress at Coco's Restaurant in Corona del Mar, and she would see Kathryn Kuhlman sometimes coming in to eat.

Kathryn was known for being very articulate, and my sister would joke about her ordering a cheeseburger while stretching out the word. I told Meg where Kathryn Kuhlman's office was, and one day after school Meg, another friend and I decided to drop in on her office. Meg dared me to do it. We acted so brave going up the elevator.

I opened the suite door to reveal a plush decorated office with a couple of large Chinese vases and a life-sized portrait of Kathryn Kuhlman on one wall over an antique table. The secretary was very polite and received us warmly. I told her my father had an office in this building and we were on the show with Calvary Chapel. I asked if Kathryn was in the office.

She said we'd just missed her, and she would have been delighted to see us. The secretary showed us around and said this office was used to store the film of all shows that had been aired. We saw the large storage room of all those cans of film, and I thought how historical it was to see years of shows in one room. We felt so special after that experience, but I never returned. Somehow, I thought it might dilute the magic. Some things just can't be topped.

By 1971 or '72, Calvary Chapel had purchased other property up the street from its original location. They purchased a large circus tent to hold services while plans were being made for a school and a new sanctuary to be built to hold the large crowds. It was exciting to experience such growth, but it seemed different from the small crowded chapel we used to meet in.

Meeting Brant for the First Time

In the winter of 1971, my sister Jenifer and I went on a weekend retreat with Calvary Chapel. The object was for me to get away from the pressure of the changes I was experiencing at home. It was there that I first met Brant Baker and his younger brother Kevin, who was my age.

It was just the three of us sharing a cabin. I arrived in the cabin first, then Kevin came barging in, out of breath. He was about my height and on the chunky side. He tossed his suitcase onto the lower bunk and started yelling out the door in a whiny voice, "Brant we are over here!"

Brant entered. He was a slender fellow, a little over six feet, and looked something like the young entertainer Donnie Osmond. He had a constant smile and a spacey kind of look.

When first meeting him, Brant appeared quiet, focused, in a state of deep thought. His connection to the Holy Spirit gave him an angelic look at times. This angelic look showed up on him during healing services and afterglow services in the early days.

But this was not the totality of his personality, I later learned. Anyone who got to know Brant saw two sides of his personality in the course of time. He would often tease in a childlike way, and he had a great sense of humor. Brant was frequently full of life, fun to be around, and he made everyone laugh. He made people feel comfortable to be with him. He was big on giving hugs, kissing women on the cheek, and often calling all of us "precious" in his teachings. He had different pet nicknames to those close to him. Brant's charisma helped him rise to a position of prominence within the church.

I looked Brant over, trying to imagine the far-off realm his eyes were looking into. "How strange," I thought. I continued making my bunk bed and tidying the room.

Kevin left to get the rest of our luggage, leaving Brant and me alone in the room. We engaged in some small talk, but nothing very deep. Then suddenly Brant asked me if I spoke in tongues.

"Oh yes, all the time," I answered. He smiled, and for a moment it seemed like the sun shone brightly in the room.

Kevin burst in through the door again with more luggage, saying the Mercedes was acting up and complaining about how hot it was in the room. He adjusted the thermostat then opened the luggage. All their clothes were brand new, still in the department store bags. I noticed the bags said *Brant B. Men's Store*. Kevin kept ripping the bags open.

"Where are the socks and underwear?" he asked. Brant told him they were in the back seat of the car. Kevin yelled at Brant for putting an extra bag in the car, complaining about what a bother it was to go all the way back to the car down the hill. Brant just smiled. Kevin huffed and slammed the door as he left.

Brant remained where he was, sitting on the bunk, smiling, holding his Bible and ignoring his brother's tantrum. I was starting to feel uncomfortable and wanted to leave. I noticed the address on the bags was 19th Street in Costa Mesa, close to where I lived on the border with Newport Beach. I made a comment that I lived near his store. Brant acknowledged the store but said little else about it. We continued making small talk after Kevin returned, watching as Kevin turned down the bed for himself and his brother.

From the first day I met them, the contrast between Brant and Kevin was stark – one was comfortably in control, the other was reactive. Though

I would become swept up in the vortex of Brant's world, like Kevin, I would never be in control of my own destiny until I came out the other side.

The teachers that weekend were Chuck Smith, Lonnie Frisbee, Ken Gulliksen, and Romaine. I came to know them all very well.

Ken was a young man in his twenties who was new to the staff during the past year. He was a soft spoken, blond, blue-eyed Swedish Bible teacher and minister. He had a real kindness about him when he talked. He also played the guitar and sang at gatherings. He wrote a worship song that became popular at the time. The lyrics came from I Corinthians 13, known as the Love Chapter.

Romaine had a direct approach to teaching. He was around the same age as Chuck. He was known for his tough love and direct, blunt answers when it came to scripture guidance. He was like the sergeant at arms when it came to the ministers and those who came to the church, protecting them against any false teachings.

Along with the teaching, there were other music groups who came from Calvary and played. They included The Love Song group, Children of the Day and other soloists. That Saturday night there was a worship period and another worship service that was called an after-glow service led by Lonnie Frisbee. It included lots of different percussion instruments, and other people were singing in tongues in a heavenly harmonic wave of music.

People were spread out through the chapel area, on the floor and in front of the stage. People were giving prophecies of all types, and I remember Brant gave a lengthy prophecy while sitting up on the stage, leaning against the wall. I was impressed with his communication style. He was quite artic-ulate, and there was something different about him. A spiritual rapture was filling the room. If Jesus would come, He could come right now.

I don't remember much more about that weekend, other than Kevin snoring at night. He and I talked a little. I picked up that he was going through some hard stuff in his personal life, and I felt sorry for him. He always seemed uptight and had a lot of nervous energy.

After that night, there was a morning church service. We said our goodbyes and exchanged brotherly hugs.

It would be the following summer, my junior year, when I ran into Kevin Baker again, He was my roommate for a short time in Hawaii with Calvary Chapel. My middle sister and I went together, a gift from my mother. It would be forty years before I would be in Oahu, Hawaii again, working in the Air Force Reserve. The later trip evoked for me the events of that week with Calvary Chapel.

Upon arrival, I had a lesson in humility. I'd just pre-judged someone I met on the plane, asking the Lord, "How come I seem to run into these strange people?" As soon as I thought that, Kevin barged in the door of my room. He was to be my roommate.

"Hi ya." He said.

"Do you remember me?" I asked him, incredulous.

"Oh, yeah. It's great to see you. I remember."

I asked if his brother Brant was with him. He said "Oh, no, he is busy with his Bible Study."

"Yes, I heard about that from a friend who is also going."

He started to unpack for a moment then left. For whatever reason, he changed roommates with another person. He said it had nothing to do with me. I felt a little hurt but accepted it.

It was a great week of fellowship, meeting new friends, daily Bible studies, music and site seeing on two different islands. It was a time of change, and I felt myself maturing with each new event.

Bearing Witness For Each Other

During the summer at the end of my sophomore year that same year, my parents separated. I was devastated. They sold our Tustin house at a loss, and I was living with my father in a small ranch house on Birch Street, close to the Orange County Airport. My father was struggling financially, working as a security guard on the night shift. We were boarding horses at the time, and we rented out a couple rooms to supplement his income.

It was around that same time in 1971 that Greg L, Brant B. and Randy. showed up at my high school. They came to Bible Study we would have outside on the lawn. I don't remember much of what was said among us. I do remember Brant had that same spacey look and had his long hair. He said a few words, and Randy played the guitar.

Randy went to the same high school as I did, and by then he had already graduated. He was a few years ahead of my class. I do remember Randy in a school play when I was a freshman. He was performing in "Alice in Wonderland" where he played a rabbit. Randy returned off and on, leading Bible Study and playing his guitar during lunchtime.

During one of the Bible Study sessions at my school, I came out in a jester costume. I was in a drama sketch we performed for each period of the day. Randy liked my costume, and we ended up talking about drama since we both had the same drama teacher. I think he admired my courage to wear this costume in public. He looked at me differently after that.

After receiving the Baptism of the Holy Spirit at the end of my freshman year, I wanted all my high school friends to experience it. However, my friends Brad, Cindy and Sue thought I was too fanatical for them at first, and they put some distance between us for awhile. Then slowly during that summer and through my sophomore year, we became friends again as I encouraged them to come to church with me. They relied on me to attend, since I was able to organize transportation through some of the members of the congregation.

I continued to have conversations with them about their experience. It seemed they all became born again at once. It was very exciting to me to see this happen for them. I wanted them to experience the Holy Spirit the way I did, and I prayed with them, so they would receive the Baptism of The Holy Spirit.

In time they did. Some of them even spoke in tongues. After I got my driver's license, it became easier to attend more of the services, and we had some exciting times together. A couple times we visit other Pentecostal churches out of curiosity. We thought some of those services were funny, with their shouting and crying out loud.

What we were used to seeing and being a part of was very different. At the Calvary Chapel services, we had a different kind of service, something more subdued, with contemporary music groups. We would have singing, prayer and talking about spiritual matters. We would get together at each other's houses when our parents were not around. Even when we went to the beach, we just continued with the same spiritual activities.

We would have our own afterglow services, like we learned at Calvary Chapel. This was a time we asked the Holy Spirit to come upon us and feel the presence of the spirit. We would speak in tongues and pray for each other until we fell backwards onto the ground. There was a great spiritual presence of feeling of love among the gathering. It was powerfully uplifting

Together, my old and new friends became part of the spiritual wave that was taking place with the Calvary Chapel movement. We were a zealous group, going to the different functions at the chapel and the beach. We would bear witness to other people, and we were constantly yelling out of car windows, "Jesus loves you!" Since Meg and a couple other friends lived in Corona del Mar, we would also walk around the beach and on Balboa Island, screaming out "Jesus Loves You!" Not everyone welcomed our message, but we were carefree and felt the call to spread the word. We knew some would hear us and respond.

One time on Balboa Island Brad, Cindy, Sue, Meg and I snuck into the yard of Buddy Ebsen, the actor from the TV series *The Beverly Hillbillies*. His house faced the water, and a group of us climbed the fence and went up on the second-floor balcony above the pool, peeking in the window. We heard a dog barking and we all got scared and scurried down off the balcony porch and jumped over the fence running down the street laughing. We had hoped to make a connection and spread the good word. All we made were fools of ourselves.

Hanging out with my Christian friends kept my mind off my parents splitting up and the changes that were taking place in my family. These changes affected me more than my siblings, since I was the youngest and last one in the house.

My father made the comment once after he had a few drinks that he was concerned about all my church activities. Why was I not being a normal kid, getting into trouble, going to parties and getting drunk like other teenagers? I thought he would be proud of me that I was not causing some of the heartaches that my older siblings had gone through with my parents.

I think he was proud of me. This strange sarcastic comment was his way of expressing his concerns and letting me know I had options other than going to church all the time and reading my Bible. I didn't say anything to him about it. I felt hurt and walked away.

As some of my older friends drifted apart, I thought they gave in to the world, and Satan was having them fall into all kinds of traps. It was sad to me. I did not blame them. I was still friendly towards them and prayed for them. I lost some of those friends one by one as they gained other interests. It was hard for me to see, but I knew I had to let them go.

CHAPTER 3:

DRIFTING APART

During my junior year, Brad and I drifted farther apart for a while when I moved from my Tustin home. We still saw each other off and on, and he would often give me a ride to school in his car with a couple other friends. We did have one class together, which was work experience. We had jobs in the school library a few days a week during our junior and senior years.

I got to know a girl named Peggy from my drama class. We connected right away. We performed some comedy scenes together, and it was great fun. The routines were for a health event at our school, so they had real value besides being purely entertaining.

Peggy had a younger sister named Cindy, and they were both quite talented. Cindy played the flute, and Peggy was a dancer. During the summer, Peggy and I were involved in a community musical play, and Brad was on the stage crew. The play was produced by, Tom, a talented classmate of mine who wrote an original musical with a girl he knew. He also played the lead role, wrote the musical score, and played the piano.

Peggy and I were in the chorus and had a blast. I talked with Peggy about Jesus, and for a time she came to church along with me. Brad, Sue E.

and Cindy and others also came, and they would weave in and out of our Christian group.

Peggy and I were good friends, and we had a lot of good laughs. She was so witty, and I adored her. Yet when she broke up with her boyfriend, Rob, I discovered she was looking for something more than a platonic friendship with me. Brad seemed to be a better fit for her, and I entrusted Peggy to him when I left to go with Calvary Chapel in Hawaii. This was during the summer of my junior year.

As a result, Brad and Peggy started dating steadily. I was hurt at first, but I got over it soon enough. We all got along well and continued to hang out as friends at my place, Peggy's home and Brad's.

Brad and I continued to talk as close friends, although I know my zealousness for God was becoming an unspoken source of tension between us. He was polite about it, but this didn't smooth things over. We had stopped masturbating together since I became a Christian, and it was no longer an issue for me for a while. I continued my Christian activities with our other Christian friends as he became less involved with that group.

Before, our conversations about sex mainly centered on the feelings and discovery of sex and masturbation. Then he started making out with the girls we met and going to church. I figured he was just exploring his sexuality while I refrained my impulses of making out with girls. I thought it was my personal mission to try and help and love him as a good friend. I think he loved me as a friend and decided to go along with it for a while. I believe the Jesus experience was real to him at the time.

While Brad and I were drifting apart during my junior year, he took on a part time job through a job referral agency for teenagers. I was using the same job agency, getting gardening jobs to help older people with their yard maintenance. Brad was hanging out with his other friends during this period, so we spent little time together. Even though we were going in different directions, I would still make the effort to extend my friendship and see him.

I did not realize it at first, but Brad was discovering for himself he was gay. He talked to me about being seduced several times by older men where he worked. One of the jobs he took was to help someone with household chores. Another job was a part time babysitting gig that was to last for about a year. He opened up to me about what was going on with him, confiding in me about the man whose child he was babysitting. Brad seemed to like the erotic excitement and attention at first. It wasn't long before he wanted to get away from it, and he quit the job.

At the time I was thinking I didn't know how I would have reacted if that happened to me. I probably would have reacted no differently than Brad. I would have been just as curious at first and not known how far I would have gone with the actions as Brad went into detail. After he told me about it, I felt bad for him.

At the same time, Brad had known all I had gone through with my parents' divorce and the emotional changes I was dealing with. In his own way, he was reaching out to me as a friend and wanted to express his feelings about what was going on with him. As his story unfolded, he pulled out his collection of male pornography for me to look at.

It was clear he was coming onto me. I could not allow myself to give in to his unspoken suggestion of wanting to masturbate together. It was arousing and confusing to me at the same time. It frightened me I was feeling aroused by those pictures since I'd never seen such a display. He played on my weaknesses, and I think he knew it.

I told him I couldn't do this, and he pulled away. He was polite and respected my wishes. We talked a little longer and I left. Brad and I would still run into each other sometimes through my senior year at school events, birthdays or during a stage production.

In my senior year, the school did the musical Carousel, and Peggy played Mrs. Mullins. I auditioned for the production but later backed out. I thought it would be too much to handle with what was taking place at home and at work. The year unfolded swiftly, and soon high school was behind me.

I saw Brad at our graduation and then at the party. He was there without Peggy, though I was not surprised. Peggy had told me she and Brad had broken up. She was still a junior, and it would be the last time I saw her until a couple years later at the college she attended. Part of me missed those high school days when the three of us hung out together.

Shortly after graduation, a tragedy took place with a family member of one of the girlfriends, Linda and Sue, which Brad and I hung out with. Cindy's 10-year-old sister Linda was abducted, raped and murdered. One of our senior classmates was first suspected, but this proved to be false and was let go. The perpetrator was not to be found. It would be forty-six years later the offender was found through a DNA website. The whole thing was horrible.

Linda's funeral was very somber with an open casket. She was dressed in a pretty sparkly dress. Cindy sat with her parents and family to one side of the casket. The funeral home was packed and included the young Girl Scout troop members Sue belonged to.

I don't recall the message, but I do remember we got a horrible case of the giggles during the service. None of us could look at each other. I blame it on being young and how we reacted to the stress of the whole situation. I was desperately biting my check, trying to control myself while tears were coming down the side of my face. It looked like all of us were crying.

It all started when Brad and I decided to go together to support Cindy and her family. We sat in the same pew. Sue said something about Linda sitting up in the coffin. We didn't know what gallows humor was, but this was enough to trigger our uncontrollable laughter.

When the service was over, all of us were ushered, along with the Girl Scout troop, to view the casket. By the time we got to the front door, hugging and shaking hands with the minister and family members, we still were fighting back tears of laughter desperately trying to show expressions of grief. We ran to Brad's car out of total embarrassment. Brad started his car and tore out of the parking lot while we let out our laughs, we felt terrible about the whole thing.

That was the last time I saw Cindy. It would be a few years before I would see Brad again. I loved him as a good friend. He went off to college for a while and further discovered his new freedom as a gay man. I furthered my involvement in an evangelical healing ministry to help save the world since Jesus was to return very soon.

What's A Shekinah Fellowship?

I first learned about the Shekinah Fellowship meetings in my junior year (1971-1972). The word "Shekinah" (pronounced shuh-KAI-nuh) means "the presence or glory of the Divine Presence." The name was different from the names of other Christian churches at the time. This word sounded mystical and magical to me.

My Christian teaching told me the word "Shekinah" referred to God's presence. It was the Shekinah glory cloud that led Moses and the children of Israel through the wilderness, and it would rest in the traveling temple tent at night.

My friend Meg was part of the Christian group I hung around with. We had a core group of people who did things together, and since I had access to a car, I could provide transportation when I was available.

Meg was the one who introduced me to Shekinah. She made it sound like it was a secret group and only certain selected spiritual individuals could come. I felt a little left out and curious. I wanted to belong, especially since the name struck such a chord in me.

The group met in a small office space in Long Beach, then as they grew, they relocated to a meeting space at a small church called Bethany Chapel. Eventually they moved into the main sanctuary of the chapel, and this is where I attended their meetings.

Before I went, I kept asking Meg about this place she was going since she treated it like it was a big secret. As I asked more questions about the group and who was leading the meeting, it finally clicked with me. This group was led by Brant and his brother – the same people I ran into over a year before at the Calvary winter camp.

They were also the ones who once came to my school campus with Randy and Greg L. When Meg mentioned the leader of the group owned a clothing store on the border between Costa Mesa and Newport Beach, it tipped me off. At last Meg invited me, and I ended up going to Long Beach with her sister and a couple other people from our group.

When I saw Brant for the second time, I thought, "What a strange, entertaining and flashy person he is!" His voice would resonate into a high pitch when he preached. He was sharing a study on the Song of Solomon that was dramatized in an entertaining way, making it both funny and dramatic.

As strange and funny as he was, I felt a spiritual attraction and I wanted to be part of this experience. The worship time before Bible Study was intimate with a warm, emotionally stirring wave of the presence of the spirit of God. It was powerfully moving. I felt this way before in some of the early Calvary Chapel services with Lonnie Frisbee. I also felt it during a couple of the Kathryn Kuhlman services I had attended, which were so spiritually rich, I became hooked on what took place in those meetings.

I remembered how the early Calvary Chapel church meetings were free flowing. Later they became almost mechanically routine and stiff, rushing from song to song. Brant's services were always powerful, and they had a natural flow of their own. I started to attend Shekinah Fellowship when I could borrow the car, and I took Meg plus a few others. My brother even came once, and he liked it.

Brant would often tell the story of how he got the name of Shekinah and when he first had the vision of the Shekinah cloud. He would refer to the time when his grandmother was very sick in the hospital. He was devoted to her since she left a big impression in his life growing up, and she was one of the influences in his Christian conversion. With his heart aching, fearing she was dying, he prayed for her and the room glowed with a bright cloud over his grandmother. She soon recovered, and it marked a turning point in his life spiritually.

Toward the end of the Bible Study lesson, there was a time of prayer when people came forward to receive prayers and healing. As Brant laid hands on the people, they fell backwards while ushers would catch them and lay them down on the ground. This was called being 'slain in the spirit.' I had already witnessed and experienced this before, so I understood what was going on.

The service lasted for several hours but we were unaware of the passing time. They would have a short break then continue with an afterglow service in the basement. This was a special time we would further invite the presence of the Holy Spirit to move in the room as we sang more worship songs. We would all sit on the floor and wait for the spirit to move.

When the spirit did move, there would be musical percussion instruments and singing in the spirit with other tongues which all blended in harmony. Once the noise died down there was a moment of silence and different people would offer words of prophecy that were uplifting. It was like winter camp with Calvary Chapel over a year before, when I first met Brant.

Brant was soon added to the collection of my "new personality" spiritual role models for my life. My personality was drawn towards the performing arts anyways, so it only seemed natural to be attracted towards those ministers with a dramatic flair who possessed the gift of healing. I saw them as "Super Star Saints," larger than life and charismatic.

I wanted to learn more, so I started to read whatever I could find on ministers who had healing ministries. However, I would later find out many of those who had healing ministries had personal struggles and tragic lives.

This puzzled me because they appeared to have found success in the Christian ministry. I did not understand the disillusion this type of spiritual success can bring, or the pitfalls these leaders can become prey to. My fascination with healing ministries was the escape I needed since my own family life had so much chaos.

The Shadows of Addiction

I was trying to understand the adult decisions my parents were making. Their choices were confusing to me. They were dealing with their divorce, financial struggles, alcoholism, and my father's gambling. I never really noticed before, because it was so well disguised until I got older. Their drinking always seemed to be on the lighter side of life, with memories of happy parties.

My father's gambling did not come to light until he got in debt over it, trying to regain some financial investments. My mother shared little by little what was going on with my father and how he'd fly to Las Vegas during working hours, then return home later that evening.

Maybe I was denial that it was my father's entire fault for the mess he got into and put his family and client at risk. I wanted to believe the best of him. I wanted to believe he was put in a vulnerable situation with one of his clients, a woman who was flirtatious towards him. She put pressure on him to invest her money, so it would get a greater return for both of them, but it would be risky. He played along with her and gave in to her game. He wanted to please his client. It seemed to work at first, but then the market went down, and he lost a good part of her funds. In desperation, he gambled with the money she had entrusted him to invest and was borrowing from others to gain back what he lost.

During this time my mother got involved with a community intervention crisis clinic and attended Alcoholics Anonymous (AA) meetings on her own. Listening to the problems of other women was her way of dealing with the problems of her own marriage.

The stock brokerage company my father worked for ended up as a local business scandal when the details became public. It was embarrassing to me. It seemed like something important to some journalists to write about in the local newspaper. My simple solution and prayer for them was they just needed Jesus, and everything would be all right. That was my safety zone – I relied on my Christian activities, going to church, reading the Bible, Christian friends, and seeing the healing star ministers. I came to the realization later how he knew exactly what he was doing. My mother was just protecting myself and the family from the reality of the decisions my father made, while prayer was my protection of the denial that kept me from facing the truth of my father's bad choices.

I recall one night, my parents' drinking ended in an emotional scene. My father had taken an antidepressant after he had a few drinks and confessed to me what was happening between him and my mom. By then, I was not totally in the dark. I had known some of what was going on from what my mother was telling me.

My parents called me into the living room and explained in a philosophical way they still loved each other but were going to separate for a time. My father was shaking and looked stoned. I was upset to see him like that and hated to see what was happening to our family. I tried to explain to them they needed Jesus in their lives.

My father just looked at me and said, "It was sad that Jesus never married and did not know what it was like to raise a family." I left and went back to my room and called my brother on the phone to pray.

Despite their struggles, it seemed like my parents were going to work it out. They were just going to sell the house to downsize and file for bankruptcy while both worked to start over. As more of my father's business practices and gambling losses were disclosed to my mother, it all became too much for her. They decided to separate, and then they ended up getting a divorce. It was out of protection for her interest they divorced so she would not be responsible for any of my father's debt under community property law in California. Divorce was the safest option for her, despite the havoc it worked for all of us.

When my parents divorced in my junior year, the large house we lived in was sold at a loss. The furnishings were sold and divided among my parents and some among my siblings. The plan was for my mother and me to move out together. However, she did not have a job yet and there was no money left after the house sold. So, I ended up moving with my father.

My mother first moved in with her friend Shirley in Newport Beach on Lido Island. Shirley had a guest apartment on her property on the waterfront, down the street from John Wayne's place. A short while later, she moved to a large single apartment complex. She got a job at the apartment complex in the marketing department. I got a part-time job there, delivering the monthly newsletters.

She later moved to Los Angeles with another friend named Weiss, whom she got to know through one of her friends. They went to AA meetings while we still lived in the Tustin Avenue house. Weiss was a black man who was blind, and he was a popular AA speaker.

He seemed remarkably intelligent to me. He was humble about it and very nice. Weiss was also a talented piano player and was really into astrology. He came to our house a couple times before my parents' divorce and our move. He gave me a few piano lessons, and he recorded them for me. I was already learning to play the piano myself, but my father could no longer afford any lessons. Having the recordings was a real help.

Weiss lived in a three-bedroom high rise apartment in LA, and my mother was going to be his assistant for awhile. I went to his place a few times with my mother. We went out to dinner together with him, and I spent the night. One time I went to the apartment after going to one of the Kathryn Kuhlman meetings at the Hollywood Palladium. I was with Meg, Brad and a couple other friends. We stopped by and shared what we just experienced at her meeting, and they listened politely. Soon we left.

It appeared my mother was dating Weiss for a while. She asked what I thought of him and how I liked the area. I said he was a nice person. I did not want to reveal what I really thought. I just was not used to seeing my mother with another man, especially one who was black. This situation was just too weird and confusing for me.

I was starting to think I had to move to LA. It seemed scary at first, but then the idea of moving to a large city and living so close to Hollywood felt kind of exciting. My mother gave me a tour of the area, and she showed me the house she lived in the 1940's. This was where she lived when she moved from Michigan with her mother and her two other younger siblings, Phyllis and Eric.

I was enchanted with the older buildings and homes, which reminded me of some of the older black and white movies in the 1930's and 40's.

My mom's relationship with Weiss ended abruptly. He suddenly turned weird with her and practically tossed her out of his apartment. My father apparently came to the rescue and helped her move to another apartment in Costa Mesa. My dad made the comment to me he had not trusted Weiss for a long time. Of course, I thought there would be some jealousy and concern on my father's part. It would only be natural.

While my mother was making her first moves, my father and older sister Meredith rented a small ranch style house in the Santa Ana heights. It was located just below the small undeveloped Orange County Airport – what is now John Wayne Airport.

The house had some land to keep her horse on, including a stall and corral. It was an older property, and it had only two bedrooms and one bath. Meredith and dad each got their own bedroom, and I slept on the small closed-in porch. For awhile we had no stove and used an electric hot plate to fix our meals. The refrigerator from our other house was too big to fit in the kitchen, so we had to go outside to access it under the eaves of the roof.

My father got a job as a security guard. He worked mainly at night and slept during the day. We couldn't afford to keep our car. The payments were too high, so had to turn it in. In its place he got a convertible piece of junk. It was embarrassing to be seen in. I drove it to school a couple times, and it did not fit in with the lifestyle of middle-class Corona del Mar.

I had to hold the top latch down while driving to keep the roof from blowing off at high speeds. My friends and I would laugh about it while we took turns holding the latch to keep it from coming undone. The car really smoked bad, and the engine would always stall. The car was an obvious sign of our change in status.

Meredith was working and going to school at the University of Irvine. She lived with us for only a short time, then moved into the house next door with a couple friends. The house had a pool, which was empty while she moved in. Brad and I offered to clean it out, which we did, and we filled up the pool for our use. It took constant maintenance, but at least it was a small luxury in a difficult time.

I must give my father credit for being resourceful in finding ways to bring in extra cash. Besides economizing on groceries, the car and housing, he came up with creative ways to generate more money. One of his projects was to build some more horse stalls and rent them out. Once they were built and occupied, it was extra income for us with little effort. It was up to the renters to clean the muck in the stalls, and all my dad had to do was collect the rent every month.

When Meredith moved out, I took over her old room. This left the back-porch empty, so my father rented it out to a college student. He also made a room in the garage and rented it out as well. We all had to be flexible in order to make ends meet, and my dad showed no lack of resourcefulness.

In spite of his best efforts, money was still tight for my father. He tried hard not to show it around me, but there were times when the stress would reveal itself in the small details of life. One time he got really upset with me when I used too many postage stamps to mail a letter.

Cooking was a mystery to him, which meant we made compromises beyond mere economy. Grocery shopping meant mostly frozen food with TV dinners. I started to learn how to cook on my own, beyond just TV dinners, and I tried new things. Friday meals were easy since I always made one of my favorites – Kraft macaroni and cheese with hot dogs. Little by little I ventured into making more complicated dishes.

I felt proud I made a Thanksgiving dinner for the whole family. I turned my bedroom into a dining room. We were able to fit the whole family around the dining table, including my grandma Edith who was living in a retirement home. It meant a great deal to her and to the rest of us.

That Christmas, we made all our gifts by hand, sometimes with questionable results. My father went a little too far with his economizing and sent out used Christmas cards, from samples pulled from a Christmas catalog he'd found at work. We took the sample cards from the catalog, crossed out the family name printed on the bottom of the card. We put our name on them and mailed them in different envelopes.

This raised a few eyebrows among our friends and family, and some of them probably would rather have gotten no card at all. When my Uncle Eric and Aunt June got their card, my uncle crossed out my dad's name on the card, wrote his own name and mailed it back to us. Though he meant it as a joke, I was pretty embarrassed by his gesture.

This was a dark time for us in many respects, and we did our best to remain close as a family. One day while my father was building another horse stall to rent, I was in the house talking to my mother on the phone. She broke the news to me her father had died. She was leaving soon for Florida to help make his final arrangements. Her stepmother, Beulah, would help her gather some of his things and settle the estate.

Memories of my grandfather flashed before me as my mom told me this. I thought of the few times I saw him when I was younger, thought of the letters we wrote to each other and the love in them. He knew I collected stamps, and he would often send me some from his own stamp collection. Now I'd lost that connection to his love.

I went out to the yard to tell my father. He paused in his work and stared. He seemed stunned at first, then said, "Oscar was a good man." He mopped his brow briefly and went back to work.

I found out later my mother had been looking forward to getting a share of her father's estate. She was hoping for an inheritance that would help her during this time because she was financially struggling on her own. But things turned out different from what she expected.

My mom discovered most of her share of the estate was already spent since my father had borrowed from it while they were married. He had gambled it away, trying to get back some of the investment he'd lost for his client. My mother discovered letters from my father with fabricated stories about her, justifications to my grandfather for why dad needed the money.

On learning this, my mother seemed to understand the position my father was in at the time and why he did what he did. The pain she felt came from the fact her father was left with an impression which was not true. It hurt that her reputation was soiled by the lies in those letters, and now she had no way to defend herself or reveal the truth. It took quite awhile for my mother to let it go and forgive my father.

It was not long after this time my grandmother Hoyt died – my dad's mother. It was only a month later when I was in the backyard and I saw my father at the back door, holding the phone and crying. This was one of those few times I did see him cry, and he was calling out to me for help. In between his sobs he said, "My mother died. Take the phone. Your mother is on the phone."

My mother told me to make some coffee for my father and just listen to him. I told her I understood. When I hung up, I made him some coffee, but my father did not drink it. He just continued crying. He explained my grandmother had Alzheimer's and he was saddened she did not have any memory of him.

His mother's passing gave him a taste of what my mother went through a month earlier with her father dying. It seemed like poetic justice for the lies he told my grandfather, leading him to believe the wrong ideas about my mom when my father wrote those letters. Beyond the loss I felt for losing my grandparents, I felt bad for both my father and mother. Mixed amid a flood of memories I had of my grandparents was the sense of my parents' own suffering. It was confusing to me, and I felt helpless to ease their pain. I could only pray.

My father's spirit was broken, and I was sad for him. Despite how I felt, I did not know how to express it. He was drinking steadily, but not enough to notice any real difference in his behavior – nothing that would affect his work schedule. He seemed to always hold his alcohol consumption to times when he was around me, and he would often appear relaxed and jovial.

My father was working a lot of hours at his security job, so I would not see him that often since he was asleep when I got home from school. Other times he would come home from drinking and go right to bed and catch some sleep before he went to work. One time he did not come home for a couple days. I didn't know where he was until my sister came over to tell me he had been in touch with her. He was in Las Vegas for those few days – no explanation and no contact with the family. After, he did not go to Vegas again, or at least, not that I know of.

It took me a long time to understand the choices my father made. He was left with picking up the pieces after the divorce. I felt angry and sad he sabotaged our family, his marriage and his career. I was mad he was being stubborn and not getting the help he needed to stop drinking and gambling. My mother tried to get him to counseling of some kind, but it seemed it was always a joke to him. He'd say, "Your mother would always try to get us to go to counselling together. I would agree to go for her but did not see the reason."

I flashed back to an earlier memory several years before, sitting in the reception area at a psychologist's office, waiting for my parents to come out.

Another time, my mother asked me if I would agree to family counselling if we all went, but it never happened.

It was my father's way of dealing with pain to hide it inside. During the events leading up to their divorce, my mother once said to me, "Your father always felt like he was the black sheep of the family, at least in the eyes of his father." I learned, regardless of this, his father always bailed him out whenever he got into a jam. This time, though, my father dug himself too deep, and his father said he would not help.

I felt there was nothing I could do. I just kept giving it to God the best way I knew how and praying for strength to find the answers. I tried to be supportive.

Where once my father had taken a lot of pride in acting and public performance, those days slowly ended. The last play he did was a couple of years before my parents divorced. I took Sue E. with me, and the play was sad because it reflected what he was going through at the time. It was about a middle age man who was experiencing a setback in his business while going through a divorce. I remember feeling a pain and a bit of embarrassment to watch him portray something so close to his own reality.

While I was living with my father, I started to go to a Baptist church a few blocks away from our house. I didn't have the use of a car very much at the time, so getting to Calvary Chapel and Shekinah, I had to be creative. I thought the Lord would want me to go to the Baptist church and mentor some of the youth around my age. I wanted to share my experiences about the Baptism of the Holy Spirit. I did get a chance to share with some of them and even got them to come to Shekinah Fellowship.

Besides going to the Baptist church and Shekinah, I would often spend time on Sundays watching Oral Roberts and Kathryn Kuhlman on television, still fascinated with their ministry. I loved their sermons and felt a kind of glow when I heard them preach.

Sometimes I would spend the night at my mother's apartment. When I did, she let me drive her 1966 Mustang to church and to see friends. As for my mother, she was making progress on her own path and going to AA meetings. My dad acted like there was nothing wrong and dealt with his pain in his own way.

Moving In With Mom

Sometime late in my junior year, my mother started dating a man named Bruce, whom she'd met at AA meetings. I saw him a few times when I was visiting my mother, and he seemed like a nice guy. After she broke off her relationship with Weiss, it was still hard to get used to the idea of my mother seeing another man besides my father. After the divorce, she had lost weight and she looked good. She was always attractive even at the age of fifty. Funny what you think is old when you're in your teens.

My mother's new boyfriend, Bruce, reminded me of the actor Jack Nicholson because of his witty sarcasm and mannerisms. I liked him well enough at first, and I was getting used to seeing my mother dating someone other than my dad. However, one early evening Bruce came over to my house when I was alone. That was a red flag for me. Something was not right with this man. I did not know how to react because I was taken aback by the way he was acting. I acted friendly but was scared inside, wondering what he was up to.

His eyes were glazed. He pushed his way into the house, not saying anything to me, and went into the back yard near the stalls, and started talking to the horses. I called my mother on the phone and asked her what to do. She told me to make him some coffee and she would be over.

While I waited, Bruce tried to make friends with the horses as he staggered around, leaning over the railing calling out to them. He said he came over to get permission from me to marry my mother because she was a really good-looking woman and special to him. I didn't say anything back to him. I was thinking, "Like I really have anything to say in the situation."

I continued to keep my mouth shut. I went ahead and made the coffee, wishing he would just go away. I was scared for my mother, thinking, "What did mom get herself into?" Bruce kept calling out to the horses, saying to them in a slurred voice, "I wannamarry your mutherrr." I gave him some coffee and he waved the cup in the air, spilling it on himself. I thought he burned himself, but he didn't seem to notice.

He staggered and said, "I wannamarry your mutherrr, and yurrnot gunna stomme."

I stammered but found the nerve to reply. "I don't know if she wants to get married." My mother arrived in the back yard and spotted Bruce leaning over the railing with the cup of coffee calling for the horse to come to him. My mother teased him about talking to the horses to sidetrack him.

"I cammmehere to asssk your sssson if youwannamarry mmme" he said.

My mother seemed embarrassed and simply said, "We'll talk about this later. Let's take you back."

Bruce kept talking to the horses, waving his coffee cup in the air, while my mother did her best to manage him. Finally, she coaxed him away and got him into her car. As they drove away, I heaved a sigh of relief. I hoped it was the last I'd seen of Bruce. My wish was not meant to be, and that evening foreshadowed a tough time ahead.

At the end of my junior year in high school, my father had a new girl-friend named Jessica. He'd met her in a bar, though he had known her years before. It wasn't long before they began talking about living together. I did not want to live with my father if his new girlfriend was there. They seemed like nothing more than drinking companions every time I saw them together.

My mother was a little more settled by then, I thought. She had her own apartment and she was building a new career for herself. She had been involved with AA meetings for a few years and was doing some counseling work on her own on the side as well. She was in the process of building a non-profit organization called "Mariposa." It was a counselling center for women struggling with alcoholism.

She offered to let me to move in with her, and I was glad to take her up on it. It meant I could finish my senior year at the same school, but I wouldn't have to deal with my dad and his new girlfriend. I didn't know then her boyfriend Bruce was part of the package, and I was walking into the same situation I was trying to get out of. When I discovered the truth, I did not say anything about it to my mother. Still I was disappointed.

Bruce was both friendly and at the same time overpowering to me. I did my best to remain neutral and stay calm. It was not until he started to drink and would get belligerent, I saw his dark side.

This was an aspect of alcohol I hadn't seen before. My parents gave the illusion of being the "happy couple" when they drank, and they were jolly. I didn't know then that it was the alcohol numbing them, masking some of the issues of their marriage. Their drinking kept them together far longer than if they'd been sober. I suppose my mother felt it was her mission at the time to bring Bruce to sobriety. She herself was not drinking, and she wanted to share the good thing she'd found. But Bruce's salvation was not meant to be.

Bruce went on a drinking binge for several weeks one time, and I shut myself in my bedroom as much as possible to avoid him. My mother did not know what to do since she went to work every day. During this drinking episode I came down with the flu. It was during Christmas break from school.

My mother stayed home that day and apologized for the situation. She said she was sorry this was happening, and she did not expect this. She tried to tell me to just shut out what Bruce said. She told me it was part of his illness from drinking.

I felt feverish and foggy, and I had a hard time understanding what she meant. I was trying to process what she was saying to me when Bruce barged into the room, swinging the door wide open. He stumbled, knocking a few items off my bookshelf. He was only wearing his bathrobe, which was untied. It kept coming undone, revealing his nakedness.

He said something about me, about how I just acted like my father by being silent. I was sitting up with my back leaning on the wall, feeling the body aches from the flu. Bruce sat on my bed and stared into my eyes, shouting and slurring his words. "Ssspeak tommme. Ssspeak tommme! You'rrrre jussslike your fatherrr."

My mother was standing behind him, telling me, "Shut it off. Don't pay him any attention. Just ignore what he says."

Again, he said, "Youdonnn't sssayanything! Ssspeak tommme! Sspeak tommme! You're jussslike you'rrre fatherrr. Youdonnn't sssayanything! Ssspeak!"

I responded with a smart remark. "Bow wow."

He paused for a moment, staring into my eyes, hate swimming in his glassy pupils. Then he lunged forward and started to choke me with one hand. I felt paralyzed, and I thought to myself, "This is it, Jesus. I'm done."

"Bruce!" my mother shouted. He released his grip, it seemed in slow motion. He got up and stumbled out of the room. My mother apologized to me and followed him out. I sat there stunned, my head swimming. I could still feel his chokehold on my throat, disbelieving what had just transpired.

It all happened so fast. He didn't bother me during the next couple days I was home in bed. It would be years before I really understood him and the source of his own pain.

Bruce was very sociable and witty when he was sober, but the underlying tension and anxiety were not easy to deal with. As I watched him interact with people, so seemingly normal, I would always wonder about the next time he would start to drink.

He had a way of building people up when he was sober, but when he drank, he betrayed us with his words. He would talk about the future and about the great things we would do together.

He would give the impression he had money and some real-estate investments in Newport Beach. He'd say we were going to move into one of his beachfront properties on Balboa Island. He would say all kinds of grandiose things, but he never followed through with them. Even worse, he would blindside me with insults, tear me down and tell me I didn't deserve his generosity.

He saw me once in one of my plays at school and was impressed with my performance. He made several promises to me about helping me go to a theater arts college. Then during one of his drinking binges he tore me down, saying I did not have any talent and would not be any good as an actor. I felt hurt about it for a long time. His words lingered and ate away at my belief in myself.

Later I asked my mother about the property he said we were going to move into. She told me it was complicated, and the future was uncertain. She confided in me she thought this was one of the reasons he drank. He did not know how to deal with it when his plans were not turning out right for him. So instead of admitting or explaining what was really going on with his finances, he would drink and try to tear down anyone in his way.

My father gave me the family baby grand piano while I lived with him. After some time, I sold it, hoping to use the money to buy a car. I needed some wheels, so I could drive to school since I lived outside the school district. Bruce did help me with this, and he managed to get me a car with some of that money. I think it was Bruce's way of apologizing and trying to be a friend.

It was nice to have wheels again. Besides driving to school, I was able to get a part time job at a flower shop in Corona del Mar. I made deliveries, learned how to do basic flower design and run the shop when they needed me to.

The job kept me from going home right after school, which meant I could avoid Bruce as much as possible. Since Bruce would often come home early, I was constantly anxious, never knowing if he would come home drunk. I tried to time it so my mother would get home first. This meant I could avoid a confrontation or an actual scene.

I watched my mother go through many more of Bruce's drinking binges and finally paid the cost to get him treatment. As I watched her struggle through his many drunken episodes, I wondered what she could possibly see in him. In time I came to have sympathy for his pain, but there were many tests along the way.

CHAPTER 4:

PARTING OF THE CLOUDS

During my senior year, my part time job at the flower shop gave me a chance to see some really nice homes in Corona del Mar and Newport Beach. They were owned by some prestigious local business owners and celebrities who lived in the area. This showed me a side of life I had never seen before. Even with my parents' occasional brush with show business and appearance of being secure middle class, I hadn't encountered this kind of glamour in my young life other than those short trips in Beverly Hills to my great Aunt Phyllis' home.

The flower shop was run by a woman named Ruth, a nice older lady in her early sixties. She had partnered with a gay man, Chad, who was in his mid-thirties. They moved from the East Coast and were living together and sharing expenses. At first, I didn't know he was gay, but I read between the lines real fast.

Chad was very nice to me. I thought he was funny, and I liked him right off. Among other things, he was a flashy dresser with polished mannerisms and an air of sophistication. Ruth often confided in me about Chad when he was not in the shop. She would tell me about some of the problems they had with his spending habits and his boyfriends.

Ruth told me Chad was married once, how she became friends with Chad, and helped him start all over again. Ruth knew I was a nice Christian boy. I shared a little with her about my faith whenever she asked questions. She would ask me to pray for wisdom and strength for her to help Chad.

Like Ruth, Chad confided in me when we were alone making flower arrangements. I would listen to him and he would share his frustrations about his love life. He shared some of his letters from a boyfriend he was struggling with, and I would feel bad for him he was a man looking for love. I would sometimes fantasize if Chad came on to me what would I do. Would I be able to resist the temptation of seduction from an older man? I prayed that this would not happen.

From time to time, Chad would ask me to pray for him since he knew I was a Christian. Then one day Chad said something I didn't understand. He told me not to be concerned or afraid of him. I wondered what he meant by that.

We would often make jokes about different customers, and he liked my dry humor. It made him laugh. Chad also told me when some of his gay business associates would come by. He warned me to stay away from the mortician up the street when he came into the shop. I would usually go into the walk-in refrigerator during my shift to arrange the flowers when a new shipment came in.

When the mortician came to the shop, it was my cue to go into the refrigerator to avoid him. The mortician would often glance at me through the window while I was in the refrigerator. Sometimes he'd walk by the refrigerator and look in while he was talking to Chad, and he'd smile at me. I would look up and smile back, then continued with my work.

I did have to deliver some flowers once at the morgue up the street from the flower shop, and I felt nervous about that. The mortician stared at me and told me to set the spray of flowers on the open casket in the next room. I did as he asked and left in a hurry. I told Chad about it, and he just laughed – said I was lucky.

Every now and then, Ruth and Chad got into squabbles about customers or money issues, and Chad would throw a tantrum. I often saw them both working on a floral design together then get into one of their squabbles. Out of frustration, Chad would tear up the flower design and walk away, asking me to clean up the mess. Ruth would then salvage the remains to add to the floral design she was working on.

Though I didn't laugh outward, their antics made me think of a TV sitcom. I wondered how they'd managed to remain together for so long.

I didn't work at the flower shop long, but I did have the honor to be invited to Chad's formal birthday dinner party. He and Ruth hosted it at their condo in Irvine, and I brought my friend Melissa T. It was a very elaborate sit-down affair with several courses and flower arrangements tastefully adorning every piece of furniture.

The highlight of the evening was when Chad made a colorful grand entrance down the staircase and went over to the organ to play. Everyone sipped champagne as they watched. He was an animated host and made us all feel welcome and appreciated.

A Clique Of Our Own

My job at the flower shop wasn't my only escape from the touchy confrontations of my home life. Just before my senior year of high school I started to become friends with a guy named Scott. I considered him to be a genuine and humble person, one who was hungry for the things of the Lord.

We ended up going to Shekinah together along with Meg and the rest of our crowd. His zeal and concern for others to serve the Lord would get dogmatic at times. He could not understand there were more sincere and mature Christians who wanted to serve the Lord first. Others felt he would get down on them for not being a more genuine Christian. The atmosphere would get tense at times, but everyone saw how zealous Scott was and we tried to understand him. Scott and I became good friends, and he helped me stay in check with our Christian beliefs.

I was surprised one day during my senior year when I saw Kevin Baker at my high school for a short time. He showed up in my gym class, but he was absent a lot. We talked very little. He did tell me he was going to move to Long Beach to be more involved in the ministry with his brother, Brant. I asked whether or not he was going to finish school, but he did not respond to my question and acted like he did not hear me.

It was somewhere in my senior year Meg told me she was moving to Long Beach to be involved with the ministry. She said it was too hard for her to stay at home any longer with her father, and the Lord had opened a door to move in with someone. I asked if she was going to finish school since she was a year behind me. She said, "Jesus is coming too soon for that." I saw her point and accepted it. In fact, I felt bad I was missing out on something myself. I would miss her since we had been through a lot of things together in the last couple years.

Listening to Kevin and Meg added to my own feelings of being lost and lacking direction. I didn't know what I was going to do after I graduated. I was thinking about going to Orange Coast College in Costa Mesa, but I didn't want to remain at home. The thought of joining the military crossed my mind. I also considered going into the ministry. Shekinah was having an effect on me, inspiring me to minister for Jesus since He was coming so soon. All of these things pressed on me, and I pondered what to do.

During Saturday and Wednesday meetings, Brant would talk about the great revival and healing meetings with the founder of the Foursquare Church, Aimee Semple McPherson. The meetings were held at the historic Angeles Temple in Los Angeles. She was known for her great healing services from the 1920's up to her controversial death in 1944.

Brant read from her biography, "This Is That". He said God was preparing us to do the same type of work if we were willing to serve Him. I was starting to get to know more of the different people at Shekinah meetings at the Seventh Street location. I wanted to become part of what was taking place, to get more involved. I understood why Meg wanted to move to Long Beach and wanted to become involved in the ministry. It seemed like a loving environment to be in and accepted.

Brant Steps Out In Faith

While still in my late high school years, those early Wednesday and Saturday services were a loose structure of singing and worship, which was always a large part of the services. The songs were led by Randy. playing the guitar and Joe. on the upright piano. Brant and a couple other elders sat on stools on the small stage, singing along with everyone else.

We would sing the traditional Calvary Chapel songs, sometimes giving a different rendition of the song or adding some hand movements to make it fun and energetic. After about thirty minutes of this, Randy or someone else would sing a solo or duet. There would be some general announcements, and an offering was given with no big push on giving money. There was some more singing while the offering went around. Brant would put on his lavaliere microphone and sing another song.

At some point Brant would sing the old gospel hymn "Great Is They Faithfulness" just before he started to teach. This eventually became his theme song. Once he sang it, he opened up his well-marked-up Scofield Bible with its crafted leather book cover. He set out his notes, read a scripture and went into his preaching and teaching style. He was able to combine both sincerity and humor, which kept everyone laughing the whole time.

Brant had tailor-made shirts for his sermons and would wear them each Wednesday and Saturday. They had puffy sleeves and a bib front which would button up to his neck. The patterns were all the same with different pastel colors and sometimes a simple print design, which looked something like a peasant shirt. They reminded me something I saw Davey Jones wear with his band The Monkees in the mid 1960's. This fashion statement was unusual, and at first it was odd to look at, but I took it as his flamboyant way.

A couple other singers would join with Randy during the worship songs. A young gifted Canadian musician named, Lilly, would play the guitar. She had her own style of Christian contemporary music that blended well into the Shekinah Fellowship group. She and Randy were soon joined by another young musician, Kelly. He played the guitar and was a good vocalist, and all three of them would lead the worship, singing.

In those early Bible studies and worship services, there was a sincerity and purity of presence we all felt. Towards the end of the Bible Study we would sing some more songs, the lights would dim low and Brant would start to use the "Word of Knowledge" by calling out different symptoms of sickness.

This practice started back when we met in the Bethany Chapel church which was behind the storefront of the future Shekinah Fellowship meeting hall. Brant explained once he felt the Lord was telling him he would start to use the Word of Knowledge when he was in his backyard at home in Long Beach. While in the backyard, he felt impressed and received insight about a young lady who was experiencing some sickness. He knew the symptoms and he received an impression of the woman who was going to be at his Saturday Bible Study at Bethany Chapel.

This was a turning point for him, stepping out in faith to exercise his spiritual gift. When he came to the end of the Bible Study that Saturday, he called out the Word of Knowledge that was given to him about this woman who fit the description. She came forward later and testified. From there, Brant exercised more of the Word of Knowledge, going sometimes into great description about a different person each Saturday.

It wasn't long before Shekinah moved from Bethany Chapel around the corner into what we now called Little Shekinah, and the Saturday meetings continued to expand. The location was a former gym in a small strip mall, sandwiched between a drugstore, cafe and a liquor store. The gym was remodeled to turn it into a chapel with stained glass tiffany lamps hanging from the ceiling. The facility had a small office as well.

After the Saturday Bible Study, there was a separate afterglow service. This was a time when a group of people who wanted to stay longer would wait for the presence of the Holy Spirit to be manifested. The group would move in a less structured way.

Before the afterglow service started, a description was given about what to expect. First, we sang as a group. Small percussion instruments – triangles, bells and wood blocks – were passed out to those who wanted them. Joe or someone else would be at the piano as well. The song leader would start a worship song while people sang together, followed with a period of silence. We had the freedom to pray for someone and speak a word aloud to them. With no cue given, someone would start a simple rhythm with one of the percussion instruments or a piano chord was played.

One by one we start to sing again by singing in tongues, which others started to follow and harmonize as different languages were sung with the instruments. The music combined with singing in tongues made a dramatic and divine effect. This mystical sound continued for awhile until it reached a crescendo. Then a reverse effect would take over, with the different voices starting to fade. The instruments became hushed until all faded into silence.

Different people would give words of prophecy, words of encouragement that sometimes sounded like an Old Testament Psalm, an old English, or modern dialect. The words uttered testified about the Lord's love for us and how pleased He is with us. They said we have been called to worship Him, and they gave all types of testimony.

Then one by one, people would start to get up and go to others in the room and pray for them. They would whisper a word of personal prophecy, which was an encouragement. There would be laying on of hands, praying for each other, and sometimes healing would take place before our eyes.

These afterglow meetings seemed to be the foundation and training ground of the early ministry, using the spiritual gifts as we understood them. They would often last for hours. Later, this training would be further utilized on a larger scale that got us ready for the Saturday healing services when the congregation grew.

Brant got his inspiration from going to Kathryn Kuhlman's services, observing how the different workers in her services operated. They were going into the congregation and pulling people out of their seats to further pray with them if they needed it. They would send them up front to the stage area, to the testimony line.

We knew what we were doing was special. We didn't know where it would lead, but we could feel a tremendous rush of energy in these afterglow meetings. We were passionate about the Holy Spirit. We were excited to spread the word and have others join us.

Transition to the Foursquare Church

During 1972, the Saturday meetings grew every week. Scott. and I saw a new development take place every time we attended. Eventually the meetings moved to the Foursquare Church on 11th and Junipero.

The pastor of the Foursquare Church was Billy Adams. Since Claudia W. knew Pastor Adams from childhood, it was her who opened the door for Shekinah to move in and use their church. When this move took place, it was becoming clearer the ministry was modeling even more after Kathryn Kuhlman's healing services. It was understood and accepted by most in the ministry, since Kathryn was one of Brant's favorite role models. She was the voice of experience for him, which appealed to his creative and colorful nature. It made sense to me and others since she was one of our spiritual mentors, besides Jesus. Brant continued to share the stories of Amie Semple McPherson with us for further inspiration.

Women and ushers were part of the afterglow services. Now they were ready to make their debut in the Saturday services held at the Four-Square Church. At first Brant prompted just a few of the elders' wives to work in the congregation, to circulate and assist individuals during the healing services. Others were added in time.

The workers were looking for a feeling or prompting to go to someone who was receiving some type of healing touch from the Lord. They would get further prayer or a word of inspiration. These workers became known as "Word of Knowledge workers."

The changes were taking place seemed to be happening quicker when the ministry moved to the Foursquare Church. The large church auditorium was oval in shape, built sometime in the late 30's or 40's. The hall was erected after the Angeles Temple was built in Los Angeles, where Amie McPherson held her great revival meetings.

Compared to the small storefront space, this was a major transition. In order to give the appearance of a smaller space and keep everyone from spreading out all over the auditorium, temporary partitions were put up in the middle of the auditorium. It gave more of an intimate look, so Brant would not have to look at all the empty seats. But as the meetings started to grow over time, the partitions were pushed farther back. Eventually we filled the space completely.

The services were never like the typical healing services you would find in a Pentecostal church at this time. The music in those Pentecostal services had a fast beat along with banging on the tambourine. People would shout out praises to the Lord, clapping and stamping their feet, raising their hands into the air, shouting, "Thank you, Jesus!" This certainly was not allowed in Kathryn Kuhlman's services.

However, this type of demonstration of the moving of the spirit was allowed in the smaller afterglow services when we ask the Holy Spirit to move through us. A wave of emotions washed over us, with speaking and singing in tongues following a word of prophecy and encouragement.

In the healing services, if someone would start to show an emotional outburst of speaking in tongues or shouting it was quickly squashed by Brant or an usher would rush up to the person to quiet them down or remove them. Once in awhile, Brant would let a person speak a word of prophecy. This was followed by the congregation singing melodic songs backed by the orchestra, offering a moving experience for many. Then the auditorium would become silent for a moment and a word was spoken. Brant would give a hand signal to the usher it was alright.

The Saturday services started to become more formal when we moved into the Foursquare Church. To open the services, first Randy. would solo on the guitar, then Joe. would join him on the baby grand piano. Soon a few others joined in with their instruments to make a full ensemble. During the worship part of the service, Mrs. Adams would play a large organ below the middle of the stage area.

The organ gave a dramatic touch when a healing testimony was given or after Brant prayed for someone and they were slain in the Spirit. The congregation responded by clapping, and Mrs. Adams pumped out notes on the organ like a chant.

When stage lights were added with a follow spotlight, Brant started to wear makeup. Some people were critical about him wearing makeup, but coming from a theater background, I understood. If he did not wear makeup, his face would appear ghostly white and he would look washed out.

It was not long until Randy. had a full choir behind him, and it grew under the talented choir director Terry B. Terry was an elder at the Neighborhood Foursquare Church and a busy businessman. He was tall, in his thirties, married and had two young children. He had an attractive, petite wife whose stature contrasted sharply with Terry's tall frame.

The choir started small and mushroomed to about one hundred members over the next couple of years. A small orchestra was formed as well from the members of Shekinah Fellowship. It expanded with violins, flutes, trumpets, and percussion instruments under the leadership of Joe. and David

K. The women in the choir wore shapeless pastel maxi dresses with puffy shoulder sleeves, and the guys wore pastel shirts with white ties.

At the beginning of the service, after the general announcements were made, the choir would sing. Then Randy. would come to center stage with his guitar and lead the congregation in singing a few Calvary Chapel worship songs. Joe. accompanied on the piano. His playing was now becoming more like the pianist Dino Kartsonakis at Kathryn Kuhlman's ministry. After Randy led the songs, the lights would dim, and he would sing along with the choir the chorus of "Great Is Thy Faithfulness."

As Randy left the stage, Brant took center stage wearing a lapel mic with a long chord. He continued to sing the chorus, then he made the transition into other worship songs, moving around the stage, building anticipation as the music crescendo, backed up by the orchestra. This inspired feelings that flowed through the congregation was phenomenal. For a moment we could step outside ourselves, escape all our cares and bask in the presence of a heaven.

A Flare for Worship

Over time, the music evolved into a grand spectacle. Eventually the prelude to Brant's entrance was the choir singing a short version of the Hallelujah chorus, followed by a transition into "Great Is Thy Faithfulness." Then Brant would enter and take center stage.

This choice was inspired by Kathryn Kuhlman, who also entered the stage on cue after her choir had sung "Nothing Is Impossible with God" followed by her theme song, "He Touched Me." The music heightened the anticipation and level of the energy in her auditorium. She used dramatic gestures and waltzed across the large Shrine auditorium stage in time to the music.

It was also during this period Brant's ministerial attire took on another change for the Saturday healing services. Instead of his Davy Jones peasant shirt with the button bib in the front, he wore a Renaissance peasant shirt pleated in front and back. It buttoned up the middle, and he had a matching bow tie. The shirts were mainly a white satin, and he wore black pants and black patent leather shoes.

Brant wore accessories that gave him a real sparkle under the stage lights. His belt buckle was a large shiny brass cross. He wore a small wooden cross on a gold chain around his neck and a brass wristband. On his ring finger, he wore a gold and diamond ring with a Christian fish symbol and grape cluster of stones. His attire was a male version of Miss Kuhlman's puffy sleeved chiffon dresses, gold belt, and gold lace sandals.

Brant told us the puffy sleeved shirts were cooler to wear since he perspired a lot while preaching. They also made it easier to pray for people because people tended to grab him as they fell back, and their hands would slip off his puffy sleeves. His wooden cross, ring and brass buckle had a special meaning to him with a story behind it.

Brant saw it was time to start grooming the elders and ushers, requiring them to wear a tie and jacket. The women who ministered in the services were required to wear long pastel granny dresses with a high collar. He felt presentation was important, and it showed respect for the formality of the occasion.

After Brant finished leading the congregation in worship songs, the transition was followed by a short testimony about a healing that took place during a previous service. At the close of the testimony, Brant would pray for the person, who would fall backwards. They were caught by the usher, and Brant would make a dramatic gesture saying, "Give the Lord praise!" The congregation would applaud while Mrs. Adams struck a chord on the organ. It underscored the moment and led into another congregational worship song.

After this part of the service, an offering was usually taken accompanied by another musical number. This usually featured a soloist, a music group, a piano solo or the choir would sing. Brant then made the transition, giving the message, which led into a worship song. He invoked the Word of Knowledge, calling out various healings that were taking place and giving a brief description of each one. The Word of Knowledge workers and ushers took their places for this part of the service.

At this point, Brant invited people to come forward for prayer. People formed a line up front, and Word of Knowledge workers screened them to verify what happened to them. After they gave their testimonies, people responded to an altar call and came forward to accept Jesus or rededicate their lives to the Lord. To conclude, Brant gave his closing remarks, which were followed by a closing worship song.

The Good Word Spreads Like Wildfire

During 1973, Shekinah experienced an incredible growth spurt. News was getting out about the services, not only by word of mouth, but also with broadcast advertising on different radio stations and eventually, soon after graduation, television shows. The anticipation for the Saturday healing services was intense. Some were curious, and many wanted to experience the anointing. They were intrigued, watching the ministry of these unusual teenagers and young adults.

Those of us involved with the ministry were led to believe we were special since this was part of the fulfillment of the book of Joel – that the spirit of God would be poured out among the young and they would prophesize. We felt a great surge of energy and a warm, loving spirit of God's presence within those services.

I wanted to be more involved in what was taking place. Scott and I would talk about how God could be leading us to be part of this ministry. The question was, how was this going to happen for us? It was only a matter of time before the answer came, and the tide of events overtook us.

In the months leading to my graduation, my life shifted in a new direction I could never have anticipated. What was about to happen was beyond prediction, and I awakened to an intense new life. But even before I graduated, the call of the Holy Spirit was deep and inviting in my life.

CHAPTER 5:

MY SECRET IS OUT

It was spring of my senior year, Scott, and I were going to the Saturday services as often as we could. We wanted to experience the excitement of the moving of the Spirit. When we could, we also went to the Wednesday night Bible Study held at the little Shekinah location on 7th Street.

Scott and I were starting to talk about the possibility of moving to Long Beach and getting involved with the ministry. We believed Jesus was returning real soon and wanted to be involved with this movement, bringing God's message to people.

On this particular day, Scott and I took turns at the wheel to make the drive to Long Beach. We were going to a Saturday Shekinah Fellowship service at the Foursquare Church. We were as excited as ever, and we talked about it non-stop the whole way there. Once we arrived and parked, we shuffled in along with the rest of the crowd. As excited as I was, I could not have anticipated the enormous unification that was about to happen within me.

In the middle of the service, Brant was making the transition from closing his message. He was calling out the Word of Knowledge for different people who were being healed and touched. The choir started to sing soft worship music as the congregation joined with them. I was sitting on the left side towards the front section in the auditorium.

Brant looked over to my section, and he said, "Someone is being healed of homosexuality. I have never said that before," Then he pointed at me. It seemed like a camera lens zoomed a close up of his finger right up to me as I looked back at him.

A surge of a type of electrical energy swept through my body. I started to shake and cry so intensely I could not control myself. I felt embarrassed at the same time, and I wanted to hide. Scott was speechless sitting next to me, staring.

A defining "Aha" moment flashed into my mind. I had personally renounced any sexual temptation to not involve myself with girls in a sexual way, other than just friendship, because of my Christian moral witness and the fear of getting a girl pregnant. I thought I had managed to suppress any thoughts or desires of entertaining homosexuality. These desires were there, as though I had some kind of abnormality

I felt there were two natures inside me, but I did not understand what it meant to be bisexual. I was embarrassed this was even a part of me. I never said anything to Scott before about my mutual masturbation sessions with Brad or my attraction to both girls and guys. I kept suppressing these thoughts to protect myself. I knew as a Christian I had to keep any type of sexual desires in check to guard myself. I did this out of fear of losing my relationship with Jesus.

While these thoughts rushed through my head, I kept on crying. Charlene C., who was one of the elder's wives and a Word of Knowledge worker, made her way into my row. She took my hand, inviting me to come with her to the testimony line. I did not want to go, but I went with her. She ushered me into the line where I waited as people were being called to testify of their healing.

If there ever was a time my ego wanted to be noticed, now was not the time. I did not want this to happen to me – to reveal something so private about myself for others to know in a public place. This was the early 70's, and sex was now being talked about more open than before. The American culture changed during the 60's, especially for those of us living in California. However, homosexuality was still not widely talked about in an open form, especially in evangelical Christian circles.

Now my secret was out in the open. It was fine to have Brant call out a back pain, sniffling nose, or a tumor. But to call out homosexuality was going too far, and it was awkward during the moment this was happening.

I felt like the prostitute Mary in the Bible. She was caught in adultery and waiting to be stoned by her accusers. Was I to be stoned here among my Christian peers? It sure felt like it. I did not think this needed this to be exposed about me, about being bisexual. My private thoughts were now being exposed openly – what I had been contemplating.

I was ushered up to the stage, waiting for my turn, standing behind Brant. Bill. and John C. were on the left and right of the stage in the testimony line. They were each using a microphone, summarizing to Brant what just happened to different people who were touched in some way by the Holy Spirit. Randy. and Robby W. were on the stage serving as catchers on the left and right of Brant.

Now I was on the stage, knowing I was going to be the main focus of attention at any moment, wearing a loud Hawaiian printed shirt. As I looked out towards the crowd in the church auditorium, I felt incredibly self-conscious. I wanted to get the whole thing over with and just leave.

I looked at Joe., who was sitting at the grand piano. His perfect blond hair was combed back and sprayed heavily with hairspray. What was I going to say? How was I going to explain? Suddenly it was my turn, and John C. told Brant in a brief sentence what happened – I was healed of homosexuality.

Brant looked at me in that moment as though we had some kind of connection and understanding of each other. Were we the same? My eyes took in his white satin shirt with its puffy sleeves, his bow tie, and his wooden cross with a gold chain around his neck. He wore black pants and black patent leather shoes.

The room swam around me, and only Brant stood out in high relief. I focused on one tooth at the corner of his mouth that had a small space between the other tooth while he smiled at me. He paused for what seemed like forever, just stared at me for a moment, and I smiled in response.

Then he approached me and began to pray for me, stretching out his hands. I started to fall back. I just gave in to the feeling to get the ordeal over with. Randy. caught me, and the congregation applauded. Mrs. Adams struck a crescendo chord on the organ. I was conscious but lying down. I couldn't wait to leave.

Brant immediately started to sing a worship song as I lay on the floor for a moment while the piano and organ played. Then I was helped up, and I returned to my seat. Scott. was looking over at me in disbelief with his mouth open. As others continued to testify, a couple other guys also testified about being delivered out of homosexuality.

When the service was over, Scott. was standing next to me, still in shock about what had just taken place. Though he and the others were surprised, my fears of being chastised were unfounded. I discovered there were no accusers and no stones to be thrown. I felt accepted and loved.

As we made our way out of the church, a number of people, including some of the elders, came up to me, patting me on the shoulder. Others hugged me saying, "God Bless you." Several guys said they admired my guts to go up and testify. A couple of them asked me general questions about their own gay sexual struggle, as if I had any real answers for them. All I could say was, "Read your Bible and pray and the Lord will guide you."

There was one young man named John. He was one of the other men who went forward to receive prayer for his homosexuality. He was a little taller than I, had blond hair, blue eyes and a fair baby-face complexion. We talked a little, and afterward he hugged me and thanked me for testifying. It was an exhausting day, and I was glad to be going home.

Later that evening after the service, I was spending the night at Scott's parent's house. We reflected about what took place earlier in the day. He told me he never knew about my homosexuality. He didn't know because I did not say anything about it, and I felt safer if he did not know this about me. I realized he may have suspected since I was into drama and other things gay men are typically drawn to.

I did tell him a little about my previous masturbation sessions with Brad, Scott didn't seem bothered by it. He said he thought whatever spirit was bothering me left. Whether or not it was a spirit, I don't know, but I accepted his answer. I was aware in a fuzzy way I was attracted to the same gender and felt guilty about it. I was ashamed, and I dared not share it with anyone. I figured it was my personal cross to bear, but now part of my secret was out after that night from the service.

Yet at the same time, I felt I was accepted and loved by those at Shekinah Fellowship. I was a Christian, and as a Christian, I thought I should not have this inside me. Yet as I was experiencing these feelings of being attracted to my sex, I tried to ignore those feelings. I had limited understanding of just what it meant to be gay. If being bisexual was a part of my nature, I figured it was part of my creative nature. I would have to learn how to use it for the good.

That night, as Scott and I talked, I reflected on how I would find out if I really did receive a type of healing at the service. I felt I would be tested in some way.

Making Our Move

The healing service brought a change in me, and it was a clear line of demarcation. I felt differently – both accepted within Shekinah and loved by the Lord. I wasn't the only one who felt this kinship.

My friend Scott was really hooked on Shekinah. He talked more seriously about moving to Long Beach to get involved with the ministry. He wanted me to go with him. We would talk about it for hours, about how God was going to use us in some way in this great work of His before Jesus came.

It all came about suddenly, and we decided to move shortly after we graduated high school. Several people in the ministry were encouraging me to move to Long Beach as well.

I was planning to go to Orange Coast College, and the next thing I knew, we moved within the month. This changed my plans considerably. Moving was also my way to get out of the apartment, away from Bruce.

Details came together quickly, and we dealt with them as the need arose. I told Ruth and Chad at the flower shop about my moving. They wished me good luck, and I managed to find them an assistant to replace me.

My car broke down and could not make the move, so I did what I could to find another one. Scott's parents gave him a car, and we found a large one-bedroom apartment for $100 a month. I told my mother about it, and she accepted the idea without resistance. She loaned me her car so I could move my stuff. This helped make for a smooth transition.

Scott and I were trying to talk another friend of ours into moving with us, but he decided not to. We were ready for God to do His great work since we made this move. So instead of going off to college and moving into a dorm or going off to join the military, I joined God's forces in the ministry. I wanted to be like a missionary in Long Beach, feeling great anticipation the return of Christ would happen any time.

When Scott and I moved into our apartment, there was a real sense of adventure and wonderment of what was going to happen next. I slept in the front of the apartment, and Scott took the back bedroom. He landed a job right away at the local McDonald's. I was getting odd jobs here and there, helping around the church with whatever needed to be done. I was there quite a bit, and people took a liking to me.

The move was hard and an exciting adjustment being on our own, but we had the faith and zeal knowing this is what we needed to do for God. Scott and I didn't know what to expect from moving to Long Beach, other than we wanted to be part of what was going on. We wanted to become ministers. Also, we both felt drawn to the adventure, to be on our own.

Almost everything in our home was secondhand, and even feeding ourselves was something of an adventure. We had to get a refrigerator, and my mother helped me with some cash to buy one at a thrift store. Since I had more experience with cooking, we agreed I would do some kind of menu planning.

There was not much to work with. Oatmeal, eggs, Velveeta cheese, bread and tuna fish made up our main menu. I did know how to roast a turkey, so I would make different meals from the leftovers. We had enough money to come up with the rent and utilities. The rest we needed came in spurts as I worked different odd jobs. There were a number of times I went dumpster diving to find food that was tossed. I found a few edible things like fruits, vegetables and some dairy products. Once a bag lady hit me with her cane. She thought I was taking her share out of the dumpster.

Despite the fact funds were low, Scott and I got along overall. He was long winded, and he would talk for hours into the night sometimes. He would expound on what he was learning, like what he was reading from the Bible and Bible commentary. Scott worked a lot of hours at McDonald's, and he was often tired. I worked around the church, and we agreed it would be best if I would continue to work different odd jobs, whatever I could get. I felt bad he had to work there, and neither of us were happy with our low-level jobs. Despite the dues we had to pay, there were many things to distract us from the drudgery, and we were fulfilling our dream.

Friends and Romances

It was during this time I casually noticed a girl named Brigid, and her older sister Mary at the Little Shekinah location. Brigid and I would make small talk before and after the service. I always seemed to make her laugh for some reason. I thought it might be due to my own awkwardness or both of ours.

Brigid went to the same high school in Long Beach as David K. and Bob L., friends and members of the ministry orchestra. They had some other school friends as well who were part of the orchestra who hung out with each other. We were all in the same age group.

David K. looked and acted more mature than the others. He had shoulder length hair and a full beard, though I still barely had any facial hair myself. He was an articulate, artistic intellectual type. I thought Brigid, Mary and the rest of that group were very musically talented, since they all played an instrument or sang. It was kind of intimidating to me. Some of them had already started college, and they worked part time while coming to the ministry.

David and Mary were encouraging Brigid and me to connect with each other. The relationship felt like it was pushed on me, and I was uncomfortable with it. I had just moved out on my own with Scott, and I was not ready to think of any kind of relationship with a girl beyond friendship.

During this time a lot of romantic relationships were starting to form between the Christian brothers and sisters of the ministry. Every couple weeks it seemed there was a new engagement announcement. Brigid and I entertained the thought the Lord had put us together for the work of the ministry, and every now and then we would laugh about it.

I did not see her much, other than at church and a couple potlucks at the nearby park. She was in college, studying music and working part time. I related to her love of music and opera. She reminded me of my friend from childhood, Melissa T. In reality, that's about all we had in common and the relationship never took root.

Shekinah had its first TV taping at the new TBN studio in Tustin when we first moved to Long Beach. The studio was not far from where I used to live with my father and sister during my junior year of high school just after my parents' divorce. It was a small studio, converted from office space. We did not have an elaborate set then, just a dull background with a coffee table and some chairs. We brought in bales of hay and Christmas trees to give the set more character.

This was during the early years of Paul and Jan Crouch's ministry, when they were still launching their new television station. Paul and Jan were a vibrant couple in their late thirties or early forties. In time, Jan would wear more colored wigs, hair extensions and extra makeup. I could never figure out in the early days if Paul was wearing a white wig since his hair always seemed perfect. For now, they were working hard at crafting their show and image.

One day I popped in to see what was taking place, and we toured the studio. I remember seeing Jim Bakker, who also was in his early thirties at the time. He just looked up at me and smiled then continued with his work.

Jim and Tammy Bakker partnered with Paul and Jan in the early days of TBN. Later they broke off and moved to Charlotte, North Carolina to start their own show, The PTL Club. These two couples where well on their way to becoming giants, breaking new ground in the Christian television arena as Televangelists.

The Shekinah taping was made into four separate interview shows, giving a testimony, song and message from Brant. Later that year, after using the TBN studio, the TV tapings moved to another studio located in Glendale across from the famous Forest Lawn Cemetery.

Shekinah Summer Camp 1973

That summer Shekinah had its first camp, and it started within a month after Scott and I moved to Long Beach. I had already secured my spot, paid for half in cash and got a scholarship for the other half. Scott was working at

McDonald's, and he only managed to come up for a few days. My friend Sue O. from high school came to the camp as well.

It was so great to be among the whole Shekinah group in the mountains of Big Bear. The rustic cabins were dorm rooms with three sections. Each section had three bunk beds, and the center room had two sets of bunk beds. There was no heat, electricity, bathrooms and glass windows. They just had windows with shutters that opened up to let in the light and air.

Each cluster of cabins had a separate building for bathrooms that included showers and toilets in them. The cabins were just used in the spring and summer months. The winter snow meant the cabins were only practical to use during the warmest part of the year.

Every morning we were greeted with a small orchestra of cymbals, trumpet, flute and other instruments. Several people sang "Rise & Shine," a fun, upbeat, spirited song. They would parade around each cabin area, waking people up with a joyful noise. Joe., who was obviously gifted in teaching and communication skills, could mesmerize just about anyone with his deep masculine voice.

It didn't take long for us to settle into a routine at camp. Sue O. and I would hang out together, and with others. The week was full of daily Bible studies from all the elders. Some of the Bible studies were better than others, depending on the different teaching styles. Mealtimes were like a large feast, with everyone gathering to sing before we started to eat.

Brant and the elders would sit at the head table, and one of them would say a prayer before we all dug in. There were announcements and sometimes a funny story mixed with some joking around, and everyone would laugh and enjoy the humor of the moment.

We had a group camp picture taken that year. We all gathered around a small outdoor amphitheater with a campfire area. Brant was front and center, holding his Bible and wearing his wooden cross. The rest of the Bakker family was next to him. I was sitting behind Brant in the shot. Everyone looked so happy and full of optimism, ready to take on the world with the mission that was given to us.

One of the big events that week was the wedding of Marla and Randy. Many people helped Brant with the flower arrangements and display. My flower arrangement experience came in handy, and I got to assist Brant. It was a fun day, and we were busy putting this event together.

The wedding was in an open meadow, and we put up poles connected with different colors of ribbons. Everyone stood in the center, leaving an aisle in the middle for the bride and bridesmaids to enter. The music group members sang a couple songs, and Brant performed the ceremony. Afterwards we all went up to the dining area and had a reception to celebrate the event.

Towards the end of the week, we had an afterglow event following the evening Bible Study. A few of the elders each shared a short message to prepare us for what lay ahead. They reminded us we were all in the mountains having this great retreat experience. We were surrounded with harmony, love and great teachings, protected in this haven experience from the outside world.

Soon we were going to leave this safe mountaintop experience and go forward with the work of the ministry. They told us to be on our guard as we came off the mountain, not to be tempted by the world. They warned us not to get dragged down when we faced our responsibilities again – told us to get ready for the work of ministering.

Brant had been reading to us throughout the week from sections of the book by Aimee Semple McPherson. The messages were from the different revival healing services she recorded. This was inspiring to all of us, as he was preparing us for a greater potential, he felt we were going to encounter. He confirmed we are moving forward to do more outreach and healing services. His desire was for people to see Jesus and His miracles of healing take place with the moving of the Holy Spirit.

My heart wanted this to be, and I know many others wanted the same thing. We knew it was going to be a great movement of God's holy spirit, and we felt special to be picked for this assignment during this time. I could sense the anticipation and excitement to be part of this message on the last day.

We were all so young to be taking on the world. Conducting these types of services would be part of the outpouring until the rapture of the church would take place and Jesus would return. We were different, unique and peculiar people. Others would want to come and see us and be part of this event of God's healing power.

Before the afterglow service that evening, we had a communion ceremony. We went around the room and served portions of bread and grape juice to each other. There was an emotional presence of the Holy Spirit and love felt throughout the room.

We then went into the afterglow service, singing in English at first. This transitioned into singing in tongues, with harmonies blending together as one voice. It reached a peak and tapered off to a silence for a few moments, then started up again. Some spoke a word of prophecy, tying together the messages we had been hearing from the elders.

They sang about ministering and reaching out to the lost world, telling others about Jesus. There where prophetic words of encouragement – about how the ministry would touch many – and also words of warning not to fall into the devil, flesh and temptation.

Brant was the first one to speak, telling us about a vision he had. It had to do with ministering to many people. There was silence, then we sang, followed once again with silence. Brant wanted to end by leading us in silence back to our cabins. He wanted the events of the week leading up to this last service to sink in as we prepared to come off the mountain experience. It was effective and soul stirring.

I was changed by my experience at the camp that summer, and I felt I was ready for my next obligations to the Lord.

Summer's End

After our retreat, life at the Fellowship resumed a steady rhythm. One week there was a weeklong Bible school with the elders and Brant. We all seemed to share the same vision of ministering for the Lord in whatever capacity was needed. The worship music and anointing from the song leaders always lifted our spirits. I was glad to be part of it.

I was doing even more volunteer work than before. I was cleaning things up at the church during the day and running errands as needed. Some of my jobs consisted of sweeping the parking lot, picking up trash and cigarette butts, setting up chairs, ushering at night, and helping to direct parking at night, both alone and with the other deacons.

I remember I got the idea to go door to door in the neighborhood and ask for odd jobs. I talked to one Christian sister named Debbie., and she agreed to go with me as I canvased for work. She would tell people we were part of a church ministry, looking for any type of household or gardening work. We looked clean and honest, but this must have looked strange to some, judging by the looks they gave us. We knocked on a number of doors until we lined up enough work to carry us through.

I spent a good part of my time reading my Bible and some commentaries while going over notes. The ministry had the whole Chuck Smith library on tape, kept at the 7th Street location. To me that was worth its weight in gold – getting to listen to all those tapes, checking them out two at a time.

This reminded me of an early time when I was in high school. I would listen to tapes and read my Bible at a Christian commune called the Mansion Messiah. It was not far from my house off of Newport Beach Blvd. when I lived on Tustin Street before my parents' divorce.

My brother, sister-in-law and middle sister first brought me there. The commune was under the guidance of Calvary Chapel, one of several they ran. They were all young hippies in a discipleship program, getting on their feet, living for Jesus. They would have Bible studies there and potluck dinners. I remember bringing Brad. and several other friends as we went to the potlucks.

It was a great time to experience brotherly Christian love and a genuine caring and acceptance from each other. This was what I'd hope to experience more of by moving to Long Beach and volunteering at the Fellowship.

Brant's first assistant was Linda T. They met back when Brant went to Calvary Chapel. She was a young woman… we were all young. When Claudia W. started to come in the early stages of the ministry, she worked with Linda and Brant as an assistant. Claudia was the same age as Brant. Linda ended up getting married to Joe., the elder and piano player. When she married Joe, she assumed other secretarial functions for the ministry while Claudia became Brant's personal assistant.

Claudia lived with her parents and she would give me some odd jobs, hiring me to work at her parent's house. It was Claudia's mother Trudi who made most of the long-sleeved shirts and pants for Brant. Trudi showed me all the detail that went into making those shirts with the puffy sleeves. I looked at those shirts gazing at them as though they were something sacred. I really thought they had a glow to them. I saw them like the holy robes a priest would wear in the Old Testament. They filled me with awe.

Kevin B. befriended me and talked me into helping him do some tasks around his house. He introduced me to his parents and a number of people as I would help him with errands for the church. At the time he was living with his father, Bob. Sometimes Kevin's mother Jo Ellen showed up as well.

They lived right across the street from the church on 7th Street. Before I knew it, I was doing different kinds of errands for the elders, mostly helping Claudia and doing fix-it jobs around the church. I ended up helping out with a couple dinner parties for the elders that were also business meetings, exhortations to minister for God.

I did not mind helping Kevin so much at the time. He just wanted some company around. He was kind of pushy, and he seemed to get himself worked up and stressed out over things at times. I found it kind of entertaining to watch him in action and wondered often why he acted the way he did.

Kevin seemed to get into a number of scuffles with his parents over something that would come up, but then he quickly made up with them. I also witnessed a couple blow ups between him and Brant. I just stay out of the way when those encounters happened. I acted like I was not even there.

I remember one of those incidents occurred at Kevin's house during a visit from Brant and Claudia. I was outside, and the next thing I knew, Kevin ran out of the house with Brant charging after him as they continued their argument. Claudia seemed to be in the middle of it, saying nothing, while I observed from the side of the house. I did not know what it was all about, and it made me concerned. Brant then stormed off up the street and Claudia followed him.

Kevin went back into the house. I entered from the back door and saw Kevin slouched in a chair, sulking. I asked him if he was alright. He mumbled, "Brant and I got in a fight." He continued to sulk, and he wanted to be left alone, so I left.

I don't know what these explosions were all about, but there seemed to be a pattern. The scuffle would happen, and then it would be all over with. Then Kevin seemed to be all lovey-dovey with his parents and brother again. It was a mystery to me.

I heard about other times when Kevin would go into one of his rages, and everyone wanted to stay out of his way. Brant shared a story once about the time he had his men's clothing store and Kevin went into a rage. He knocked over some of the apparel displays and racks of clothing. "But the Lord has worked on Kevin since, and he's gotten better," Brant said. I thought it must be hard on Kevin when his brother is the star and the center of attention.

Prior to moving to Long Beach, the ministry started to have outreach events in San Diego at Balboa Park auditorium. On Wednesday night Bible studies, Brant would read about the great revival and healing services that took place in Balboa Park under Aimee Semple McPherson ministry during her time. We would all pray with earnest anticipation to go and minister in that city, expecting God to move in the healing services that we were about to start.

Scott. and I would pack his car or get a ride with someone else down to San Diego for the services. If I had worried once about belonging or being useful, those days were long over, as I had my hands full of duties at these events.

Somehow, I ended up running the stage lights backstage since I had some theater background. Just before my first event, Brant came up to me and smiled. Then he started to talk really fast, giving me instructions on adjusting the colored lights to match the mood of the music. He would say "when this song begins, give more red then bring in the blue."

Scott ushered, as well we both worked the healing prayer lines while Randy. carefully orchestrated the traffic flow. When I would help out with the lines, sometimes it was a real balancing act. It was like an obstacle course, trying to maneuver around and avoid tripping over someone.

Claudia had me take care of the anointing oil that was being used in the prayer line. There were two small vials that once held an Avon product and were now filled with olive oil. I felt so privileged to be entrusted with these items.

I got an aerobic workout, rushing back and forth trying to keep up with the action. Brant would zig to the left and zag to the right as he laid his hands-on people. They would fall backwards, and the ushers would catch them as they fell. People would then help them to their feet. They scooted to the side as the next line of people came up to be prayed for.

Brant went back and forth again to pray for the next line of people while the choir and congregation would sing. This would last for a half hour or more, then he transitioned into hearing testimonies of healings which occurred. Many times, I almost got knocked down from the rush of people who would come through the prayer line. But this wasn't the only pressure I was feeling at the time. Soon I was getting pushed from all sides.

CHAPTER 6:

CAUGHT IN THE PRESS OF EVENTS

As I became more deeply involved with the ministry and our revivals, my social life revolved totally around my Christian brothers and sisters. By now Brigid and I had dated a couple times. There was not much of a romantic connection between us at the time. We just enjoyed each other's humor, too young to know much else. We hardly knew each other, but we both wanted what we thought God wanted.

After some prompting from David K., we thought about getting married. We believed we were supposed to get married and minister for the Lord until the rapture. I didn't really have anything to offer her at the time. I was more focused on being involved in the work of the Lord. Still I felt pressure from my peers and the elders.

Brigid appeared to be more involved with college and her job. She worked part time at her stepfather's drugstore. She remained occasionally involved with the ministry, but it wasn't her focus. The only thing we had in common was our faith. Because of the push we felt from the outside, we seriously considered becoming man and wife.

Brigid's sister Mary participated in the ministry more than Brigid did. It was obvious to me she was talented, and her sister were very smart. They were from a middle-class family, and I understood their status since I was once middle class too. I enjoyed that lifestyle before my parents' divorce, but as a young man fresh out on my own, my fortunes had changed considerably. It made me feel inferior, and I was intimidated by their lifestyle.

I really did not know what we were getting into since we were both being naïve about our relationship. I talked it over with Scott about Brigid and me – what I thought maybe the Lord might be doing. He did not say much, only commented, "Make sure it is the Lord."

Brigid and I talked about marriage, but no plans were made beyond that. Only a few people knew about us getting married which was her sister, David and Scott. David and Mary were happy for us, but Scott was more cautious. It was David K who thought prophetically "God told him" we were meant to be together.

Brigid was waiting on me to make the next move. Rumors got out about Brigid and I getting married, but nothing was ever said about when. We both just continued to be involved with what we were doing, and in time we just started to drift apart. None of us really said anything more as Brigid and I saw less of each other.

Incidents and Accidents

During that summer, Scott and I took in a roommate named Kent, who was Hispanic. He slept in our large walk-in closet off the living room. We asked our landlord about having Kent live with us, and he raised the rent an extra fifteen dollars.

The apartment owner was grumpy most of the time and uncomfortable to talk to. Kent was very zealous in the Lord. He was an usher and catcher in the ministry. He also liked street witnessing. We nicknamed him "John the

Baptist" since he went to the beach with a megaphone and would stand on his car preaching. He later married a girl named April who went to Shekinah.

Scott and I had a couple of other roommates during this time, though they didn't stay long. One was John J., and he seemed to have some kind of mental disability or brain injury. He had boundary issues, and always wanted to hug the girls longer than appropriate. He didn't stay long.

We had a very short-term roommate. This one stole our rent money. When we confronted him about it, he admitted his guilt. This strained our relations, and he moved out after that.

During this period, I was reading information on different healing evangelists – whatever I could get a hold of. At about that same time, there was a movie that came out about someone named Marjo Gortner. He was a young child evangelist, groomed by his parents, and they made a movie exposing different types of corruption in evangelism. I thought the movie was evil at the time, sent from Satan to stain the name of Christ. Later, I made the connection Shekinah was conducting services at Marjo Gortner parents' church in San Diego.

Also, during that summer of 1973, the ministry had purchased some property so all the elders could live in a communal situation and save money. The property consisted of a house and adjacent two-story apartment duplex. In the back was a garage that had been converted to a sound studio for the radio and music practice. There was also a small graphic studio in one of the rooms.

The house had several rooms added to it. One addition was a large sunken living room. Right off the living room, outside in the gated back patio area, there were stairs that led to another large rectangular room which was not finished. The staircase had a chair lift that went up the side. The room had been intended to be a large recreation room or studio of some sort.

Brant lived in the large upstairs room off the living-room. Other core elders occupied the property including newlyweds, Kelly and Lilly G. along with Jeff and Ann S.

There was a lot of work to do before everyone could move in – lots of spackling and painting. Claudia W. was busy orchestrating the project with the elders' wives. Since I had the time, I got to know everyone in the house while working there. We shared several meals together, which was a real treat. I felt honored to be in their presence.

A Messenger Arrives

There was an older single lady in her late fifties named, Loraine, who went to the Foursquare Church and worked part-time as a secretary for Pastor Billy Adams. She was kind, wise and had a great sense of humor. She had long black hair, and for some reason she reminded me of a traveling gypsy woman.

Loraine had several children. Her youngest son, Bob, was around my age. Bob was in prison – the same prison Pastor Adams was ministering to. He was later released and went on to become a minister himself.

Loraine befriended Brant and Kevin and earned their respect. I got to know her better one day when I went to Kevin's house, across the street from the Little Shekinah Church on 7th Street. I told her I wanted to be a minister. I asked her if she would be my spiritual mom and pray for me, and she agreed to it. She was one of the prayer warriors for Shekinah along with a number of other ministries she held in prayer.

Loraine seemed to be the insider when it came to information about who was considered the evangelical spiritual status quo of the time. She also worked with the Kathryn Kuhlman ministry off and on, and later with the Benny Hinn ministry.

At the time I met her, she loaned me a book of hers about a man who had a healing ministry in the late 1940's early 50's in Long Beach. His name was William Branham. He started his healing ministry after his first wife died. He saw angels in the congregation near people who were being healed.

Branham himself died at the height of his ministry in a car accident. I often wondered if it was God's way of removing him before he headed down the wrong path. I also wondered if Loraine's gift was intended to have a deeper meaning for me. Whatever her intentions, I soon found the winds of change blowing through my life again.

Attack In the Night

During this time, I was getting depressed from the stress of being on my own for the first time and having to continually look for work. It was demoralizing, constantly having to find food from the dumpster behind one of the local markets. Sometimes Scott would bring back groceries after visiting his parents on the weekend. The stress was coming out of my skin, and I was breaking out with acne and boils on my back to the point they would bleed. I wondered if I had made the right decision, but I didn't want to move back home.

Scott and I had long talks into the night over scripture and what was happening within the ministry. It was a time we reprimanded each other about our carnal nature getting in the way. We talked for hours about how we could be better ministers for Shekinah.

After these talks, I felt I was getting beaten up inside. It seemed similar to those Catholic monks who would beat themselves until they bleed to cleanse themselves. I found it interesting after having these cleansing talks, I was given more tasks to do at the church. At the time, Scott didn't have a problem with my working at the church and finding part time work as I could. He knew I was ministering at the church, which was our reason for moving there, and I was also doing the cooking and laundry. However, his feelings about this would soon change, and so too did our living situation.

In fall of '73, Scott and I decided to move out and go our separate ways. Tension was building between us (at least it seemed that way to me). I think Scott was just tired. I don't know what the real issue was, and I didn't know how to talk about it with him. I think he was getting frustrated, feeling tired from his job, and trying to make it to all the services. I was getting worn down from hearing his long talks and feeling guilty all the time, trying to be a better Christian. I loved him as a friend and brother, but it was time for a change for both of us.

We nervously told our grumpy landlord we were moving. Scott moved in with an usher named Peter. I got an offer to live with a deacon, Ron W., and John, who was an usher and a counselor. (People nicknamed him Baby Face John because of his smooth complexion.) My room was actually the dining area, and Ron and John had their own rooms.

It only took a short while for me to settle into my new residence, but it was far from smooth. One night our apartment had a break-in, and they cut Ron W. with a knife. We were all astonished things escalated out of control so quickly.

It all started when the neighbors below us kept blasting their music every evening, late into the night. This kept Ron up since his room was directly above theirs, so he came into the living room to sleep. Ron had made several complaints to the apartment manager before, but the neighbors continued with the noise. John just covered his head with a pillow and slept through the noise, and I followed suit. We didn't want to confront the neighbors directly, so I told the manager. He and I went to the tenant's downstairs to talk to them about the situation.

The music was loud when the manager knocked on the door. The tenants answered the door, acting belligerent. It was obvious they were drunk and on some kind of drugs. They were two beefy men who cussed at me, saying, "We are going to get you faggots." I saw the anger and evil in their eyes, and it made my back shiver and my stomach upset and tight. The apartment manager yelled back at them, and they slammed the door. They turned down the music, but I did not have a good feeling when I went back upstairs.

I told Ron and John what happened, though they were half asleep. I felt uneasy, and I was praying. Ron went to sleep on the couch in the living room. I went into the kitchen, continued to pray, and I fell asleep.

A couple hours went by, and I heard footsteps coming up the stairs. I peeked out the kitchen window door, and I saw our neighbors standing next to our front door, holding some kind of knife. There was another door in the kitchen which exited the front porch area, but it was sealed shut. I reached for a cast iron frying pan for defense.

The two guys busted in our glass front door, I broke through the screen in the kitchen window with the frying pan, jumped out of the kitchen window and ran downstairs.

The men threatened Ron with a knife and pulled a chunk of hair from his head. They scraped Ron with the knife a couple of times. By then, John woke up and grabbed a large abalone shell to use as a weapon. He made some noise coming out of the bedroom, and the men took off.

By now I was downstairs, banging on our manager's door, telling him to call the police. He saw me waving the frying pan and quickly dialed the operator. By the time the police arrived, the two men had already run off. I ran upstairs to check on Ron and John. I was happy to see they were alright, but I was shocked by Ron's wounds. Thinking back, it could have been a lot worse. The angels were protecting us that night.

The apartment manager apologized for the incident. We had to cover the front door, and we barricaded it in case they came back. We were all wired by then and could not go to sleep. We kept recounting what had happened and half joking at the same time.

I had a feeling those guys were going to come back after we all went to bed again. Sure enough, in a few hours John came out in the living room and said he could hear them downstairs. We looked out the window and could see them carrying some luggage along with two rifles as they took off. They must have sobered up and realized the seriousness of what they had done. They came back to grab their things and split to avoid any more trouble.

The next morning the manager and I went into their vacant apartment. They had left it a mess. The manager was still apologizing for what had happened. I was sure we were not going to hear from them again.

I called the Shekinah office that morning and spoke with Diane., who worked in the front office of the church as the secretary. I asked her to put us on the prayer chain. She was shocked by the story, and we were both half laughing over the incident as I summarized what happened.

Word got around fast, and different people from the church called us out of concern for Ron. They wanted more details of the incident, and they promised us their prayers. Though the incident left us all shaken, I truly felt supported by the church and the congregation. It brought everyone closer together.

A Rash of Weddings

By this time, the church members were coming together as far more than Christian brothers and sisters. Even though the elders had said they would not get married and would choose to remain single, they were now pairing off and getting married. Like any growing church of young people, the natural progression was people connected together, formed relationships, and before you knew it, there was a flurry of weddings. It seemed like an epidemic between 1973 and '74 with all the weddings that took place.

All those weddings meant showers which were hosted at the church. It was getting hard to locate enough people to be in the wedding parties since this was an expensive role to fill and most of us only worked part time. I could not afford it myself when I was asked, since a tux had to be rented each time. I was sad to have to turn down the many grooms.

Some of the weddings were more elaborate than others, depending on who had more resources. I thought elder Steve's wedding was one of the more dramatic ones, since it followed directly after the Saturday night miracle service. What a way to bring friends and relatives to church – a healing service followed by a wedding! Brant made a quick change from his puffy sleeve shirt into a suit. I don't know what the wedding party thought.

Kelly and Lilly G., who were in the Shekinah band, used their talents in their wedding. They added a unique romantic touch when they both sang to each other the song Lilly wrote called "The Wedding Song." It is still widely used in weddings to this day.

Brant often shared in his messages the dangers of getting married since it would sidetrack from ministering full time. But it is hard to control the passions of physical attraction and young love in a thriving group like ours. Brant started to change his mind when he saw the benefits of couples working as a ministerial team, since ministry was the main focus for everyone involved.

But Brant was losing his loyal subject elders who said they would all remain single and minister for the Lord. As the elders were married off, he slowly detached himself from them. This allowed them to run the ministry more on their own and not depend on him so much.

If there was a pecking order among the elders, it did not really show that much. It just seemed they knew their place after Brant guided them along. Sometimes I would hang around just to hear conversations between him and the different elders. They didn't seem to mind I was hanging around to listen.

By this time, it was obvious to me Brant was starting to feel lonely. He would stay on the patio area under his room where there was a fireplace, reading and meditating into the night. A fire was going to stay warm as he read, prayed and fell asleep.

I was at the house late one night, helping clean up, and I went outside by the fireplace. I swept up the ashes and poked at the fire. Brant was awake.

There was kindness in his eyes as he said "thank you." It was an encounter I wouldn't soon forget.

CHAPTER 7:

THE CALLING

Towards Thanksgiving I was helping to decorate the Foursquare Church. Our crew consisted of Claudia, Brant, Bill K., John and Charlene C. We used large ornaments and ribbons we were hanging between the arch ways towards the ceiling.

Brant wanted to add some more color to the church auditorium, so he had Randy S. paint the large arches in the church a sky blue and gold trim. Randy S was the deacon, but he earned his living as a painter. His confidence with the craft really shone through in this case. Some members of the Foursquare church congregation complained about the color scheme, but I thought it gave a heavenly look to the space.

We finished decorating the church that week. It was the following Saturday during the service I was approached by Robbie. He said Steve was looking for me. I thought he wanted me to work on a project or something similar since I had already done a couple of small projects for him.

I found Steve, and he wanted to talk to me privately. This made me nervous, and I wondered why. Steve gazed into my eyes for a moment with that penetrating look he had with his dark brown eyes and oversized mustache.

It was as though he was looking through me, and he seemed to be at a loss of words.

A moment later, Steve explained that Brant had taken a liking toward me, and he was looking for someone to help him. I asked what he wanted and what I was supposed to do.

Steve continued, saying Brant thought I could be trusted as a friend. He wanted someone for friendship – a companion to be with and travel with. I didn't quite understand what he meant. Nonetheless I was stunned and at a loss for words.

Steve said, "Don't make a decision now. Pray about it and think it over, then get back to me next week." He was always so practical in his decision making, and I appreciated the way he handled my response.

Steve gave me one of his gentle long hugs that he often gave to others before I left and gave me that penetrating look again with his dark brown eyes. I was kind of in a daze and mulling over in my mind what was said. I knew something was about to change in my life soon. I just didn't know what. After a lot of reflection, I agreed to take the job.

Claudia W. was instrumental in preparing me for the position I would soon take. She knew how I always wanted to help and be part of the ministry. She knew I had a heart that was eager to serve the Lord, like so many in the congregation who were already involved.

Her perspective was that I was well groomed and appeared intelligent, unlike some of the others Brant knew. Many of them were hippies – free spirits but tending toward the unkept side of grooming. Brant began cleaning up their image to fit the mold he was shaping for the ministry he wanted. Claudia saw I was different. She and I had developed a friendship, and she knew me well.

Of all those involved in the ministry, Claudia spent more time with Brant than anyone else did. He would listen to what she had to say about various people. She was his assistant and they had become close friends.

She was the spokesperson for Brant, relating his intentions and instructions to the elders and their wives. Not surprisingly, Claudia often served as the mediator between Brant and his brother Kevin. There were times when Kevin would push Brant's buttons to the point of exploding, and Claudia's buffering helped keep the peace.

Claudia was a couple years older than Brant, and she came from a diverse church background, mainly Pentecostal. She had acquired some leadership skills as a result. She spent all day and hours into the night, sitting and talking with Brant. He had visions and told her what we he was seeing. He asked about people they both knew, and she would give him her input. It was during one of these times she put in a word about me.

Claudia was a big influence when it came to opening doors for the ministry and for other people who wanted to get involved. She was instrumental in Shekinah's move to the large Foursquare Church rent-free. She's the one who opened that relationship for us with Pastor Adams and the ministry.

Claudia had attended the Foursquare Church when she was a little girl and had known Pastor Adams through the years. She gave the idea to Brant, and in response, Brant asked Steve to contact Pastor Adams. Before we knew it, Pastor Adams opened the door for the ministry to move the Saturday services to the Foursquare Church. It was located at 11th Street and Junipero, just a few blocks from the Little Shekinah facility on 7th Street.

Claudia was also instrumental in getting one of the key singers involved in the ministry. Lydia was a hippie and a free spirit who had a heart for the ministry. She sang so well, but it was hard for her to conform to the mold Brant was shaping for us. She couldn't seem to let go of her hippie ways.

I never saw myself in this light, but according to Claudia and Brant at the time, I appeared better educated than most in my peer group. They considered a few others for the position, but like Lydia, they didn't fit the image Brant was cultivating.

Their decision to recruit me for this position was based on a few factors, but my image definitely played a role. My clean good looks helped, plus I was tall and in good physical shape. I had a polished look and seriousness about me. Being extroverted and creative was a plus, and they appreciated my personal flair.

Claudia influenced Brant to get to know me because, for some reason, my background intrigued her more than the others. I seemed more independent, and I could think for myself. I didn't seem like a groupie, and I had the leadership qualities they were looking for. They saw me as being more open to people, accepting them wherever they were coming from.

It seems funny to me describing these qualities, because I did not really see myself this way at all. I was just trying to find my place in the world and in the ministry, and I felt insecure. Evidently it didn't show.

This is where I found myself on the night Steve. approached me about taking the position with Brant. I didn't know the reasons I was offered the position as Brant's personal assistant. I was young, naive, and eager to please. I knew the decision I made would impact me for a lifetime.

Brant Picks A Wife

It was at this time Brant and Claudia were making plans to marry. He was twenty-five, and she was twenty-seven. She saw the marriage as an opportunity to promote and run the ministry with their friendship serving as the foundation.

Claudia was not looking for a husband in the traditional sense. She had suffered through an abusive relationship with her first husband and was healed from that marriage by coming to Shekinah and getting involved. She had no physical desire whatsoever for Brant. She felt she was supposed to take the role of his wife because there was a need to serve Brant in that way – therefore serving the Lord.

Claudia saw how this man was so tormented inside, haunted by his past and his own insecurities. He did not have any peace and could not sleep at times. He needed a companion to console him.

Brant agreed to marry Claudia and felt she would meet his need for a companion. In fact, they both felt they were companions to each other already.

Brant got Claudia to agree they would not consummate the marriage, even though they agreed to sleep in the same bed. It took her awhile to agree to those terms – to have a sexless marriage. Ultimately, she felt she was not sacrificing anything by mothering him instead of filling a role as his mate. By getting married, they would be closer, and their needs would be taken care of.

The two of them went to look for a wedding dress together, and Brant was planning the rest of the wedding. They met with Pastor Adams of the Neighborhood Foursquare Church to get his counsel and blessing. He said the marriage would probably work. However, they didn't tell him everything. They left out the part about not being intimate with each other. Had he known; he probably would have offered different advice.

Claudia was naïve and did not realize how foolish it was to even attempt this. As an outsider, I can only say she should have seen what was coming. She rationalized a sexless marriage with Brant would be great, since she survived a sexually abusive marriage with her first husband. She thought she would be better off because she would no longer be raped by a violent husband. She was going to be a nurturing saint to Brant, providing him with companionship in the name and spirit of the Lord.

It was the fall of 1973. Pastor Adams suggested Brant and Claudia should wait to get married until after the Easter-In Gathering at the old Long Beach Auditorium in April of 1974. Since tension was already building around preparations for this big event, it was best to postpone their wedding until spring. Brant and Claudia agreed, and they kept their betrothal quiet for the time being.

The only other people who knew about their engagement were Joe and Linda. They were really excited for them. Joe thought it was the Lord bringing them together. The couple quietly forged ahead with their plans, eager for the spring and the time when they would take their vows.

Jo Ellen Steps In

Once they were sure, Brant went to Palm Springs, excited to see his mother, Jo Ellen, and tell her the good news. The meeting did not go over as planned.

Jo Ellen completely freaked out when Brant told her about his betrothal. She called Claudia right away and went ballistic on her. Brant's mother did not want the marriage to happen at all, and this got Brant stirred up.

Claudia held her ground. She felt it was the Lord at work, bringing them together, and she would not let Jo Ellen bully her. She thought their marriage was intended to serve the ministry.

But it wasn't long before Brant began to cave in, capitulating to Jo Ellen. He could have been influenced by his mother's money, or it's possible she threatened him. She is the one who took care of Brant when things got hard for him during his young life. With her holding the purse strings, she really controlled Brant. His mother's sharp tongue gave him cold feet.

Jo Ellen liked having Brant dependent on her. She saw him as the Pope or something and the idea of getting married was too removed. Claudia did not fit the mold she wanted for her son, the star. She saw Claudia as a threat, someone who would cause her to lose control over her son.

Instead of Brant confronting Claudia with his decision, Steve was tasked with breaking the news to her. He was told to convince Claudia to accept the story that this was all her idea, and she was to blame for spreading the story. The rationale was it would make Brant look good to say she fabricated the whole thing. Claudia agreed to take the fall and let Brant save face.

Steve was loyal to Brant, and he wanted the best for him and the ministry. He overlooked the fact it was Brant who took the ball and ran with it to begin with. Brant was the one who was making all the wedding arrangements, and he had not been reluctant at all.

This meant Claudia was forced out. The church car was taken away from her, and her responsibilities in the ministry were passed to Brant for the time being. He needed a replacement for her as soon as possible, which led to his search for a clean cut, young companion. Kevin B. was out of the question.

At this point, Brant must have talked to Steve about me, which led to that fated conversation between us. Once I accepted the offer, Brant had Steve inform the rest of the elders and wives what had happened with Claudia. They played up the story about what she did, and they suggested what could be expected by replacing her with me. I didn't suspect a thing.

Since Claudia worked the prayer line on Saturday nights, they figured they would need a replacement to hold the anointing oil during the service. However, Brant and the elders were stunned when Claudia showed up that night and worked the prayer line. She had a bright smile and held her head high. Even though her heart was broken then, she knew it was the Lord who had laid this path for her.

What she couldn't know at the time was the Lord had other plans for her. If not for her broken engagement to Brant, she would not have been open to another man who came into the picture a short while later.

In the meantime, I prepared to fulfill my duties as Brant's constant companion. I contemplated the offer before me. I knew it would require growth and commitment. It would mean stepping into the role of personal servant to a healing evangelist. I contemplated my own worthiness.

Answering the Call

I don't remember much of the week I was offered to work with Brant. I was praying over my decision about the offer that was proposed to me. This was an opportunity I'd been looking for but didn't know it. I knew I desired to minister and even have a healing ministry someday myself. That is one of the reasons Scott and I came to Shekinah – to get the training and exposure. We knew the rapture was imminent before the return of Christ.

I didn't have time to go to Bible College, and since the elders did not go, I thought it was a waste of time. Bible College seemed to be discouraged in some of the Bible Study messages. Brant didn't go, and my teaching from Calvary Chapel was that Bible College was like getting a funereal degree.

At the time I did not realize spiritual development would take years, and I was too impatient at eighteen for such a long path. I thought these were the last days of Mankind and the spirit of God was being poured out upon the youth. Somehow, I had attracted this opportunity to come into my life and needed to go through the open door right now without hesitation.

After that week, I saw this could be part of my training as a minister. I talked about this idea and the opportunity privately with my roommates, Baby Face John and Ron W. I told them I was scared about it, but Ron seemed perplexed by my mixed emotions. John spoke up, saying what an honor it would be to help Brant this way.

Finally doubt left me, and I decided: Yes.

Yes, I would be the servant to Brant, as Elisha was to Elijah the Prophet. I would learn from their model and emulate them. I realized this opportunity was an honor, and I was willing to do what I had to do to be trained by the prophet himself, to witness the man of God – Brant – firsthand. I was nervous about the weight of this responsibility, but I accepted it with all my heart.

When I spoke to Steve the following week, he seemed pleased. I was not sure if this was going to be a volunteer position and felt embarrassed to ask about a salary for such an honored position. However, I needed an income, I needed to cover my share of the rent and food. Still, I didn't know how to raise the topic.

Somehow, I stumbled with the request, and he asked me something to the effect of how much I would need. Before I could answer, he went on to say, "You will be living at the Shekinah house, if that's alright with you, and everything will be taken care of."

That was indeed a load off my mind. We agreed I would receive an extra $15 dollars a week allowance for spending money. Even though it was a modest amount, I thought I'd slipped and fallen into a pile of luck. At least I would not have to look for food in the trash dumpster anymore.

Steve asked if I could meet him at the Shekinah house after the service with Brant. So, quietly and without much fanfare, it all began.

I was dropped off the Shekinah house, as we agreed. I was sitting alone in the living room, wondering what was going to happen next. Various elders were coming in and out of the room, returning from the evening service. They seemed to know why I was there, and we exchanged smiles. I had the feeling everything was prearranged and discussed.

Suddenly I heard Brant's voice – "Oh, you're here. Good." He gave me a quick hug. I was surprised to see he was at a loss for words and a bit nervous. That made two of us.

"Claudia will have to fill you in, but I need to show you where my shoes are to clean." That seemed reasonable.

He seemed reserved, and his movements were a bit stilted, not at all the charismatic minister whose presence filled the auditorium. I felt awkward. It was strange to see him so diminished, so... human.

"You need to get some clothes," he mused. "You can use the community closet. It's the one the elders use." He opened the closet doors, and it was filled with an array of shirts from his clothing store. There was every color, pattern and style imaginable.

"When can you start? I need your help. Can you start tomorrow? I have to be at the church tomorrow with pastor Adams, and I have a TV appearance interview with Steve early Monday morning. I need you here early to wake me."

I said, "I'll need a ride. I don't have a car."

"You'll have to take the car then," he tossed out casually. "Steve will make the arrangements to do that."

There it was. My first assignment. I was to wake up Brant in the morning to get him ready for church at the Foursquare Church with Pastor Adams. It was to be the breeze before the whirlwind, and I was excited to meet the challenge head on.

Brant and Claudia Don't Talk

I hardly slept that night. I was very excited, nervous and insecure. I ended up talking with Baby Face John in his room and fell asleep on the floor. Somehow, I managed to wake up in time to start my new position.

I arrived early at the house and knocked on Brant's door with a cup a coffee. I heard his voice say "OK," and there was a bit of shuffling inside the room. I stood there for a moment, and he opened the door, smiling with a morning beard. He took the cup of coffee, said "thank you," and shut the door.

I waited patiently in the living room, half asleep, while he got ready. Later I sat in the front row of the church with him. I was half in a daze until the service was over. We went out to breakfast with the Adams' and Terry B. It was the first of many Sunday breakfasts to follow.

The following day, once again I woke Brant early with coffee, getting him ready for a morning TV interview show in Los Angeles. I drove the three of us to the studio. While Brant gave his testimony and told how the ministry started, I sat in the green room with Steve watching the broadcast on the TV monitor.

Through that week, Brant found other clothes for me to wear from the community closet. He would add to it once in awhile as he came across shirts he liked.

He was frequently driven by impulse like this, or at least by influences that had no rationale behind them which I could see. I thought the fault must be mine.

My job description seemed to be made up as we went along. Basically, I was to follow him wherever he went, clean up after him, and delegate responsibilities as needed. Beyond this, there was no master plan.

I had a small portable typewriter I carried with me all the time to type scripture notes. I was lucky I took typing in high school, so I knew well enough how to type, though I was slow.

His shoes all had to be shined regularly. All his clothes needed to be dry cleaned, even his jeans and the community closet of shirts worn by all the elders. The local dry cleaners loved to see me coming in once a week. I would get a check from Robby for the weekly bill, and it went straight to the cleaners. Brant's belt buckle needed to be polished for every service, using brass cleaner and his brass bracelet and rings.

Throughout the week, Claudia would come in and out, giving me tips about what to do. She and Brant told me what kind of make-up he wore. I already knew Brant wore makeup, since he told everyone on the Wednesday services a couple times because it would wash out his face under the lights. We all accepted it and did not have a problem with it.

Since my background was in theater, the fact Brant wore make-up had little meaning to me. However, I did think it was strange he would wear makeup during the week in public. He used it to cover his stubble and the tired look under his eyes. I chalked it up to him being especially concerned with his public appearance.

Besides helping Brant keep to his schedule and helping him with his wardrobe, I also became the babysitter for his small dog Joy, a Pomeranian. This was Brant's closest companion, and she meant the world to him. He would often talk about Joy in his Bible studies in his early days – how she ministered to him and kept him company.

A couple days after I'd settled into my position, Claudia came to the house to fill me in on more details about what needed to be done. All the elders knew what was taking place, and they acted like nothing had happened.

Claudia seemed to feel kind of awkward. I picked up there something amiss, but I did not make the connection with what was going on.

Brant and Claudia kept their distance when they were in the same room, and she would communicate with me only. I thought it was strange. I didn't know all the details about what had transpired between Brant and Claudia. It took me awhile to understand I was picking up, reading between the lines as the elders' wives made comments about her.

"How the mighty have fallen," I thought. I felt bad for her and the way so much had turned against her. I pushed the thought to the back of my mind and carried on with what I believed was God's work – serving Brant, the healing evangelist.

CHAPTER 8:

THE HUM OF SHEKINAH FELLOWSHIP

Beyond helping to spread the grace of the Holy Spirit, there were practical matters to consider in my new role as Brant's personal assistant. I would get my weekly allowance of fifteen dollars, and Brant would get a draw of petty cash every week. I held it for him, and the amount was based on what we thought he needed at the time.

Later, when he moved out of the Shekinah house, Brant's schedule increased and so did the amount of cash he needed. It started out around fifty-dollars a week and increased as time went on. My pay remained the same.

I had a credit card to be used for the car. I would hand in the weekly receipts to Robby for safekeeping. Later I passed them on to Claudia, who took care of some of the bookkeeping. I'd put in my request, and I would get several checks for items we needed.

I would also get a petty cash check for Brant, which was cashed during the weekly service after the offering. Robby and Steve would do the book work, recording the offerings and writing checks for the different accounts to be deposited. Robby would tease me at times about how much was needed, since the amount kept increasing. It got to the point I was handling several hundred dollars at a time. We went out to eat quite a bit, and he liked to entertain the elders as well. To me, it was quite a lot of money. All the same, my weekly allowance remained a modest $15, which I managed separately.

During the first Saturday service in my new position, I felt so important when I put Brant's Bible on the black wrought iron podium and placed the scripture notes next to it. When he first handed me his Bible to take to the podium, it was like time slowed down for a moment. I clearly remember his red leather handcrafted Bible cover and the heft of the book. It was as though I was handling something so sacred, I needed to guard it with my life.

From that moment on, I was caught up in the hum of a well-oiled machine that was the Shekinah Fellowship. I was constantly running back and forth from Brant's dressing room, getting people he needed to talk to, and standing watch by the dressing room door. It was my job to pre-screen people before letting them into the room, where they would be inspected by the security personnel. Security was not a matter of vanity – it became a matter of necessity.

There was an incident during one Saturday service when someone lit a firecracker outside the Foursquare Church by Brant's dressing room, which was vacant at the time. During the service it sounded like a loud gun-shot. Everyone in the congregation heard it, and a murmur went through the crowd.

"That is the devil!" Brant shouted while preaching. "That is the devil!"

Some of the ushers rushed outside to find the person responsible. Ever since then, extra security was added around Brant, including personal bodyguards. John C. and a couple of deacons determined the placement of security personnel. Randy. monitored the prayer line for security, and he directed traffic. For Saturday services, I would park the car behind the locked fence at the Foursquare Church, or at other secured areas for the different outreach services.

Adding security meant a change in tone around the church and the ministry. It also marked the beginning of what would eventually become his isolation. For now, it meant adding time to routine activities to allow for security measures.

As the security increased around Brant, crowds started to surround him even more than ever, which made it hard for him to move. He explained in the small services on Wednesday it was part of Jesus' disciples' task to protect Him as he walked among the crowds. Brant expected us to do the same for him. We just accepted what he had to say, and we were conditioned to protect Brant. At times the crowds would start to press in to be closer to him. This made him feel more anxious and nervous than ever. People didn't just want to hang around him – they wanted a piece of him.

Brant Seeks Some Privacy

Within the first couple weeks in my new position, Brant and I went looking for an apartment for him. Brant thought it would be best to separate himself from the elders. He wanted to see them work together as a team and not depend on him so much. It also meant he would keep to himself more, guarding his privacy.

After the added security personnel, getting his own apartment was his next step in separating himself from his people. It would be the first of a series of residential moves Brant would make that year while I was working with him.

We ended up locating a one-bedroom apartment that was in a newer complex north of Long Beach. It turned out the woman who managed the complex used to be an Assembly of God preacher. She'd heard of Brant. Because he was on the radio, his name circulated among denominational groups. When his TV shows started to air later on, he became an even bigger name.

As far as the apartment rental, there was a problem with Brant's small dog Joy – they had a "no pets" policy. Still, the manager said she'd overlook that, and she waived all the security deposits as well as the last month's rent. It was indeed a professional courtesy. Brant would see a lot of unsolicited favors like this in the months and years that followed.

I gave the rental paperwork to Steve. to fill out, and I arranged the financing with the manager. Brant's brother Kevin was already orchestrating the move, getting people to help with packing and carrying. Brant's move left an opening at the Shekinah house, and I was given a new room upstairs. Everything came together within a couple days. In many ways, Kevin was a real help in making all the details come together.

When he first found out I was Brant's personal assistant, though, Kevin was standoffish toward me. He saw me as an obstacle between himself and his brother. It wasn't long before he started to warm up to me again, wanting to help me in little ways. Yet there were still awkward moments between us, and I sensed he was jealous of my position. He would step in and try to take over situations in little ways, and these petty power plays bothered me. I tried to be patient and overlook them.

After Brant had settled into his new apartment, he would call upon me for small personal things. I was no longer merely tending his wardrobe and making his business arrangements. He wanted me to come over to take his dog out for walks.

This task wasn't as simple as it sounds – there were ample logistics involved. To start with, it took time out of my day to go to his apartment and come home. I was never able to get in and out quickly, because Brant always wanted to chat. Plus, Brant's dog Joy was not a good dog. She was spoiled, and she did whatever she wanted. It wasn't a fun job for me. At the same time, I was compelled to do it. This was just the sort of task, if left to his own devices, Kevin might use for his own political gain with his brother. I had to do it and do it well.

Joy was finding it hard to get used to her new surroundings, and she tried to get away from me whenever I took her outside. She managed to slip out of her leash a couple of times, and I almost lost her. She would run around and hide, scaring the daylights out of me. I'm not sure what Brant would have done if I'd lost his dog, but thankfully that never happened.

Brigid Has Second Thoughts

Just before my new job started and after Brigid had been away at college for a while, we reconnected further. The idea of us getting married was still being entertained on her end. I believe she wanted me to be the one to make the move in going forward. My new position was starting to take a toll on my personal life. I was so caught up with the responsibilities involved in taking care of Brant, I put Brigid on the side, thinking she would understand the importance of what I was doing.

I remember calling her on the phone, telling her I'd accepted a position working directly with Brant. She already knew about it, which stole a bit of the excitement of my news. Brigid was concerned about when we could see each other. I told her this would be a good experience to learn about the ministry. She said she understood, but the tension lingered.

Brant expressed concern about my getting married, wondering how it would impact me as his personal assistant. He seemed to think my loyalties would be divided. Once he accepted the idea, he embraced the situation and said we could work together for him.

At about this time, another man came into Brigid's life and swept her off her feet. I did not know about it until someone told me, and I was crest-fallen at the news. Even so, I went to see Brigid and her new boyfriend Rick D. at his apartment. Some of my friends who lived up the street from the Shekinah house came with me.

It was obvious from the first moment we arrived I was out of the picture. Seeing the two of them together made it all clear. Rick was a better match for Brigid. He was a young, tall, intelligent, handsome college student.

Brigid seemed nervous about being confronted this way, but Rick was cool headed. Brigid snuggled even more closely to him for support. I must have looked like a fool.

My concern was they were both missing out on what God had in store for them in the ministry. I talked about what the Lord was doing and encouraged them not to be left out. Neither one of them seemed interested. I don't remember much of what I said to them when my friends and I departed that evening. I just remember feeling let down and sad.

I went back to the Shekinah house, and the elders were having a meeting and prayer time. We went around the room praying for needs. I made the announcement that Brigid and I had called off our engagement and she had found someone else. They all stared at me with concern. Some held back laughter, apparently uncomfortable with their own feelings and my somber tone.

Brigid left the ministry, but her sister Mary remained involved. It was not until about a year later Brant wanted me to get a hold of Brigid and Rick to ask them to come back. She did return to the ministry, though I don't know if it was because I asked her through her sister Mary, or if it was because of the encouragement of her friends.

That Christmas of 1973 was a rush of activity. I was running around for holiday shopping, buying presents with Brant, and being introduced to people on a different level than before. It set the tone for the coming year and the many people I would meet and observe as Brant's assistant.

He was the Pied Piper. He played the music, and like so many others, I followed along. Brant cultivated the rest of us – sometimes as a congregation, sometimes as a celebrity entourage – and we stayed for whatever personal reasons and agendas we had at the time. The dynamics were sharpening, with higher highs and lower lows yet to come.

The Heart of the Shekinah House

After Brant made the move out of the Shekinah house, I felt honored to be there with all the main decision makers, the elders of the ministry. For the most part, we ate together in the evening. All the wives contributed, sharing the meal preparation in the evenings. We would often joke and tease each other, and we had a clear sense of community.

I felt like I was living with the disciple's wives who supported their husbands during Jesus' time. The only difference was they were the wives of the disciples of Brant and the ministry that was growing.

My memories of that time and place fill my heart. The Shekinah house was constantly full of people. Between the sound of the piano practices in the early morning, guitar chords playing, the radio shows being edited together, elders working on various projects for the ministry with the sound of Chuck Smith tapes playing in the background, people on the phone working on some kind of ministry deal and the hubbub of the wives; there wasn't a moment of silence to be missed.

The house was a busy place. There were always chores, including daily cleaning and running errands back and forth with supplies being dropped off. I pretty much knew what each of the elders did before. Now I witnessed what was taking place behind the scenes and how they handled their appointed roles. It was fascinating as I got to know the different characteristics each of them had and the way they approached their jobs.

I got to know each of the elders and their wives at different levels. I spent some time with each of them in a small way as we interacted with each other. There was a lot of laughter, and I learned something from each of them. None of them were much older than I was, though I respected them as elders.

It was challenging sharing one main bathroom among all those people in the house. Time in the bathroom was at a premium, and it was carefully orchestrated when it came to timing getting ready for the services. I don't remember any arguments among any of us, and everyone seemed to get along. We respected each others' personal space, since we lived in such close quarters.

The head of this household, of course, was Brant. I would pick up Brant and bring him around to the house, and suddenly the air was abuzz. Everyone gathered around him, waiting their turn to talk to him, get his attention, and share what needed to be done.

Brant would often joke and tease them, meandering around the property and making mischief, or cajoling us at the dinner table when we ate together. Sometimes he would chase someone, and there would be a sudden yelp or a screech of a surprise, followed by laughter from the next room. Besides his natural charisma, he had a way of bringing people together through his playfulness. He could be so uninhibited, and it made for high spirits in everyone around him.

One-time Lilly G. and Brant got into a water fight. It started when Lilly said something sarcastic, teasing Brant, which shocked him. He reacted by splashing some water at her. Lilly tossed a glass of water back at him through the kitchen window, but it didn't land squarely. Then Brant got a bucket of water, went into the kitchen, and dumped it onto Lilly. She screamed. Lilly tried one more time to retaliate, and this time her weapon met its mark. After that, Brant knew Lilly would not back down, and he respected her even more because she stood up to him.

By then, all the original elders had become ordained, except for Kelly G., who was part of the music ministry and newlywed Jeff.

All the elders were married by the time I was living in the Shekinah house. Of course, what usually follows young love and marriage is a baby. I think it was Stacey. who got pregnant first. Through Claudia W., Brant sent a message early on for the elders' wives that having a baby would be a distraction from the ministry, and he encouraged them to remain on birth control. When Stacey. became pregnant, this was especially emphasized. However, Brant said the Lord told him it was alright for Stacey. to have a child. Still, he did not want the rest of the elders' wives to follow suit and anyone else who got pregnant, would be at their own risk at the disproval of Brant.

But that is what happened. Over the course of the next couple years, various deacons' wives and other members of the ministry started having children. Once kids became part of the scene, there was an unstated social pressure that pushed out the growing young families. As a result, one by one they would slip away. At some point, Kelly and Lilly moved down the street from the Shekinah house into an apartment when she became pregnant.

I Get Promoted to Scribe & Hack

Sometime after Brant moved to his apartment in North Long Beach, the ministry purchased a used limousine. It became my job to drive him around in it. I became known more as Brant's limo driver and assistant, and I was often teased about getting a chauffeur's hat. People thought driving Brant around was the only thing I did. Little did they know I wore a number of hats while taking care of Brant's personal needs.

Robby W. found the limo for Brant. It was an older '60's limo that looked more like a hearse. I nicknamed it Job because of the mechanical problems it had. The justification for getting the limo was so Brant could rest, pray and read during the drives to the different outreaches. The limo held more passengers, so Brant could have meetings on the road with different elders in the car.

All the elders seemed pleased as Brant showed off the car, and they took turns riding in it. In spite of its popularity with the elders, the limo did not go over well with the general ministry. There were a couple meetings with the rest of the ministry team, asking why the limo was necessary. Brant explained to them why the limo was purchased, and it became generally accepted after that.

There was a problem with parking the limo at the different outreach locations, since Brant didn't want to keep explaining to congregations why the church had a limo. I would have to drop him off at the church where the meeting was, and John C. was the lookout person for a place to park it.

In between duty calls, I would type scripture references for Brant, working either in my room or at his apartment. Brant would say, "I stay prepared and stay in communion with the Holy Spirit." He would call this living in the moment.

It seemed this was how he delivered his message to the congregation. He never wrote out a sermon or message when I was with him. His messages were all scratched notes of scriptures with colored markers, or the scriptures were typed out along with a newspaper article or current event. He watched television news and interview talk shows, and he listened to Christian radio programs to get ideas.

Brant had a small collection of Bible commentaries. He mainly read from the Mathew Henry commentaries, Torrey and Halley's Topical Bible, as well as other Bible translations. He also had access to the whole collection of the Chuck Smith teaching tapes of Calvary Chapel. He compiled all this to incorporate in his preaching while being spontaneous as the spirit moved him.

Brant's style was a mix of expository and topical preaching. He would have a theme and follow it, which would carry over from week to week. It would last several months as he went from place to place, traveling on various outreach missions. The repeated emphasis of the theme was the presence of the Holy Spirit. That was always tied into the main message, compelling those in the Christian church to wake up to the genuine movement of the spirit.

After Brant moved out of the Shekinah house and we got the limo, it was clear he was beginning to feel isolated. He told me he felt guilty about the decision to move out, and he was lonely. He wanted to get together with the elders and spoil them in little ways as much as he could. One of the ways this manifested was in the outings he would put together for us. We got all the stuff for a barbecue with the elders and brought it to his apartment. We had a feast, and everyone laughed a lot.

Afterwards we all piled in the limo – at least most of us did – to go to the movies. We saw "The Three Musketeers", which was both popular and critically acclaimed at the time. I was struck by the movie's theme, "All for one, and one for all!" And how it seemed so perfect our group watched this together.

I looked over at Brant, projection light flickering on his face. Even though his gaze was fixed on the screen, I could tell he was miles away. There was a wall around him, even as he sat in the crowded theater. I wished I could help him, but my service to him lay in another direction. For now, it was all I could do to help him with the mundane tasks of running the ministry. The loftier issues remained between him and the Lord.

The Dew Is Off the Flower

The year of 1974 saw another growth spurt for the ministry in outreaches of healing services, radio expansion, and now television tapings. I was very busy that year behind the scenes with Brant, and working with all those who volunteered their time to support the growth of the ministry.

The Shekinah Fellowship was in full flower. We were all on the same page. We believed with full faith the rapture would take place any moment, removing us from Earth to be with Jesus. The seven-year tribulation was going to take place while the anti-Christ would rule the world until Christ returned to set up his kingdom. Any plans for a career were not important, since this was not in harmony with the goal of the ministry or Brant's perception of what was taking place in the world.

Given my excitement about the upcoming rapture, 1974 was a real rush for me. I was traveling to many of the outreaches with Brant, making his personal arrangements when we got there. I had never been a personal assistant or secretary before, but I did the best I could.

Brant moved five times that year. It always involved a quick decorating turn around and a buzz of activity from unpaid recruits. Claudia and Kevin would make most of the arrangements, while volunteers would help with the painting and moving. I met a number of interesting well-known personalities that year who were attending the ministry and met with Brant in private. I was often an observer of the conversations that took place in those meetings.

One of those personalities was Brant's role model, Kathryn Kuhlman. He and I attended a number of her services together. Although we never met her personally, we always seemed to get a good seat in the large Shrine Auditorium by going in through the side door. Sometimes we would be on the main floor or on the first level balcony.

During one of these services, I was wearing one of Brant's double-breasted dress coats he gave me. It was white with gold buttons, very flashy. A worker must have identified me as one of the TV evangelists, and he asked if I was on the seating list of ministers. He wanted to know if I needed a seat. I told him I was already with Brant, and he nodded humbly, backing away swiftly like a butler serving a nightcap.

At many of the meetings I attended with Brant, I always had a hard time staying awake during Kathryn Kuhlman's messages. Usually I had been up late the previous night, and it was difficult to remain alert through the hypnotic rise and fall of her voice. I was more awake during the healing part of her service, but even then, her words relaxed me to the point of embarrassment.

Sitting in those meetings with Brant as he studied her, I could not help thinking I was sitting next to the only man who rivaled the preacher on the stage. I truly felt privileged, though never quite satisfied. Brant always wanted to leave before the service was completely over to avoid the crowds. I would shake the fog from my mind as we stepped to the side door, out into the fresh air and back toward the car.

One of Kathryn Kuhlman's services was going to be held in Pittsburg, Pennsylvania. Brant wanted to fly there. Travel arrangements for his return trip got mixed up, and it meant he could not be on time for one of his own meetings. This made him so upset he wanted me to talk to Steve. and Linda., telling them how disappointed he was in them. He felt they should do a better job in working around his preaching schedule.

He kept harping about it to me, his voice getting higher in pitch the more excited he became. He said he was disappointed they were so insensitive about his schedule. I wondered why he couldn't tell them himself, since he knew them far better than I did. Nonetheless, I agreed to talk to them. This was one of those tasks I could not have anticipated when I signed up for the job of serving Brant. I would not have chosen it, but I agreed to do it.

I was nervous about confronting Steve and Linda because I'd never done anything like this before. Besides my inexperience, it just didn't feel like the right thing to do. I thought since Brant was a man of God, he must be right about this. I figured Steve and Linda would accept it as such.

I didn't know it at the time, but it was usually Steve and Claudia who did the speaking for Brant. It turned out when he wanted to get his point across to someone, he would have a trusted ally relay the message for him. Now I was in that awkward position where I was the one appointed to speak for Brant. I felt I didn't have the skills to verbalize that kind of message, especially knowing Steve's position in the ministry. This made it very awkward for me. I gathered my courage and braced for what surely was a coming storm.

After the Saturday service, Brant left the church with one of the elders to get something to eat. I gathered Steve and Linda into one of the rooms in the Foursquare Church and sat them together across from me. I remember I was wearing one of Brant's stylish red coats, one with shoulder pads and fancy buttons, paired with a bow tie. The coat must have come from his men's store. I felt rather stylish, and it gave me a much-needed boost of confidence.

I explained the reason for the meeting and repeated Brant's words several times, driving home the point about how disappointed he was. I spoke in a calm, clear voice. Steve and Linda looked at each other for a moment, puzzled, and Linda smiled. She said something about the schedule, and she apologized.

Steve had a more serious, hurt look, as though he was going to cry, and it scared me. He said he did not know. I repeated Brant's message several times, how disappointed he was. I felt as though I was scolding a child, and I felt really stupid while saying it. Linda said something to the effect we needed to be more careful in arranging Brant's schedule.

It was all too much, and I had to backtrack. I said, "I'm sorry. I never had to do something like this before." Linda asked if there was anything more, and then she excused herself. Steve said he would catch her later and told her to close the door when she left.

There was a moment of silence that passed between us. I knew I was in for it now, and I could sense his anger and hurt welling up inside him. I felt ridiculous, like the shoulder pads of my jacket where slipping down and my bow tie was falling off.

Then Steve started to talk. I felt myself shrinking in my chair as Steve vented his feelings in a low voice. His words seemed so powerful to me; he might as well have shot me. What he said was a blur, but the impact was crystal clear. I do remember apologizing again for the fact I never had to do this before, explaining I was only repeating what was told to me as the messenger.

Steve seemed to believe in my sincerity, and then his tone changed. He wanted to express his concern for Brant's wellbeing, and I believe he felt hurt. Since the move, he and Brant were not as close as they used to be. Steve said we both needed to talk more since we both shared the same concerns for Brant.

We seemed to come to a better understanding of each other, and he gave me one of his long gentle hugs he was known for. After that meeting,

Steve was friendlier toward me than he had been before. But that night was a turning point for more than just my friendship with Steve.

Many things were not the same after that night. It was as if a trickle of water had found its way into a hairline crack in a granite slab and turned to ice. With such a divisive force at its core, no foundation could withstand such pressure in the course of time, no matter how solid the rock might appear.

The chilling voice of dissent had whispered, and it was only a matter of time before it became a loud chorus. From my position at Brant's side, I would soon hear it the loudest.

CHAPTER 9:

TRAVELS WITH BRANT

Brant and I would go to the Lake Arrowhead cabin once or twice a month after a service. It was hard to drive up the mountain pass late at night, but Brant used the trips as a personal retreat. He said he needed to recharge after giving so much to the congregation.

The cabin had two bedrooms with a loft. It was used as a getaway for the elders, however they hardly used it. Brant was quiet during most of the time we were there. I brought the recording equipment for Brant to tape the radio shows. After the sound technicians showed me how to do the recording, I would operate the equipment for Brant whenever we went to the cabin. The equipment included a reel-to-reel tape deck, a microphone and a portable mixing board. After a few tests for volume level, I would signal Brant to start his talk.

He was good at it. He just had his Bible, and a few notes or something with other material to read from. Afterwards we would go for walks and talked little, only making comments about the surroundings. I thought I must have been really boring to him, yet he told me he wanted the space to remain quiet. I didn't have a problem with that and kept my thoughts to myself.

We would drive into town to get food and supplies, and we took turns doing the cooking. There was an ice-skating rink not far from the cabin we both went to. He used to ice skate quite a bit before taking up the ministry, and he had even aspired to be an Olympic skater. His mother pushed him to do it, but nothing ever came of it.

I could barely ice-skate myself, wobbling around the rink and barely staying on my feet. Once Brant warmed up, he would glide across the ice like a pro, jumping and spinning with ease. I was surprised to see how good he was. He thought it would be good exercise if we would go more often, but once he realized how sore he was the next day, he did not seem as eager before.

After a week at the cabin, we'd drive straight to an outreach or back to Long Beach for the Saturday healing service. I would have his ministry clothes already to go, and the typed scripture notes from the portable typewriter. After awhile, he stopped having me type the notes. Instead, he wrote down the scripture reference using color markers. He'd make some highlights and write in his own style. Brant often did this with the television on, watching his role models for inspiration.

Besides the scripture notes, Brant took inspiration from articles and current events. Steve. would cut out articles from the newspaper to share with Brant before a service. Sometimes he would find a magazine article that tied in with a Biblical message, or he'd find something funny to share.

In the beginning, Brant and I shared the same hotel room when we went to the San Diego area. We would either go out to eat or I would get something and bring it back to the room. One night as we came back from dinner, we caught a man who'd broken into our room. He was walking off with Brant's long white trench coat and briefcase. Brant yelled out to him, and his commanding voice must have put the fear of God into him. The man dropped the stuff and ran off.

One of the more memorable hotels we stayed in was at the famous Hotel Del Coronado on the beachfront near San Diego. This Victorian hotel is the largest wooden building of its type that's still standing. The lobby of "the Del" featured many pictures of celebrities who'd stayed at the hotel over the years. Our trip was during the off-season, so it was too cold to lie in the sun, though the beach looked wonderfully inviting.

Once again, Brant and I shared a room while we stayed at this hotel, and I remained quite most of the time to give him his privacy. Still I was privy to the little things no one else ever saw.

For instance, Brant's complexion always appeared to be so smooth, even after cutting himself shaving. Though he had thick stubble in the morning and late afternoon, he never seemed to have razor burn. I was still in my teens, and my own facial hair was just starting to come in, so it made me wonder.

I already knew he wore make up to cover up the flaws in his complexion. To get that fresh baby face look, he used different types of facial masks. I'd often noticed he took special care of his skin, but that weekend he let me in on his facial secrets, showing me the facial masks, he used. He said his main trick was to use petroleum jelly on his face – a technique models used. He also had a variety of moisturizers to keep his complexion fresh.

From there, we went into a health food store by the hotel and read the labels of different soaps. I picked up a bottle of Aloe Vera juice and read the label. It said it had healing properties and was good to put on the face. He had me buy a bottle, and we both put it on our faces. It stunk, and we started to laugh. I pointed out that you can drink it as well. He was skeptical, so he let me try it first. I swallowed some straight from the bottle without diluting it. It tasted terrible, and we laughed again. I offered him some, but he refused.

It seemed like such a small thing at the time, sharing moments like this with Brant. Yet I was keenly aware I knew things about him no one else did. There was an intimacy in these little incidents, and I felt like I'd been given a special privilege to be near him. A bond started to develop between us.

Within that week, we drove south and crossed the border in Mexico. We parked the limo on the other side of the border and hired a cab to take us around the city of Tijuana, a town notorious at the time for its poverty, beggars and thieves.

As could be expected, Brant did not blend in like a regular tourist would. He wore his long trench coat, patent leather shoes and flared pants. His flashy dress made him an easy mark, and he was constantly approached by beggars asking for money and peddlers pressing him to buy something. The pressure and attention stressed him out, and I had to shoo them away.

Despite the unwanted attention, Brant did buy a number of gifts for friends along with a couple of rings and gold necklaces for himself. With my $15 a week allowance, I could afford little but a handful of Mexican jumping beans. Still, it was enough for me to spend time with him in Tijuana. It was the most exotic place I'd been up to at that point, and Brant was the most flamboyant person I'd ever known.

Enter: Bill Laskey

Back in Hollywood, Brant began to collect colorful characters. One of them we entertained was Bill Laskey. He was a delightful man in his sixties who came to the services and pursued Brant. His father was a former Hollywood producer at one of the studios during the golden era of Hollywood.

Bill was fascinated with Brant, and he boldly approached him several times to talk to him and try to get to know him. Bill followed Brant's speaking tour for awhile, attending the different outreaches. Brant gave him his phone number, and ultimately Bill befriended him. They routinely talked on the phone for a long time.

There were many times the three of us would go out together after the service. I think Brant respected him as kind of a father figure. The first time we went to Bill's apartment, it left quite an impression on me. I finally got to see his pet raccoon he talked about and many other oddities. My eyes scanned around the room of all the old Hollywood pictures of his father's work. Brant and Bill also went to North Hollywood Assembly of God Church together as well. It was obvious they were becoming close.

I don't know how or why, but suddenly Brant broke it off with Bill. I think Bill was disturbed about rumors that were starting to get around, saying Brant was gay. It was true Brant spent an unusual amount of time around gay men after he moved to the Hollywood area. But gay men weren't his only dinner guests, and many of the characters I chauffeured around with Brant were immensely colorful.

Madame Bilquis Sheikh

One of my most memorable events in the limo was when I chauffeured Brant and Madame Bilquis Sheikh. She was a prestigious woman whose family had previously been in a high governmental position in Pakistan. This was before her conversion to Christianity.

Madame Sheikh gave her testimony at several of Kathryn Kuhlman's meetings and on her weekly television broadcast "I Believe in Miracles." Madame Sheikh came to Shekinah a number of times to share her testimony at the services, and she was featured on one of the Shekinah television tapings. She always referred to us in the ministry as "God's flowers in His garden."

When I chauffeured Madame Sheikh and Brant, we were on our way to dinner at the Beverly Hills Hotel. As we drove down Hollywood Boulevard, I noticed there was a police car behind me with his red lights on. I didn't think he was flagging me because I was going rather slowly during rush hour traffic. Then I heard the siren go off, so I pulled over. All of us in the car were puzzled at what was going on.

That's when Brant turned around to look and gasp and said in an excited voice, "They've got guns!"

I said, "They do?"

Our royal visitor said in her deep, aristocratic voice echoed me. "They do?"

The police called out over the loudspeaker, "Driver, throw the keys out the window and keep your hands in sight."

I did as they said, as we all stared, stunned and speechless. Then they told me to open the car door from the outside and get out slowly with my hands up. As I did, I noticed there was another officer behind me with his car door opened for a shield. He was pointing a weapon at me as he talked into the megaphone, instructing me on what to do. He told me to walk toward the sidewalk in front of the limousine.

As I did, I was startled to see four other officers with their weapons drawn, pointing them right at me. One officer was holding back traffic, and another was barricading the busy sidewalk. Two others crouched in firing position with rifles aimed at me. I looked up and there was a helicopter hovering above the buildings.

As an officer began to frisk me, the deputy with the megaphone told Brant to stick his hands out the window. Brant was wearing several diamond rings, and they glistened in the late afternoon California sunshine as he stuck his hands out the window. Then he was told to get out of the car slowly with his hands raised. He emerged, and he looked like quite the spectacle, wearing his double-breasted white suit and shiny shoes. As he got out with his hands in the air, he demanded, "What is the meaning of this? I can't believe it…I just can't believe this."

It must have looked like a scene from an action movie to the spectators. As the officer checked Brant's ID, they proceeded to open the back door to let Madame Sheikh out.

Brant was flustered at this point. He kept saying, "Be careful with her. She is Madame Bilquis Sheikh from the royal family of Pakistan."

Madame Sheikh was elegant, as usual, and very composed as the officer assisted her out of the car. Her sequined sari and matching white sequined purse glistened in the sunset like they were under a spotlight. The crowd pushed in closer, trying to get a closer look, gasping and whispering among themselves, trying to guess who she was and who we were.

Keep in mind this was the time before 9/11. Terrorists were not a threat on American soil and Muslims and those from India were not as common to see among the public, especially in Hollywood at the time.

When the officer reached for Madame Sheikh's handbag she said in her rich, aristocratic voice, "You will not find any pistol in the purse."

I was nervously laughing to myself, thinking this whole scene was not for real. As it turned out, two different license plates were on the limo, and no one had ever noticed. A limousine had been reported stolen earlier that day, and it was similar to our description.

Brant asked one of the officers to let me go so I could call the hotel and tell them we would be late. They agreed. I walked in the cafe behind us as all eyes stared at me. I called the Beverly Hills Hotel and told them who I was calling for. I said, "We are being held up at the moment," not realizing what I had said. In a moment the irony struck me, and I got a case of the giggles.

When I walked outside the café, the police were apologizing for the inconvenience, and they let us go. We went on our way. We continued our drive down the boulevard laughing over the adventure we just had. I dropped them off and returned later to pick them up, taking Madame Sheikh back to her apartment in Glendale. Even at that hour, we were still talking about what happened earlier in the evening, laughing helplessly about it. There were a number of dinners with other people but the one with Madame Shekinah was one of my favorite times.

That evening I drove Brant in the limo to Palm Springs. He had to get ready for a service later that week. It was late by the time we reached Palm Springs, and another police officer pulled us over. We explained what happened about the two license plates. At least he did not pull us out of the car with our hands up this time, and just as before, he let us go.

I pulled the limo away from the curb and muttered something from the 23rd Psalm about the valley of the shadow of death. As I looked in the rearview mirror, I could see Brant smiling faintly in approval, nodding and looking out the window while the world sped by under the midnight sky.

The Sun Lamp

When I first started working with Brant, I was tasked with reading his letters. I would get his mail after it was already opened. Any money sent to the ministry had already been taken out. If the money was specifically directed to Brant, it would go to him. He saved this and used it towards gifts for people.

Often the letters would request prayer or give testimony about what the ministry was doing for that person. When I got Brant's mail, I would read it to him, and he would tell me what to say. I took some notes with the little shorthand I knew from high school and typed the letters. Brant and I read his mail between the services, and he'd sign the letters that were ready to send.

I was not very good with this task. Brant realized how slow I was, but he was polite about it. He figured I had enough to do already.

One Saturday night after the service, I took Brant to his apartment. I was reading Brant's mail and making notes, and I got the idea to read those letters under his sunlamp. There were a lot of letters, so the job took a while.

I went to bed that evening, but I woke up with pain around my eyes a few hours later. It was dark. I stumbled toward the mirror, and I had to force my eyes open. When I did, I saw my face and eyes were red. I was scared. I realized I burned my eyes from the sun lamp.

I was too embarrassed to make my way downstairs and wake up the elders. I managed to look up a number in my phone directory, and I called Lydia, who served as the ministry's nurse. I realized I had fallen asleep with a green mud mask on my face and had to wash it off before she came over. I had a bowl of water and a towel and washed it off the best I could, feeling my face with my eyes closed.

Lydia came over with another sister, Elaine. Lydia asked what that green stuff on my face was. I told her, and we laughed about it. She finished cleaning me up, then the two of them took me to the emergency room.

The ER doctor looked at my eyes and said I was lucky I hadn't gone blind. He said my eyes should be wrapped for a couple days, and I had to apply ointment to them every few hours.

Lydia stayed with me that night. I had her call Brant for his Sunday morning wake up call. Then she went downstairs and told the household one of the elders needed to pick up Brant and take him to the Foursquare Church. Lydia made me breakfast and stayed with me through the day.

I could tell my eyes started to feel better and felt I could begin to open my eyes, but the doctor wanted me to remain with my eyes bandaged for at least a day. I felt self-conscious, and I was sure I looked funny with a bright red face and bandaged eyes.

After Sunday church, Brant came over. I heard him joking around while he was coming up the stairs, saying some people will do anything to get out of work. I told him what happened, and he joked with me about it. He wanted to know when I could get back to work. I told him it would be a day or two, and my eyes just needed to rest.

I felt embarrassed and wanted to forget about the whole thing. Brant was kind to me, even though I felt so foolish, and he was very accommodating. On some level, I think he might have felt some responsibility for my folly – I was reading his letters with his sunlamp.

Kevin came over and jumped right in, offering even more support than Claudia had. My face was red, and it peeled a few days after that. The rumors got around I'd burned my eyes, and people were concerned.

Later, Brant talked to Claudia about getting someone else to help him with his mail. I missed reading the letters and working with Brant on his replies, but I never did miss all that typing.

The Easter-In Gathering

In early 1974, preparations were underway for the Easter-In Gathering at the historic Long Beach Municipal Auditorium on the waterfront. The facility was built in the 1930's, designed to hold up to 8,000 people. In its day it had seen many famous performers, including Judy Garland, Elvis Presley and Bob Hope.

Just a few years earlier, my middle sister and I went to a concert sponsored by Calvary Chapel of Costa Mesa. Calvary Chapel put on the Maranatha concerts as an outreach for the youth. Chuck Smith often gave a salvation message and have an altar call. These were much smaller events than what we had planned for the spring of 1974.

It was a leap of faith for Shekinah to hold a whole week of meetings in such a large auditorium. Compared to the Foursquare Church weekly healing services, the Easter-In Gathering was enormous. Nonetheless, we all took on the task of promotion with a lot of zeal. We promoted the event with all types of advertising. We made posters to hang in public places, passed out flyers wherever we could, and put banners on city busses. We even made radio announcements to build anticipation.

Besides the promotion, what seemed like an army of volunteers spent months preparing for the event itself. Dozens of volunteers made decorations for the backdrop behind the stage. It took them a number of months to make enough tissue paper flowers to decorate the hall. The flowers were used to spell out "Jesus" in large letters behind the choir, and they were also scattered everywhere throughout the auditorium. Posters with different quotes from scripture were hung in the hallways that wrapped around the building leading into the main auditorium. There were also fresh flowers for the podium and other typical church decorations.

The weeks leading up to the gathering were incredibly busy, and they went by quickly. Brant hovered around every part of the preparations but never stayed in one spot for long. He kept morale up among the elders and the volunteers, meanwhile planning his own presentations. Keeping up with him nearly wore me out.

The week of the meetings arrived, and immediately there were concerns about crowd size. Things weren't going the way we'd hoped, but we weren't sure how to generate more buzz than we already had. We'd pinned our hopes on the radio promotions, bus banners and word-of-mouth. The results were uninspiring, but we all poured energy into the gathering and put on the best event we could.

We opened with a concert by the Maranatha Christian rock groups from Calvary Chapel. The music was first rate. An evening concert combined Shekinah's own music group and the piano player from Kathryn Kuhlman's ministry, Dino Kartsonakis.

I met with Dino and his manager before the service to get instructions about the lighting for the music pieces he was going to play. Having played the piano myself, I was a little in awe to meet Dino personally, face to face. He was really talented. Just a few years earlier I saw him at the Calvary Chapel television tapings with Kathryn Kuhlman, and I also watched him perform at her meetings at the Shrine Auditorium at her meetings.

The crowd for the Saturday healing service was a little larger than the previous nights. I was preparing for Brant's clothing changes and sending messages to different people for Brant, keeping busy and doing work I felt privileged to do. Suddenly amid the hustle, I paused and looked out the window.

Just across the waterfront from the auditorium, the Queen Mary ocean liner was docked. A wedding was being held aboard her that very night. I was missing out on the small celebration as my mother married Bruce. My brother and sisters were there, and I was sad I was not. I don't know how I would have taken it if I was there, watching my mother marry another person. I would have wanted to wish her every happiness, I'm sure. I just didn't believe she would find it with him.

I only stopped to reflect on these things for a moment. By then the healing service had started and the choir had performed their songs. Brant was delivering his message, and then he paused abruptly. He put his hand up to his forehead to block the light, and he peered past the follow spot. Looking into the front row he said, "Is that Lonnie Frisbee?"

Lonnie answered Brant with "Hi." I knew Brant and Lonnie were friends from way back, during the Calvary Chapel days. I wondered what Lonnie might be thinking about Brant in his position as a minister, his style so obviously inspired by Kathryn Kuhlman.

When the meeting was over, Lonnie came backstage. He met with Brant in his dressing room privately for awhile, then Lonnie left through the dwindling crowd.

It was the first time Brant met with Lonnie. I saw Lonnie meeting with Brant other times privately during the years I remained with the ministry. These meetings always puzzled me, but I could only guess at their content. I don't know what they talked about, and Brant never told me. I can say before the Easter-In service, I had never seen Brant stop in the middle of a meeting to call out to someone in the audience the way he had that night. Lonnie pulled a lot of weight with Brant.

Building up to the event, there was great anticipation and excitement among everyone for the gathering. We hoped the Easter-In Gathering would kick off some kind of revival within the city of Long Beach. The whole event was like one large staged dress rehearsal. The only thing missing was the large crowds.

The crowds just did not come as Brant had hoped. Standing outside the auditorium by the car in the dark parking lot, I heard him say, "I really thought the Lord told me to have this event." He was expressing his disappointment to Pastor Adams and Mrs. Adams after the final meeting. Pastor Adams put his hands-on Brant's shoulder and said, "You were obedient to the voice, and that's what counts." Mrs. Adams hugged Brant goodbye. They got into their car and drove off. I took Brant back to the apartment in the limo, and he was very quiet the whole way. We were all tired from the week and all that led up to it. Now it was time to shift focus to the next big thing. I didn't know what that would look like, but I was sure of one thing: Brant had a plan.

TV Tapings

It didn't take long for Brant's spirits to bounce back after the disappointment of the Easter event. Just as spring turns into summer, Brant was following through with his plans to model his path and style based on Kathryn Kuhlman's own ministry. There was a Christian television studio in Glendale across from the famous Forest Lawn cemetery. He planned to tape sermons at the studio and air them on TV.

For the tapings, Brant modeled the format after Kathryn Kuhlman's shows. There was a testimony, a short message and a song from the choir or one of the soloists. Before we could begin production, we had to prepare.

In order to get ready for the earlier tapings in Glendale, Brant and I worked on a concept for one of the sets. A crew of volunteers would put together what we decided upon. To get some ideas, we went to a craft store and looked around. We came up with something inexpensive, using cardboard cut into the shape of large grape clusters. We'd used spray paint and a stencil to add the grape design. It was cheap to produce but gave the set a lot of visual impact. We decided to go with it.

Coordination of the project fell to John & Charlene C., and they worked with many volunteers who helped pull it together. They met at the Shekinah house several times, once again creating a buzz of activity. Brant added a plan to have a large painted canvas as a backdrop. The backdrop design changed several times as different tapings were scheduled.

It made for a long day to get the set ready and hang the lights. We taped four to five shows a day, and guests would sometimes have to wait for hours. A number of takes had to be done over because of technical difficulties.

During these times, Brant got tired and irritated. He didn't like it when his train of thought was interrupted, and the lights were hot. He smiled, but his voice betrayed his true feelings. Once he made a remark to Robbie., who was in the control both, telling him to get it together. It was an awkward moment, because everyone in the studio heard him, including the studio audience. This put all of us on edge in an already tense situation.

In between tapings I prepared Brant's wardrobe for him. Claudia helped me get his clothes ready, and I would help him freshen up. Once while putting on his makeup, he got very tense. He stopped for a moment and looked at me and said, "I just cussed under my breath."

I was always amazed by the musical talent that came out of the ministry. Now it was being showcased on television. Brant's skill to interact with the guests was always entertaining, and I held him in awe. I couldn't believe I was working this close to Brant on a television set similar to the one I was on several years earlier with Calvary Chapel, hosted by Kathryn Kuhlman. He was every bit as charismatic as she was.

After the tapings, all the elders and some select individuals went with us to the same nearby restaurant. The host was always gracious to us. He had come to several of our services and was involved in Kathryn Kuhlman's ministry himself.

These times at the restaurant were special. I loved the camaraderie we all shared, and the food was great too. I'd order the filet mignon, since Brant had first suggested it to me. Bit by bit, he was guiding me spiritually and influencing me socially. I felt like I was being groomed for something greater, something that would take a long time to unfold.

Chuck Smith and Lonnie Frisbee "the seeing prophet" at a
baptism at Pirates Cove in Corona del Mar 1971

Brant 1972

Brant Baker 1973

Brant Baker during a healing service

Brant preaching

Brant & Linda D, summer camp 1973 making flower arrangements
for Randy and Marla's wedding. Jud is behind Brant.

Claudia W & Brant summer camp 1973

Shekinah Summer Camp summer 1973. 1st row middle is Brant. To his left sits Jo Ellen, Georgette & Kevin three over. Jud sits behind Brant.

Shekinah Worship Band: Randy., Lilly G., Joe., Randy S., Kelly G.,

Shekinah Ministry Choir, Terry B director, Easter-
In Gathering, Long Beach Arena, 1974

Foursquare Church Saturday healing service

TV Taping 1974 in Glendale Studios

Shekinah Singers Album, 1975, Kevin Baker 4th from the left, Jud is far right

Foursquare Church during a TV taping, 1976-77

Pastor Adams and wife of Foursquare Church

Brant & Madam Sheikh at Foursquare Church

Angelus Temple healing service

Jud, Elaine, actress Barbara Sigel ("Time to Run") and actor Wendell Burton ("The Sterile Cuckoo") at a Christian media banquet award ceremony, 1976.

Judson acting profile picture 1976

Fox Theater, Long Beach, CA

Inside Fox Theater

Brant praying for the sick in a service

Madge, Brant and Rocky at Fox Theatre healing service, 1977.

Brant and his mother Jo Ellen Baker after a service

Brant signing Christmas cards, 1977

Brant and Jo Ellen, 1978

Judson at Eric & Claudia wedding

Judson & Kristy Wedding 1979 with pastor Mike

CHAPTER 10:
BRANT FALLS IN LOVE

Shortly after I became Brant's assistant, one of the people who came into Brant's life was an attractive, toned, blond young man my age named Kyle. I believe the development of their relationship was one of the turning points in Brant's life. It planted a seed of gay desire that grew in the shadows, pushing him back toward his former decadent lifestyle.

Before meeting Kyle, Brant had continued to feel lonelier and more isolated from people. I tried to understand Brant at the time, but I didn't get it when he talked to me about these feelings. He always seemed to be surrounded by people, and he was the center of attention wherever he went. How could he be lonely? I just listened to him and let him talk it out.

When the meetings were smaller, he said, it was easier to connect with people. This is something I'd seen for myself – he was more approachable and easier to talk to before the ministry really took off. He was part of the group. As the ministry grew, he felt more nervous and self-conscious around others on a personal level. The need for added security measures didn't help, and he started to isolate himself. He became more selective about who was around him.

Like many performers onstage, Brant's spiritual persona took over while he was preaching. Once the service was over, his charismatic personality would go dormant, leaving him with an empty inside. He would withdraw into himself to recharge his battery.

Just before Kyle came into the picture, Brant and I were in Palm Springs for a healing service the next day at a local hotel. We were staying at his mother's condo. While watching the news on television in the living room, there was a story about a new church called the Metropolitan Community Church. It was a community gay church that was forming in the Los Angeles area.

The news story featured clips of the service, and we saw the people in the church singing the same worship songs we sung during at the Shekinah and Calvary Chapel services. When people sang praises to God and raised their hands in worship, Brant became very quiet. He leaned in toward the television, mesmerized by the broadcast.

I was thinking this was weird for a Christian church. How could the Holy Spirit move in a church service like this? It puzzled me, especially after I had been outed in church for my homosexuality and healed by the Holy Spirit. Brant turned his head toward me, his eyes wide open, and we looked at each other. I thought, "what was he thinking?" Yet, I knew this would be a turning point for him as though he found an answer he was looking for. Neither of us said a word.

Kyle

Soon after that night, Brant started to notice Kyle at the Saturday meetings. A Christian girlfriend of Kyle's brought him to the Shekinah house the week we prepped for the Easter-In Gathering. We were all busy, working on the decorations. Kyle approached Brant with a question, and Brant answered Kyle casually. Right away, Brant took him around the house and introduced him to some of the elders as his friend.

Not too long after that, Brant had me invite Kyle to come with Brant and me on a retreat for a few days. Kyle accepted, and so it began. The three of us would get away regularly in between the weekly services.

Kyle was fascinated with Brant's healing ministry, like many of the onlookers and those who played a part behind the scenes. He wanted to be close to Brant in some way, like many others. He wanted to get his attention, be a part of him and the ministry.

I don't know how long Kyle had been attending the services before he approached Brant that evening at the Shekinah house. I do remember once when Brant mentioned him in the car. Kyle had eyes on him for awhile. I don't remember the question he asked Brant, but it worked to get the conversation started. From that point, Kyle was with Brant wherever we went.

Brant's brother Kevin was already jealous of me for all the time I spent with Brant. When Kyle came into the picture soon after I did, Kevin was not happy with the situation at all. He tried even harder to get his brother's attention.

Kevin befriended Kyle and remained on Brant's good side. He played along so he would still have access to Brant and hold his attention, despite Brant's increasing isolation. This was an ongoing theme with Kevin, a dynamic that played out between him, Brant and their mother Jo Ellen.

It was all he could do to get a share of attention to be noticed as his brother became more renowned. In many ways I didn't blame Kevin for acting out and manipulating people the way he did. It wasn't my place to judge him or get involved in the family dynamic, and I just went along with it.

The first place Kyle went with Brant and me was a beach house in Ventura, about two hours north of Long Beach on the other side of L.A. The church was renting the house at the time to be used as a retreat for Brant and the elders. I knew about the place, but I'd never been there before. All three of us were planning to take off in the limo right after the Saturday service.

Just before the service, I noticed the car's oil pressure gauge was low, and I added some oil. I did not realize the limo was leaking oil, but I felt something was wrong. I should have followed through and acted on my instinct. That evening, after the service, when we had been driving for nearly two hours, I noticed the engine light was going on and off.

Brant saw my reaction, sensed something was wrong, and he asked about it. I told him about the oil gauge, and how I had already added oil earlier. Just then, the limo stalled, and I managed to coast to the offramp. I guided the car off the freeway, coasting until it stopped in a dimly lit parking lot. We noticed a sign that said State Prison.

The limo had rolled to a stop near a payphone. It was dark and very foggy, and the prison made the scene especially spooky.

Just as we were looking for change to use the payphone, a car pulled up, and we were blinded by the head lights. Then a tall figure of a man appeared and approached the limo. We didn't know what to make of the situation.

Brant told me to call the Shekinah house and ask someone there for help, explaining we were stranded. I got out of the limo and walked past the stranger. I couldn't see him, but his vibe was heavy. My heartbeat fast.

The man asked if we were all right, wavering slightly where he stood. He seemed stoned or drunk. He said he just got out of prison and again asked if we needed any help. I told him I was just making a phone call and left the explanation at that. The man followed me to the payphone, but I just ignored him, sensing his presence behind me.

Kyle, the zealous young Christian he was, got out of the limo and approached the man. He started to witness to him about Jesus. I was holding my breath, clenching the phone as I started to dial. Randy. answered my call, and I told him the situation. He said he would be there as soon as he could. We could only wait.

Kyle managed to get rid of the intruder, and we felt relieved – at least temporarily. Kyle seemed confident during the confrontation. He was cocky about the fact he knew martial arts and was sure he could have handled the guy. It was not too long afterwards, a police officer showed up and asked what we were doing. Three guys in a limo on a dark foggy night by the state prison must have looked pretty strange. The only light showing through the fog was the payphone close by.

Brant explained to the officer who he was and what happened. He told him that we were waiting to get help with the car. The officer told us to be careful, and he added there was a nearby coffeeshop up the road. We decided to go there to get something to eat then come back to the limo in a couple of hours. Just as we got back to the limo, Randy, Robby and their wives shortly showed up in two cars. We took the church Impala car, while Randy and Robby decided for the limo to be towed back to Long Beach to be repaired. Later on, a second limo, sleeker and less hearse looking, would be purchased.

It was early morning by the time we got to the beach condo. I slept in the living room while Brant and Kyle slept in the bedroom. For several days that we were there, Brant and Kyle would be gone for several hours at a time. When they got back, the three of us would go out to eat. I don't remember what we talked about.

Kyle was on an emotional high and shared about a couple visions that had to do with angels he and Brant saw while on their walks. I did not know what to say and so said nothing – just smiled. Brant seemed to be happy, and I was happy for him. Toward the end of the week, I drove us back to Long Beach with Brant and Kyle in the backseat of the Impala.

The following Saturday after the service, the three of us went out to eat. After that we went to Brant's apartment, and I took Joy the dog out for a walk, as was my accustomed task.

When I got back, there was a tangible magnetism between them, and Kyle was silent as Brant pulled me aside. Brant told me Kyle would be staying at his apartment that night, and he was sending me home. He asked me to phone him in the morning with his usual wake up call, then pick him up for the Sunday morning service at the Foursquare.

Brant told me how he appreciated Kyle – that he was so sweet and kind, and he comforted him like a little puppy. He added that last night in the back of the car, as I was driving us home, Kyle held his hand. Brant said it was a gesture of deep friendship and kindness.

Kyle ended up staying at Brant's apartment off and on for a couple weeks. At one point I was tasked with helping Kyle get his things out of the halfway house where he was staying. For a short time, he was to stay with me until other arrangements could be made. He also spent time as a guest of other members of the ministry.

Kyle was starstruck. From his perspective, Brant came to his rescue at the right time, and he felt that Brant could do no wrong – just as many of us did. He would sit in the service watching Brant with puppy love in his eyes. Clearly these feelings went beyond gratitude or mutual admiration. This looked like a romance.

The Elders Lose Patience

It all happened so quickly, it seemed, and I felt pushed out of the picture. It was my job to assist Brant and be his companion. While Kyle was temporarily in the picture, I ended up as a valet, driver, and assistant to both Brant and Kyle. I accepted the situation and went along with it, keeping my mouth shut. The elders and others just accepted it as well. If there was any judgment about it, they kept it to themselves, not questioning what was taking place between Brant and Kyle.

I thought it was strange, like they were dating each other. Kyle stayed late into the night at Brant's apartment. I tried to rationalize it and told myself it could be brotherly love, like John and David in the Old Testament. That's how Brant and Kyle would sometimes talk about it between themselves. But the deeper undercurrent of feeling between them spoke of another kind of love.

The time Brant and Kyle were spending with each other was beginning to wear Brant down. He said he wanted to break away from it, feeling that it was breaking his focus on his relationship with the Lord. Brant told me "I don't know what to do with him. I can't seem to get away from him." He started to feel smothered. Brant told Kyle he needed space to be with the Lord, and it was hard for him to be around Kyle so much.

Kyle was needy, clinging to Brant's companionship with a desperate desire. He showed his feelings openly more than Brant did. Soon Brant tried to distance himself from Kyle several times, telling him it was not healthy to see each other so much. This began a battle between them as they talked about breaking it off. I was witness to the entire struggle, back and forth.

Brant loved Kyle and clearly felt sorry for him because he had come from a rough home life. Brant accepted his bold, vain, cocky sweet way. He melted when Kyle's feelings got hurt and he'd look pleading at Brant with his puppy dog eyes. So many of the young people in the congregation came from dysfunctional families. I wondered what made Kyle any different to deserve the extra attention.

Kyle would hold Brant's hand in the back of the car as I drove, and he would cuddle up to Brant like he was a teddy bear. I remained the silent, loyal servant who drove the car and took care of them. I wondered what was really going on with them, and it confused me. I kept getting mixed messages.

There were times I felt resentful about taking care of Kyle's clothes, since he was now sharing Brant's wardrobe. Under ordinary circumstances, this was beyond the scope of my job. But my job entailed taking care of Brant, and so I felt obligated to take care of someone who made him so happy – even if the happiness was only intermittent.

Kyle was so forward with me, expressing openly how he felt about Brant. I felt like the jealous servant, and I could relate to the way Kevin must have felt. It seemed Kyle was the one who got all the attention, even though I was hired to be a companion for Brant. This love between the two of them was hard for me to watch and accept, no matter how they tried to explain it.

At the same time, I was thankful for my position and what I was learning. I believed I was learning from a master teacher and held my doubts about him inside. Yet I was feeling lonely myself, since my position required me to be separated from everyone else. Most of my time was consumed with taking care of Brant's needs, making Kyle feel happy and welcomed into the fold.

Kyle was given full access to the Shekinah house and Brant's dressing room. The elders didn't say anything about it, but I could tell they were all watching what was going on. I was questioned by some of the elders about what Brant was doing or why Kyle had so much access. It all seemed suspicious.

I remember so clearly the moment I realized Brant had lost the elders' patient understanding about Kyle. He was talking to Charlene C., one of the elder's wives, just before I was to take him to the church for service. He told her he felt that Kyle was just what he needed, so young with such a fresh perspective.

Charlene C listened politely, smiling and nodding as he spoke. But after Brant left to get into the car, she told me she felt that Kyle was sent by the devil to bring Brant down. Whatever the truth of that, it was a long drive for me as I took him to the church.

During the drive, Brant told me once again that he was getting more concerned he had strong feelings for Kyle, and he did not know what to do. He said he knew he was the one who created this mess, and he wanted to figure a way out of it.

Brant wanted Kyle to become interested in someone else and get involved with other members of the church. He felt Kyle's company was hindering his ministry, and it would be best if they broke it off. It was hard for Brant to say "no" to Kyle when he was around him. They both felt God had a plan for their friendship in some way, but it was getting out of control. The kind of attention Kyle demanded from Brant went beyond affection, and he had become clingy and possessive.

I think Kyle picked up on Brant's feelings. He confided in me that God told him to leave, to go into the mountains to pray, or something spiritual to that effect. Kyle said he was used to being to himself, having survived the abuse of his family, and he intentionally portrayed the image that he was tough.

Part of this tough image involved his skill with martial arts. It gave him the satisfaction and confidence he needed to cope with life's many struggles and upsets. He also used it to flirt with Brant. At times Kyle would show off, pulling some kind of karate move on him. Brant would scream and laugh with delight. I think part of Kyle's charm was he treated Brant in a way that no one else could, physically overpowering him and challenging him.

Brant and Kyle broke off their relationship a few times. The first time, Kyle left for a few weeks, and Brant was relieved, though was also silent and concerned for him. Kyle came back, but once again, they broke it off. The second time, their dynamic was more intense, and it seemed harder for Brant to break away.

Kyle became involved with other members of the Shekinah group. By then, the ministry body knew who he was, and he was accepted by others, fitting into their cliques. He even dated some of the girls for a short time. One was Lisa G., Kelly's sister. She was a new Christian herself, and she was not only kind but gorgeous. Her long blonde hair and model figure led people to talk about her, calling her the perfect Barbie doll. No matter how ideal Kyle and Lisa appeared to be as a couple, the relationship between Kyle and Brant was far from resolved.

I later thought how confusing it must be for Kyle as a new Christian to look up to Brant. He told me more than once that he cast Brant as a superstar, saint and hero all at once. Though he didn't say as much, it was clear to see

Kyle was vulnerable. I know he loved Brant, and he must have been confused about whether Brant used his position to manipulate him.

Their relationship as companions had romantic attachments that were intense and out of control. I didn't know whether they were sexually involved – Brant never told me, and I never asked. Kyle would not have said anything to me about it directly since he wanted to protect Brant's position or Kyle was scared for himself. Still I knew something was going on. No one could deny it.

A Test For Me

While I watched this unfold, I struggled with a secret relationship of my own. Jeff and I had become close, even though he was married. The social climate of the time was strongly anti-gay, but same-sex love was even more taboo among evangelical Christian circles. I could not bring myself to tell Brant about Jeff and me, though I deeply wanted to. Maybe he already knew, or at least suspected. Maybe he saw something in me I couldn't see in myself.

The night I had the spiritual healing from homosexuality at Shekinah, I figured there was going to be a test for me at some point. Not too long after that, it became clear: my strong feelings for Jeff was just that test.

I happened to notice Jeff because he had several positions in the ministry as a deacon, usher, and a Word of Knowledge person. I was strongly attracted to him, and I confused those feelings with what was considered a healthy Christian brotherly love. I thought I'd had a healing. How could I continue to have the desires that grew inside me? I did not have the maturity or understand the hormonal chemistry that was taking place in my head and body.

Neither did I know how complicated it would be to confront my same-sex feelings and attractions to men when it came to my Christian beliefs. I thought I understood what my boundaries were and what was healthy for me spiritually.

During the fellowship services, Brant would often talk about the time he first saw the Shekinah cloud as he prayed for his grandmother. I myself got impressions about people, but I had no visions at the time. I remember Jeff saying during the healing services he would see a pink cloud like bubble gum or cotton candy come over the congregation, and he'd have visions of a cloud like formation of a hand pointing to different people in the congregation for him to pray with.

Jeff's ability was alluring. I thought it was strange, and I was impressed with him. I was attracted to him. Beyond this brotherly affection, he inspired attraction from all sides, not just me. To me, he was extremely masculine with his blond hair, toned shoulders, a strong chin and a soothing voice. He overpowered me with his influence, looks and strength. It made me melt in his presence.

I happened to notice him in the summer camp of '73 where he often wore a tank top. He was athletic with trim, muscular arms and firm pecs. I just started to talk to him making small talk. We cultivated a causal relationship at the ministry meetings.

At the church that summer of 73, I happened to notice Jeff seemed distant, keeping to himself. I sensed he was struggling with some burden, but he put on a front and tried not to show it. I came up to him and told him I was praying for him – that I sensed he was feeling a burden. He seemed struck by what I said, but he only said thank you and walked away. Even though I took this as a rejection, I continued to approach him.

Out of the blue, he came up to me at the church after the service and hugged me then walked away. It was not until I moved to the Shekinah house, we started to get more involved. We would see each other after I was done attending to Brant's needs. He lived next door, downstairs from the duplex with his wife Ann, who was pregnant at this time.

One Sunday night after I came home from Brant's, I noticed Jeff was out on the flat part of the roof near my balcony window. He'd been praying and looking out at the city. To get there, he must have entered my room or climbed the tree or fence next to the balcony that led to the roof top. I remembered when Brant talked about being on the roof and Jeff was standing there gazing out into the night sky at the lights of the city below.

I went to stand next to him, but he did not respond. When he noticed me, he seemed a little startled. I put my arm around him and said, "I have been praying for you... It seems the Lord has given me a burden and love for you."

He responded that he felt he was under pressure and needed the prayers, then he put his arm around me. We were silent and decided to go inside my room and sat on the coach. Then we prayed for each other as we held hands.

After that, we embraced each other for the longest time, it seemed. Before I knew it, we were on the floor, still embracing each other with my back on the floor. We never kissed, just held each other. He was rubbing his hands up and down my body, on my chest and arms, then he held his face close to mine. I was confused and excited at the same time inside while my heart was racing.

He seemed to be in a daze, as though he was drugged, as he continued to caress my upper body. He held his face close to mine while his breathing got heavier. Then his hands started to rub my lower abdomen. My stomach was twitching with excitement, and I was thinking, "Is this right? Is this okay?" His hands then reached lower into my pants. I thought, "This can't be right."

Jeff pulled his hand out and snapped out of it. He apologized – "I'm sorry. I'm really sorry about that."

I said, "It's okay," at a loss for any other words.

He pulled away for a moment then embraced me again. We caressed each other and held our faces close, but we never kissed. We held each other in silence, neither one of us wanting to let go. We just took in the moment of closeness and warmth.

I never felt this heightened feeling before toward someone in that frame of compassionate love and sexual excitement. I was confused, yet it felt so gratifying in that moment. I figured as long as we did not have sex and kiss each other it was all right.

"Am I gay?" I thought. I don't know if I was or not, but I dared not say anything about it to anyone. This was very different from two guys wanting to explore their bodies and fool around. This was far more intense than a quick mutual masturbation like I experienced before with Brad. The feelings I was having for Jeff were more romantic than I'd ever experienced before. It was frightening to me and exciting at the same time.

This situation was foreign to me. Was this love? Was I in love with a man – a married man? Was I having an affair? I thought he must know what he is doing since he's in a leadership position.

We remained in that embrace until we both dozed off. It was about dawn, and we were still on the floor. Jeff said he had to go. He got up and left, and we did not say anything more. I went to bed and fell asleep for several hours.

The Morning After and Beyond

Jeff came to my room late in the morning and asked if I was all right. I said everything was fine. Neither one of us said any more, and he left. The rest of the week I was mulling that night in the back of my mind, staying busy at work with Brant, my usual reading of the Bible, and prayer. I prayed for guidance.

My relationship with Jeff was developing further at the same time that Brant's relationship with Kyle was quickly escalating. That was fine with me. I thought Brant also might be struggling with an inappropriate love relationship with the same sex. I thought this is the way it was with David and Jonathan in the Old Testament – two men who cared for each other and were closer than brothers.

The following Saturday at the service, I saw Jeff again. I did not go out of my way to run into him during the week. We glanced at each other at the church, and I went on attending to what I normally did throughout that evening service.

That Sunday, I picked Brant up to attend the morning Foursquare service and spent the day with him. Afterwards I dropped him off at his apartment and walked his dog once again. Brant usually let me have Monday off with the car unless he wanted me to call him for something.

I went back to my room and noticed Jeff was on the roof again. He was standing there again, like before. I hesitated to go to the roof to meet with him, but I couldn't help myself. I felt overpowered by him, and my heart was beating fast. He put his arm around me like before, and I welcomed it.

He said, "I know you are praying for me, and God has given you a love for me." I was touched. He said he was under a lot of pressure, and I felt bad for him. I wanted to comfort him. We went back into my room and sat on the couch again. I let him talk it out.

Jeff went on to say he was under pressure about the ministry, and he'd come under spiritual attack because of his work and Ann being pregnant. He wondered if Brant liked him, and he wondered what Brant thought about him in general. He said, "Maybe that is why God gave you this love for me." I agreed.

I felt overwhelmed and concerned for him as he went on. I was still trying to understand these feelings I had toward him – trying to decide what to do about them. I felt it was okay since he was older (by three years), and he seemed more mature and wiser than me. I respected the fact that he had a position in the ministry. I was passive in the relationship, although emotionally we depended on each other in the beginning. I let him take the lead, do what he wanted to do. He asked if I would pray for him.

We started out holding hands, praying earnestly, first to bless and strengthen Brant and the ministry. Then we prayed for each other, binding the devil and asking for God's comfort for each other and strength together. Again, I prayed for Jeff, asking God to help him deal with the pressure he was feeling and resist any attack he was coming under in the ministry. I prayed God would give him strength as a husband and new father. Then we comforted each other. This went on for a long time, embracing each other.

Our intimacy continued for a couple months it seemed, always following a similar pattern. Sometimes I would go to his apartment. Ann would go to bed, leaving Jeff and me together, alone. Sometimes we walked in the night around the neighborhood. There was a school yard nearby, and we did pull ups on the monkey bars.

Afterwards we'd head back to the apartment and talk some more. That would lead into our prayers. We always embraced each other into the early morning. This was getting tough to deal with. My heart raced, desiring more. I am surprised we had the self-control we did with each other. I was exhausted, confused and guilty, but I could not stop myself. I figured he would be the one to put a stop to it.

Turbulent Attractions

I think Brant trusted me to be discreet about his own activities, and he left it at that. He knew I would not say anything about what went on between him and Kyle; I always went along with his wishes. But he never asked much about my personal life. The conversation was almost always one way. I knew Brant felt lonely inside. It was part of my job as his companion to help allay that. Now that this part of my job was taken over by someone else, I was the one who felt lonely and isolated.

I thought if I opened up to Brant, we could be more honest with each other about the things hindering us. I had the best of intentions. That frank discussion didn't happen.

It could be that neither of us was mature enough to handle this kind of openness, since we both were still very young. I was only 19, and he was in his mid-20's. We were each struggling with our sexuality at different levels. Maybe we were protected from each other by a higher power. Brant had Kyle and I had Jeff. These involvements kept a barrier between Brant and me and prevented us from having a relationship that went beyond brotherly Christian love.

I was not attracted to Brant romantically, other than an honest, open caring for him and a desire to serve him in the Lord. I wanted to learn from him and take this opportunity to better myself. I can't speak for Brant, and I don't know if he was attracted to me. I was hired to be his companion and assistant, yet Brant needed something more – something he must have known I couldn't give him. He was secretly planning a way to fulfill that desire and justify it in his mind, whether or not I was his employee.

As a spiritual leader, Brant's homosexual desires would not have been tolerated among the kind of evangelicals the church was ministering to. That night in Palm Springs when we saw the news clip about the gay church was a turning point. It awakened Brant's long-buried, latent desires he struggled with in private. His wistful wishes played all over his face. His wide eyes told me everything. I had not known he found a way out. He could be a gay man and still hold onto his Christian beliefs.

For the time being, it appeared that Kyle fulfilled the desire and attraction Brant was looking for, though their affair was a poorly disguised secret. Even in a Christian church, two grown men holding hands could not be interpreted as mere brotherly love. As young as I was – as naive as I was – even I knew that.

There were clearly hints of flirtation in what Brant was saying to me from the start, and he may have picked up the undercurrent of feelings I had for Jeff – the feelings I was struggling with and was so confused about. It would only be a matter of time before Brant had to find an outlet for his own gay feelings. He needed a way to express his sexuality without the guilt he was feeling or the responsibility to the ministry he'd created. Bonding with Kyle was a natural outcome.

I don't know how I would have reacted if he was franker with me. I believe Brant knew that propositioning me could have ended badly for him as a man and as a minister. He was masterfully balancing our relationship, keeping me in the loop about how he felt toward Kyle. My role was to serve as a sounding board, someone he could trust.

It was obvious Brant was pulling farther away from the original core group of men who worked together, the friends who had laid the foundation of the ministry for Brant. Yes, it was the work of the Holy Spirit that brought people together attracted to the vision. Now these men were married and were starting families of their own. Their desires were changing, their goals were shifting, and Brant could not follow in that mold.

Later on, this all made sense when I looked at the changes Brant made by separating himself from the Shekinah house. I realize now he was wrestling with his homosexual desires. He knew he had to be discreet about his feelings, what he could say, and to whom he'd say it.

He wanted more, though he hid behind what he created with the inspiration from his mentors, Kathryn Kuhlman and Aimee Semple McPherson. Their model helped him become a channel to be used by the Holy Spirit to develop a healing ministry. He had to find his own voice and style of leadership as he struggled to be honest with himself about who he was.

Brant wasn't the only one growing and changing during this time. The ministry went through an immense transformation from 1973 through 1975, and the core of elders who helped him start the church could not handle the swiftness of the changes taking place. One by one, they left on their own or were pushed out. In time, all were replaced. The path of the ministry could not escape Brant's own turmoil or his losing wrestling match with his temptations.

In the early years when Brant first started his ministry, he vowed to himself he would denounce his past life. He seemed to overcome his earthly desire for the pleasures of drugs and gay sex. Since the ministry was experiencing rapid growth within just a few short years, the pressures from the church, his family and his inner struggle were having an effect. Separating himself from others seemed logical to him, and he could justify his distance from the elders by saying they needed more independence from him. In essence, he was giving them the autonomy to operate on their own, using that as a cover while he pursued his own agenda.

This was a lot for a young minister to take on. The pressures and disillusion brought on by rapid spiritual success seemed light years away from the other Christian churches that had grown more slowly and supported his ministry.

Kyle fell for Brant's attraction, but it soon became too much for him to handle. Kyle felt trapped and confused. He must have been wrestling with it in his own mind, trying to reconcile his relationship to Brant and how he understood scripture when it came to homosexuality. Kyle had to keep what was happening between them a secret. Brant told him no one would believe him, even if he did say anything. Brant did not want to sabotage the ministry after working so hard up to this point. He knew such a disclosure would disappoint many people and create a crisis of confidence among his congregation.

Brant must have known about Lonnie Frisbee's own homosexuality at the time, and he periodically dropped hints about it. Based on what he knew about his own homosexuality, Brant understood Lonnie's gay tendencies would not be accepted among evangelical circles, and it too had to remain a secret.

From the things Brant said to me about Kyle and how he felt about him, I knew Brant was hurting inside. Yet it seemed I was experiencing this same situation simultaneously with Jeff. I dared not ask Brant any further questions since I was feeling guilty about my own involvement with a gay lover. I was wrestling with the question about whether what I was doing was right or not. I felt out of control, and I was constantly trying to figure out how to break away from Jeff. It was especially awkward since we lived under the same roof at the Shekinah house.

The night before the Easter-In Gathering, Kyle stayed with Brant at his apartment. Brant told me privately he needed to be separated from Kyle so he could focus on the event, but he could not bring himself to say no to Kyle.

He must have felt confused and vulnerable, since he could not bring himself to leave Brant's side. Had I suspected they were having sex or that Brant was putting pressure on Kyle, I don't know what I would have done. I think Brant wanted to say something about it, judging from the hints he was giving me. I was too inexperienced to broach the subject, and Brant didn't follow through on the topic.

Instead he did what seemed like the next best thing and talked to Pastor Adams. Several times he opened up about his feelings for Kyle and how he cared for him. Pastor Adams seemed not to pick up on the subtext of Brant's confessions, and the pastor's advice was unfortunately irrelevant as a result. He said the young man had a hard life and that Brant was to be commended for helping him through a hard time. Even this approach wasn't bringing Brant closer to his desired outcome.

The Romance Gets Rocky

Brant wanted me to call Kyle and break it off. It hardly seemed fair that Brant should put this task onto someone else, and I thought about protesting. But in reality, I asked myself how many difficult discussions I would have if I could hire someone else to do it. In fact, I was thinking I needed to do the same thing with Jeff and break it off. I decided to tackle one demon at a time.

Kyle was staying with me some of the time, and the rest of the time he was someone else's guest. I tracked him down, called him up, and we had that talk. I told him that Brant needed space from him for now. The whole conversation was awkward, especially over the phone, and Kyle said little to me in response. From his point of view, the whole thing boiled down to the fact he was being dumped by a man of God. It was a struggle to separate his healthy spiritual feelings from the romantic feelings that two young guys had for each other. Brant should have known better than to pick up on a young man that was still a teenager and the responsibilities he had running this type of ministry.

Kyle did not stay long with me after that. Lydia found another location for him and his brother Danny. The brothers' house had a number of deacons there. Brant encouraged Kyle to be involved with other people in the ministry. It was not long before Kyle and Lisa G. were dating, though it did not last long.

While Brant was spending time with Kyle, he started to have me lay out a white sheet on the floor in his dressing room. He said he didn't want to get his clothes soiled when he prayed on his knees for a short time by himself after the service was over. I would block the door or one of the guards posted until he was ready.

When he opened the door, I immediately gathered the sheet up off the floor, folded it up, and put it away. Sometimes there were tears or mucous on the sheet from his crying, and his face betrayed his private struggle. Were they tears of gratitude he was being used as an instrument of the Holy Spirit? Or were they tears of repentance and strong sense of unworthiness, despite his inner struggles? I wondered why he felt he needed to do that and why he felt so horrible inside. What was going on with him? It concerned me.

I really think he felt his unworthiness most strongly after a service, and he was having a struggle within himself, facing the thoughts and desires he was battling at the same time. He would often comment about how hard it was to be among many people who were expecting something from him. He had to make the transition by being alone in a hotel or at his apartment. Brant said he knew how hard it was for some celebrities when they were in crowds – how masses of people looked up to them and wanted a piece of them. He understood what it would do to their psyche to have that kind of pressure then to be pulled away and taken to a small room after a performance.

Without a strong sense of self and a firm grounding in his own worth, Brant could hardly have confidence that his supporters' adoration was justified. This explained why he was often quiet after a service, delving deeply into his own private thoughts.

There was a short episode I thought was interesting when Brant was in his silent mood. Shortly before Brant broke it off with Kyle, the three of us went to the Foursquare Church alone in the limo. The sanctuary was empty and still. I had a large key ring I often carried for Brant, and he wanted me to unlock the lid of the organ. He started to play a classical piece I recognized, though I did not know the composer.

Kyle and I sat in the auditorium. Brant must have played for an hour, so expressively. The poignant music seemed to go with his thoughts and all that he was contemplating. After he was done, we got up and left without words. Brant was in the back seat of the limo with Kyle, and very little was said.

I believe it was then when Brant decided to find a way to break it off with Kyle and separate himself from Kyle's brother, Danny. I took Brant home, then dropped Kyle where he was staying. As I drove back to the Shekinah house, the limousine felt cavernous and empty.

Shedding Kyle and His Brother

Gradually, the personal time I had with Brant was disappearing. I thought it had to do with my distraction with Jeff. I couldn't break away from him, and I was addicted to our relationship. Like anyone in love, I was finding it hard to focus.

Kyle's younger brother, Danny, was another cute blond kid. Danny was staying at a camp for troubled teens, living in one of the dormitory bunkhouses.

Early on, Kyle told Brant he wanted to help his brother and get him out of the place he was staying. He wanted him to get involved with the ministry and live at one of the brothers' houses and become involved with the ministry. He was sure the move would help Danny. Kyle said that his brother was saved but he just needed guidance. Kyle helped convince Brant to help with the plan, adding that since Brant was a minister, he could sign the release forms.

I drove Kyle to the camp – somewhere in L.A. County – to pick up his brother. I remember seeing a bunch of counselors sitting around in an office, telling us where to go. We followed their directions out to the dormitory to get Danny when we got our first taste of things to come. We got the stare-down from a group of teenage boys as we entered the room to get Danny and his things.

Danny did have a sweet spirit about him, but it would be a roller coaster ride to watch over him. I was already taking care of the needs of Brant and Kyle. Now I'd be taking care of Kyle's brother too. The hostile attitude from his fellow roommates at the halfway house was a chilling dose of reality.

By then it was decided all the elders were to move out of the main house and get their own places. Linda. had made the case to Brant about letting the elders move on their own. It cost about the same amount of money. In return, a group of deacon couples and some other brothers moved into the Shekinah house.

This shuffle meant I was living in the downstairs apartment next door to the Shekinah house, living with another deacon. Danny and Kyle stayed with me off and on from that point, with one of them sleeping on the couch, the other in an extra bedroom.

For awhile I had to keep track of Danny's whereabouts since he had a tendency to run away. Kyle would know where to find him, and we'd use the limo to bring him back.

As a matter of routine, Brant was now accompanied by Kyle, his brother Danny and me. Danny seemed bored most of the time, and I had to find him something to do. He felt out of place, I'm sure. He was like the adopted child that everyone had to accept among the main ministers.

Danny was soft-spoken and shy. He would read his Bible and listen to messages about scripture, but he would wander around during the services, out of place and disengaged. He had a habit of taking things and would return them if he was found out.

When the ministry was at an outreach in the Riverside area, Brant told me privately to watch his large key ring he had with his car keys. By then, the first limo was traded in for a sports car Brant had. He left to take his place in front of the auditorium. I left his dressing room to get something, and when I returned, sure enough the ring of keys were gone. Danny was nowhere to be found – he had taken Brant's sport car!

After the service I got a verbal lashing from Brant while Claudia and some of the elders stared at me with frank disapproval. That's when Kyle came in and told us he knew where Danny would be. Kyle borrowed the church's Impala to go find his brother. Meanwhile I drove Brant, Lisa G, and Claudia to a party in the Hollywood Hills, hosted by the cousin of Desi Arnaz Jr.

The Spanish style home formerly belonged to a silent movie star I don't remember. I was excited to go – it was my first real Hollywood party. It turned out to be a bit of a disappointment, not the big bash I had envisioned. I wandered through the house, admiring and curious. In one of the bedrooms, there was a picture of Desi Arnaz, Jr. and his sister, Lucy.

Kyle found his brother and returned the car the next day. They both were sorry for what Danny did.

Brant was so consumed with Kyle and Danny, he defended his relationship with both of them. Yet I don't think he realized the kind of impression it was making on other members in the ministry. Brant was soon to be tested.

The test came when there was some kind of misunderstanding between Danny and Baby Face John. Something John said to Danny made him run away, as he would often do. This time, somehow John got the blame.

I was getting Brant's clothing ready in the dressing room at an outreach service. Kyle was telling Brant about the misunderstanding, and Brant got wound up. He said, "We will have to do a Mathew. We'll rebuke John in front of the others to teach him the lesson."

I silently protested, thinking to myself, "But the scriptures say go to your brother in private first to correct the matter, then take two or three witnesses." Brant jumped straight to the hard lesson.

He asked John to get Randy. and bring him to join us in the meeting room at the back of the church. Randy came into the room, as requested, and Brant asked him to call everyone together. Just before the service, Brant called an emergency meeting with the ministry core. Then he had Baby Face John come into the room.

Brant exhorted the group about the importance of loving each other and getting along, or something to that effect. He then called Baby Face John to the center of the room and told everyone the story about Danny and what John had said.

Brant said Danny was a weak sheep who needed our help. He said John's remark to him was dangerous, that it would make Danny stumble – would make him run away and take some drugs.

John tried explaining what really happened, but Brant would not let him finish. He cut him off and rebuked him for being disrespectful. John protested he was not being disrespectful but was just trying to get the story straight. I could see Baby Face John start to tremble.

Everyone in the room was in disbelief about what was taking place before their eyes. Some just stood there with their hands at their sides or clasped in front of them. A number of the girls were crying. A frustrated Baby Face John started to cry.

Once Brant was done with his tongue lashing, he left John there – his heart bleeding – and quickly left the room. I followed him out. Slowly, people started to leave the room and go back to their positions. When I entered the dressing room, Brant was getting dressed. He asked if I thought he got the message across, reminding me that's what the scriptures tell us to do when a brother is in error.

I said, "He got the message." I didn't say anything more. I felt bad for Baby Face John, especially since we were roommates once. Throughout the service, people were still talking about what had happened. Some whispered about how careful we should be, stunned and embarrassed. There were few chances for any of them to speak with Danny after that.

Brant was feeling the strain of his relationship with Kyle and his brother. Danny was found again and lived in several different locations from those in the ministry. Soon he left on his own to become involved in another church. Kyle also left the ministry, along with a broken spirit after his roller coaster ride with Brant. At the time, we all believed it was the last we would see of Kyle.

These events marked a turning point for all of us and a true test of Brant's leadership. We could forgive. But it was hard to forget.

CHAPTER 11:

SUMMER LOVE AND LOSS

So Many Moves

When I worked for Brant, he never could settle down to stay in one place very long. He kept moving every few months, increasingly uncomfortable and paranoid about people watching him.

Once he was in the apartment, it was clear Brant wasn't satisfied. Eventually Brant's dog Joy became problematic. The dog wasn't happy living in a small apartment, and neighbors complained about her yapping.

Brant was dissatisfied with the apartment itself, and he wanted a different view. He liked the location well enough, despite the issues with the dog, so he rented an apartment on another floor. This solved the issue of the view, but not the problem with the dog.

Things got further complicated with the limo and its sheer size. At first, I picked Brant up with the church's Impala to take him shopping and to the services. Once we got the limousine, though, it was difficult to park in the underground parking or on the street. The car's length made it hard to maneuver or even find a parking space.

There were times I would simply have to double-park and wait for Brant to come downstairs. This made for a lot of stress and conflict when traffic would back up on the two-lane street. It meant that sometimes I had to drive around the block until Brant was downstairs, waiting for me with his gear. This fed into his fears about people watching him, and it became clear the location wasn't working for him.

After Brant and Kyle broke apart, Brant decided to move back to the Shekinah house. He took one of the rooms in the garage, a sound studio, and convert it to a small apartment. The remodeling was done by one of the elders John C, Toby B. and a couple of others. The new apartment had a bedroom and a bathroom with a walk-in closet. The plumbing of Brant's room was never really approved by the city inspectors, and the sewer line was above ground, attached to the apartment next door.

As for my quarters at the Shekinah house, I moved from Brant's old room into a smaller room off the kitchen. Robbie and Dodi W. shuffled into the room I vacated since they were a couple and needed the space. Robbie got the okay from Brant, and it did give them the room and privacy they were looking for.

Brant had only stayed in his apartment in the garage for a couple months when he decided to move again. The decision was made because one of the deacon's wives, Stacey., got pregnant. She and her husband Bill were living in the main house, but now they needed more room. Brant and the elders decided Bill and Stacey would take Brant's room, since it was large enough for a nursery.

This time Brant moved across the street from the Shekinah house, behind a family-owned market on the corner. The lady who ran the store lived on one side of the market, and she had a home for rent on the other side. Brant negotiated a month to month agreement for the rental and once more got ready to move.

This time Brant had the whole house painted and had part of the kitchen and living room remodeled. Kevin handled that project. He went a bit overboard with the remodeling. He put crown molding on the ceiling and painted different colors on the walls, decorating the place like Brant's dressing room at the Foursquare Church. Brant and I went to a furniture rental place to pick out furniture for the house. He thought it would be cheaper than buying furniture. It spoke to me of his feelings of impermanence and rootlessness.

Brant was only in his new house for a month when he decided to move again. He felt he was getting too many interruptions there, since he lived so close to the deacons. He also complained the house was too hot. He moved in during the summer months, and the place had no air conditioning. After all that work done to remodel the house – the time, care and expense – Brant told me to start looking for another place for him.

I began the search as he instructed. After only a few days I happened to find an apartment close to the water, and Brant decided to take it. It was in an older fourplex. We moved him in, but once again, the apartment didn't satisfy him. He believed the landlord was spying on him and was suspicious of him. Besides this, when he went to the café up the street, he felt people were staring at him and whispering behind his back. Maybe they recognized him from the TV shows. Maybe he was becoming paranoid. It could have been a bit of both.

From there, Brant decided to move to an apartment complex in North Hollywood. He was already attending and speaking at the North Hollywood Assembly of God Church, and the apartment was closer to him.

I think this move was a serious mistake on his part. It further separated him from the ministering body and was another way for him to escape the responsibilities of the ministry. He was already in over his head, both in terms of his duties and the consequences of becoming a public figure and TV personality. But it was easier for him to keep moving around. Other people shouldered the responsibility of moving his household goods.

This move meant I would have to go to Hollywood to drop of things Brant needed through the week. Often, he was not home. When I did connect with him, we would just see each other in passing as he was getting ready to go out. I could tell I was being replaced when Claudia and Eric worked together to assist Brant. They were taking over more and more of Brant's personal needs, and my days as Brant's personal assistant were numbered. It was a natural progression that was taking place.

Claudia got what she wanted, which was to be ministering next to Brant again. Eric was the right match for Claudia to work as a team to assist Brant.

Jeff Is Let Go

When Brant lived by the family-owned market on the corner, he and I were at the Shekinah house in the dining room, talking with Randy and Marla., Robbie and Dottie W. The conversation turned to talk about Jeff. Brant was thinking about letting Jeff go because he could not justify his paycheck any longer. I felt bad.

I believe Jeff had already received some kind of warning from Bill., who was speaking for Brant at one of the Angeles Temple meetings. It had to do with seeing some improvements in Jeff's outreach ministry in Riverside.

As this conversation was taking place in the kitchen, we could all see Jeff in his own living room as we looked into his windows from across the driveway. It was awkward and voyeuristic at the same time.

Brant felt Jeff was not that focused on what he was doing. Jeff was in charge of the monthly Bible Study in Riverside, and it was not growing. In fact, Brant was not seeing any growth from him at all. I felt it was because of me and it was my fault. This scared me. No one seemed willing to question Brant's reasoning about the situation since they wanted to hold onto their jobs as well. I certainly wasn't going to admit anything about our intimate moments.

By this time, some of the deacon wives were pregnant. Marla spoke up about Ann's pregnancy during her third trimester. Maybe Brant thought letting Jeff go would send a message: you could not have children and be in the ministry at the same time.

For whatever reason, Brant was looking for ways to save money, and Jeff seemed to be the one he singled out; Brant sensed something was not right. I wanted to warn Jeff since I knew the conversation was taking place. I felt it was not my place, and I wanted to keep Brant's comments about the others to myself. I knew a secretary was a keeper of secrets. I remembered that tip from the shorthand class I took in high school.

I knew Brant trusted my discretion about what he said around me, although it was hard to take at times. Letting Jeff go was up to Brant, whether the others wanted him to stay or not. Brant knew Jeff's wife was expecting, but he figured they could move back home and live with Jeff's parents. Jeff would brag about his wealthy grandmother – how she would spoil him, and that someday he would get her inheritance.

It became clear that Jeff would not be allowed to stay in the apartment. Someone had to tell him, and it was not going to be Brant.

Randy. spoke up and said he would break the news. Randy thought the news would have been better coming from him. With little preparation, Randy went over there to talk to Jeff. We saw him answer the door. Through the window, we saw them talking, then Jeff looked down. We continued our own conversation, and I don't recall what was said since I was feeling so bad inside. I tried to hide it.

It did not seem Randy was there very long. After he returned, he gave us a report about what took place. Randy said that Jeff had started to cry. He said he felt the Lord told him this would happen. After Randy came back, we all broke up the conversation and started to go about our business.

I went ahead and walked with Brant across the street. While we walked, he told me to go over and talk to Jeff. He wanted me to see how he was doing since Brant knew we were friends. I thought it was strange for him to tell me this. I thought maybe he was doing me a favor since he was still trying to break it off with Kyle.

What seemed like several hours later, I went over to Jeff's and he told me what happened. He said he talked to Ann about it already. She seemed upset and went on to bed. He asked if I knew about this, and I denied it. I did not want him to feel any worse.

I ended up staying for several hours again. We prayed and embraced each other, comforting each other in what was now the usual fashion. He must have known this would break off our relationship, but nothing was said.

Later on, Brant asked if I'd talked to Jeff and asked how he was doing. I said he was taking it all right, and he did not comment any further. It did not seem long before Jeff was moving back home to his parent's house as a temporary measure.

Jeff continued to come to the ministry and kept some of his involvement, though he let go of some responsibilities. One of those jobs was doing the monthly mailing of the newsletter. It required organizing the labor to have all the newsletters folded, stapled, and labeled then put into mailing bags. He did continue to work in the Word of Knowledge and continued his monthly Riverside Bible Study for a little longer.

Later on, Jeff got a part time job working for Kevin Baker's father, working one of his janitor accounts at a laboratory in Orange County. I ended up helping him with his night job sometimes since I wanted to be with him. I met him at his parents' house and go to work with him. Afterwards we'd come back and talk late into the night. Often, we'd end up holding each other and being close. It was comforting, no question. But inside I felt deeply conflicted. I was in turmoil.

I wanted to break it off with Jeff. I wanted to talk to someone about this, but I did not know who. Jeff's mom was always nice to me. Nothing was ever said or suspected. Yet I couldn't talk to her about it, despite the fact I wanted so much to talk to someone. Her kindness made it awkward, especially when I had promised to help Jeff with his work.

Time rolled on, and little changed in our intimacy. I took Jeff to the Lake Arrowhead cabin, knowing I should not have invited him. I knew what this would lead to, but I could not stop myself. I wanted to be close to him. He must have wanted it as well otherwise he would have stopped it himself.

We never really talked about what we were doing with each other and what this was leading to. We prayed and embraced each other for hours, not wanting to let go of each other. It was exciting and nerve wracking at the same time. Neither one of us made any further moves with our body to go any further in our actions with each other, although we could have done so.

Jeff was constantly on my mind and I wanted to be there for him as a supportive friend. Were we lovers? I don't know. It was just confusing. I wanted to stop myself but could not.

I kept justifying my actions, telling myself that Brant was doing the same thing with Kyle. He never really questioned me about Jeff, except once. He wanted to know what we did. I was vague and said we talked, prayed and felt close. He did not say anything or question me further.

Catalina Island

My relationship with Jeff continued unchanged for the time being, mostly centered on prayer and a frustrated passion. We could never allow ourselves to go beyond a certain point, but neither could we resist the bliss of our embrace. But this is the only thing that didn't change at that time. I needed a break from Jeff but could not bring myself to stop our affair. The thrill of being with him was irresistible, and I thought it was godly. My inner conflict and the weight of my responsibilities were getting me down.

Brant saw I was tired, and he decided to give me a few days off. It was a generous gesture. He paid my way for a weekend excursion to Catalina

Island. I thought of asking my friend Scott. to go with me as a way for us to talk and patch some things up. I had good intentions. I asked Jeff instead.

Jeff liked the idea of getting away, and on the surface it seemed logical. Inside I wondered what I was getting myself into. I wished I had not asked Jeff but Scott instead. Maybe I should have gone by myself. Nonetheless, the day arrived for Jeff and me to head across the channel a weekend of solitude and anonymity.

That morning Ann dropped us off at the boat dock. After a bracing cruise on choppy waters, we arrived in the quaint historic town of Avalon. When we got off the boat, there was a sense of celebration in the air mingling with whispers of famous past visitors and residents of the island – Clark Gable, Zane Grey, Marilyn Monroe, and so many others. Immediately I felt a sense of relief, like a huge weight had been lifted off my shoulders.

We checked into our bungalow that day then walked around the town. We came across some other Christians and talked for some time. It turned out they were holding a small Bible Study at their house, and they invited us to join them. We attended that night, and both Jeff and I enjoyed their company and some lively discussion. Afterwards, Jeff and I went back to our place, tired from a long day of sightseeing and meeting new people. We ended up going straight to bed.

Our single beds touched each other at the head, so we talked softly. It wasn't long before our faces were touching each other, cheek to cheek. The rough feeling of his unshaven face was comforting and exciting.

We laid there for hours saying little. When we did talk, our conversation wandered to the covenant between David and Jonathan in the Bible and the depth of their feelings for each other. It wasn't just the nearness of Jeff's body so close to mine that excited me. We had so much in common, and I was emotionally connected to him.

There was something bittersweet about our excursion. I knew we could not continue like this, and I'm sure he felt the same. This was going nowhere.

I was expecting him to be the one to make the move and break it off. We continued to lie there for a long time when finally, he broke the silence. He said we couldn't continue like this even though he loved me.

I remember I didn't respond – just agreed then said nothing. He continued to cuddle, pressing his cheek to mine throughout the night as we fell in and out of sleep. We said very little to each other the next day as we got ready to return. He kept his distance from me on the boat ride back to the mainland.

I did not sleep well the night we got back. He came to my bedroom window and asked to see me. We visited briefly, made some small talk, and he said he was sorry. Beyond that he did not know what to say. I said it was okay, and I was glad to see him. The talk petered out, and the conversation ended with an awkward silence.

I felt really detached and confused for a couple days until the following Saturday when I met up with Brant in his dressing room. He asked how I was. I said I was fine, and we continued to get ready for the service. Even though we didn't say much, it was grounding to be in his presence, and I started to feel better being around him.

During the service, Jeff and I would glance at each other from time to time. I thought it was over, and I was glad – relieved. But before I knew it, we were talking to each other again, falling into our same pattern, holding each other close and feeding our intimacy.

It was getting more difficult to see each other as time went on. Ann had her baby, and Jeff was a father now. They soon moved to an apartment in Long Beach, and Jeff became less involved with the ministry. I visited him a few times to see how they were doing, and it appeared Jeff was happy in his role as a new father. I couldn't help feeling left out, though deep down I knew the way things had turned out was for the best.

Several months went by, and Jeff and Ann moved again. I got word their baby was lost to crib death. Besides being sad news, this sent a jolt of fear into many in the ministry. Some thought it was God's judgment on Jeff and Ann for pulling away from the ministry. I remember Brant did make the comment to me that maybe it was God's way of getting Jeff's attention since he left the ministry. Then Brant told me to send flowers to Ann and Jeff with his condolences. Chuck Smith did the memorial service for the baby. I did not attend.

After that, Jeff and Ann moved to a cottage in Long Beach that his grandmother bought him. I visited a few more times at their new home. He had changed since they lost their child, and he was even more distant, acting cold toward me. I don't blame him. Perhaps he blamed me for the loss of his first child, and now he was being more careful. If he didn't think it, I did.

I think he was only protecting himself and his family, wanting to hold onto what he had. I understood. Even so, I felt hurt, rejected and alone. I could tell no one about my affair. I still cared about Jeff and his family. I wished him well. As my position changed with Brant, I was getting more involved in other areas of the ministry. It put even more distance between Jeff and me.

Ann was soon pregnant again, and not long afterwards, Jeff and Ann moved out of state. The whole affair left me feeling empty and confused. Answers were no closer, and my place in the ministry started to unravel.

I'd often wondered how love affairs or addictions affected the personal lives of those who were evangelists or had healing ministries. If they survived, it seemed their public image and their ministry were never the same after the scandal became known.

I remember what Kathryn Kuhlman often would say about this. She had an illicit affair when she was younger, and she gave up her marriage as a result. She would often say she paid everything and had to die to herself daily – putting aside her ego for the ministry. She would say, "God will not share the glory with anyone."

It was twenty years before the churches would accept her again as a preacher. She lived with the pain from the marriage and committed herself to the fellowship of the Holy Spirit. She dedicated her whole life to the healing ministry. She lived a life of celibacy, keeping herself for God according to the way she understood scripture.

Even with Kathryn Kuhlman for inspiration, it was a long time before I got over Jeff.

Another Camp Picture

It was the summer of 1974. Another year had passed, and once again we made the trip to Idyllwild Pines Camp in the San Bernardino Mountains. On the road there, I thought back to the time when I first met Brant and Kevin years earlier at the Calvary Chapel winter camp. I could not have predicted I would now be with Brant as his assistant and companion, sharing a cabin dorm room with him.

I sat at the head table next to Brant and the elders and looked out at all the other tables that filled the room. Those of us from the ministry were having a great time and enjoying each other's' company. Brant himself was childlike at the table, laughing and playing silly jokes while passing around the food. We all sang a couple songs, prayed and dug into the meal.

The dorm room Brant and I shared was large enough, I had one section to myself, and he was in another area next to mine. My section had three bunk beds in it, and they went unused.

Little about our routine had changed from the previous year. Early in the mornings, we were awakened to the tune of "Rise and Shine" played on a trumpet, a flute and the sound of banging trash lids together. The whole week was jam-packed with Bible studies, hikes in nature, and just good fellowship. The camp renewed our spirits and reminded us how far we had come in a year. Still there was more work to do to continue to grow and reach out to people with the ministry.

Another camp picture was taken to commemorate the event. Unlike last year, I was now sitting behind Brant, between Jo Ellen and Kevin. I felt very privileged to be holding Brant's Bible and sitting by his side.

My friend Sue O. from high school came to the camp, and I found time to connect with her a few times throughout the week. I spent most of my time by Brant's side, assisting him with whatever he wanted, listening in on his conversations as he talked to people.

Jeff showed up for one day, and my heart ached to see him. He kept his distance from me, and he acted like I was not even there. I felt hurt that he ignored me that way, but, I thought it was for the best. I played along with his game and pushed off the hurt I was feeling inside.

The week was filled with Bible studies, leading up to the last night with an afterglow prayer service. Again, we renewed our faith in what the ministry was doing and the direction it was going before we went back down the mountain.

Eric N. and Claudia W.

Eric N. started to come to Shekinah toward the end of 1973, around the same time Lisa G. arrived. Eric was in college and taking a break from his last year. He was a dark-haired athlete with a mustache – handsome, intelligent and self-assured. He looked like a preppy when he put his sweater around his neck.

During high school, Kelly G. and Lisa were friends of his. Claudia got to know Eric around the time of the Easter-In Gathering event at the old Long Beach auditorium in April of '74. Claudia had no interest in him at the time and did not even really like him because he seemed conceited.

During Easter week, Claudia noticed he was stranded without a ride from the Long Beach Auditorium, where the meetings were held. She offered him a lift. After that, their friendship developed.

He started to ride with Claudia regularly, and helped her with her duties during the services. Claudia assisted me in getting Brant's room ready before he arrived at the church with me.

Shortly after the first time Brant broke with Kyle, Eric met with Brant. I was driving the limo for Brant, leaving the Shekinah house. As we pulled out of the driveway, Eric came out of the downstairs apartment and looked over at us. Brant rolled down the window and asked Eric, "Do you need a ride?"

Eric ran up to us and popped his head into the limo. "Yeah! Wait here. I've got to get my things."

Brant grumbled. "I didn't mean for him to get a ride with me. He sure is forward."

Eric N. came running back. He jumped into the back seat next to Brant. I saw Brant's eyes grow wide in shock, and Eric told me where he needed to go. Eric was renting a small cottage behind Georgette and Elaine, not too far from the Shekinah house. When we got there, Eric invited us in. I thought we were all going in and Brant said to let him off and for me to leave. He would get a ride back later or call if he needed a lift.

The next day Brant told me he enjoyed an intellectual conversation with Eric. They both sat on floor cushions, listening to Eric's record collection as they talked. Brant and Eric became good friends for a short time – but only until Eric and Claudia got to know each other.

Others in the ministry commented that they liked Eric better than Kyle, and that he seemed more stable and polished compared to Kyle. Many commented how Eric came across as intelligent, and jokingly said he acted a little conceited as well.

Brant liked Eric well enough, but he kept remarking that Eric was too arrogant. Brant wanted to put a limit on the amount of time he spent with Eric. Brant talked to Claudia about it, and she agreed that Eric seemed egotistical. But Brant thought Eric was still new to Christianity, and he wanted to help him. In the end, it was Claudia who talked Eric into cooling it with Brant and backing off.

From that point forward, Eric's relationship with Brant turned more professional. At first, Eric would ride with us in the limo. Later, he would catch a ride with Claudia in her Volkswagen bug.

I don't know what Eric did for money. He may have worked outside the ministry, or maybe he was living off some savings left over from college. Whatever it was, he found ample time to help out at the church.

At some point Claudia gave Eric the tasks of answering Brant's correspondence. His writing was polished, and I was really impressed with his communication skills. Between Brant and Claudia, they started to transform Eric's preppie college wardrobe, adding some of Brant's clothes. The two of them were the same height, and Eric's confidence allowed him to wear his new clothes with flare. Eric started to fit in.

As Eric and Claudia spent more time with each other, Kyle started to come back into the picture. Brant was on the defensive, and he was still willing to help Kyle and listen to him. When Eric heard about Kyle, I wasn't sure how events would turn. I was surprised and relieved when there was no conflict. Eric seemed to stay out of it.

Eric and Claudia opted not to go to the summer camp of '74, and it was during that week their relationship got more serious. Sometime after camp, Brant took Claudia out for her birthday with Eric and Lisa G. Soon they started talking about marriage. Shortly after that, Claudia and Eric announced their engagement.

From that point forward, Eric and Claudia worked as a team, setting up Brant's dressing room and clothes together while I did the driving for Brant. I would come in to do the finishing touches after their preparations.

Eric always seemed to be professional and upbeat with me, and he remained cordial. It was obvious Eric had greater intelligence and better skills to be Brant's personal assistant.

CHAPTER 12:

THE EXODUS BEGINS

I had gotten to know all the elders and their wives fairly well while living at the Shekinah house. All the original elders had become ordained ministers and formed a tight group. They got along well with each other and worked closely with Brant while things were in the early stages of the ministry. The hierarchy included Brant, Steve., Robbie., Randy., Joe., Bill., Bob W. and John C.

Though they each had their own set of responsibilities, it seemed that Steve. and Robbie. worked most closely with Brant. This was mainly because of their administrative duties such as: managing the finances, organizing outreaches, and overseeing media productions for radio and television.

There was another elder, Greg L, who was one of the original charter members. He came on board as an elder when the ministry was just part of Brant's Bible Study group, before it was named Shekinah Fellowship.

Greg L had a surfer look with long hair and a beard. He looked similar to Lonnie Frisbee when Lonnie was at Calvary Chapel. Greg L teaching style was modeled after Chuck Smith from Costa Mesa with a dash of Lonnie Frisbee's style. He had an independent spirit and with confidence he followed his instincts.

I remember when Greg L came to my high school with Brant and Randy. By the time I went to Shekinah, Greg L was no longer part of that group. He ventured out on his own, developing a separate Calvary Chapel in Riverside, California.

That church mushroomed into a large organization that became known as Harvest Ministries. As of this writing, the ministry draws large crowds when it holds its outreach programs.

The Shekinah elders respected Brant, and I'm sure in the beginning they saw him as larger than life. He was very much a visionary when it came to expound on scripture, teaching, guiding the elders and molding the ministry.

Bill and Stacey.

One of the elders I got to know well was Bill., along with his wife Stacey. Bill was a tall, slender man with receding long red hair, freckles and wire framed glasses. His Bible studies were well researched, and he impressed me as an inquisitive intellectual type. He liked to read and quote Charles Spurgeon, a Baptist preacher who had lived in the 1800's.

Like so many others, I liked to listen to Bill when he talked about his studies. It looked like he was on his way to be a good Bible teacher. I don't think Bill ever wore a suit before Brant started to groom the elders' dress code for the services, but he always looked sharp and played his role well.

When we started to go to the Angeles temple services in 1974, the elders were wearing tuxedo jackets for those services. Bill's wife Stacey was seated with the rest of the elders' wives during the services in the Word of Knowledge group and testimony lines. Bill seemed to go along with the changes happening within the ministry, and so did the other elders.

John and Charlene C. were an encouraging couple to talk to on a personal level. Charlene C was in the choir as well as serving in the Word of Knowledge group during the healing service.

John worked with the logistics of coordinating some of the set up at the different outreaches. He decided how the layout should go in the auditoriums. He also secured Brant's dressing room and configured the parking.

During the regular services, John and Bill stood on the sidelines with microphones, and they would emcee the testimonials. People giving their testimony would line up to the right and left of the stage, and the emcees summarized the person's testimony. They would sound excited and put a lot of enthusiasm into their words. This helped the testimonies go smoothly and kept the person from rambling on. It was especially necessary if members of the congregation were excited or it was difficult for them to talk because they were overcome with emotion.

It wasn't long before I noticed a shift in Bill's thinking started to take place. Some of the indirect questions he asked when I was working with Brant hinted at a deeper meaning. I think because of Bill's inquisitive mind and conservative values, he saw the direction the ministry was going, and he did not like it. The things he was observing seemed to be upsetting his peace of mind, and he wrestled with those thoughts.

Like many of us, Bill came from the Calvary Chapel Gospel tradition that offered a simple message format. The Shekinah ministry started out with the simplicity of worship and Bible studies. It quickly morphed into a full-scale dramatic production with a healing service modeled after the Kathryn Kuhlman ministry.

Making the transition was difficult for Bill, and it was getting to him. Seeing Brant wear extravagant costumes and witnessing his behavior changes was a lot for Bill to take in. Compared to our simple Jesus People Calvary Chapel days, the weekly services had become highly stylized. Bill could no longer go along with what appeared to be the direction of the ministry.

Besides these factors, the changes in Brant's lifestyle were going against Bill's personal moral code and eating at his conscience. With his wife Stacy expecting a child, they discussed the situation privately and felt it was time to move on.

I don't know if Bill ever confronted Brant on any of the issues he did not agree with. After they came to their decision, Bill made the comment how he felt like a heavy burden was lifted. What I later learned is that when Brant talked to Bill, he told him to pray about his decision – whether to stay or leave. He gave Bill a couple weeks to think it over.

After this happened, Bill did not come to services for a week. When I went to his room to visit him and Stacy, Bill said he was feeling better. Though he returned to the ministry for a couple weeks, both of them just suddenly seemed to vanish. No one really talked about them after that, as though they never existed.

It felt strange to me there was no formal going-away party or ceremony for them. There was no "God bless you." No pat on the back, no thanks for all the work Bill and Stacy did, or no acknowledgment for their service. They just left. That must have been a very brave move for them to make at that time. They simply left and shut the door behind them on what was once very much a big part of their life.

Joe and Linda.

Joe and Linda. were another elder couple involved in Shekinah. Joe became part of the ministry shortly after he finished high school in Long Beach. He graduated a year ahead of me. Joe was a handsome looking blond with a great radio voice and a dry sense of humor. Even so, he was shy and reserved, a little on the pent-up inside. I didn't know much about his background at first. After I found out he was involved in theater in high school, it made more sense to me.

I always felt he had strong emotions inside him that he kept bottled up. He released those feelings through his music and in his teaching style. He seemed very self-disciplined and structured to me. I thought he was much older than I because of his maturity. His wife Linda was Brant's assistant before Claudia W. came into the scene.

When the ministry moved into the Foursquare Church, they had a grand piano and an organ to play. Other than accompany the worship songs with the orchestra, Joe performed solo pieces during the service. Brant would tease him sometimes by saying "Kathryn Kuhlman had her Dino at the piano, and we have our Joe." Joe even combed his hair the same way as Dino, slicked back with lots of hair spray to keep it in place.

Joe practiced for hours at a time in the sound studio, and he rehearsed with the rest of the music group. He was always well prepared when he did share a message. He and Linda were friendly toward me, and he was always very respectful toward Linda. It seemed, though, they never really talked as a couple when I observed them from a distance.

There were a number of times I wanted to talk to him on a personal level since he gave me the impression he wanted to open up. A few times in between services he embraced me with a hug and asked me how I was doing. I smiled and said, "Okay."

He must have sensed something was going on with me since I was always running around, multitasking errands, being the "go to kid" for Brant. I dared not risk confiding what was really happening and what I was thinking. I was balancing my position with the ministry and the relationship between Jeff and me. I felt trapped.

I knew Joe had dabbled in the gay lifestyle in his teenage years. I also knew he came out of it like many who approached the ministry looking for love, acceptance and purpose. It would have been best if I had not known he was wrestling with his sexual feelings and with his own personal thoughts. He was making choices at the time, deciding which way to go and how to navigate through the challenges in his life.

There was a time when I saw him watching me from a distance at an elder's retreat. It appeared that way. I almost shared my own situation with Joe, spelling out what was really happening with me. I chose not to.

Brant and the rest of the elders were at a week-long retreat at Lake Arrowhead, staying in a cabin we rented for them. Joe, Linda and I stayed at the cabin where Brant and I usually vacationed at Arrowhead.

We had a group meeting and then broke for dinner. Afterward, we enjoyed different types of recreation while Brant played cards with some of the other elders. It was early, and I decided to take a walk with Joe and Linda under the night sky, gazing at the stars. Joe and Linda were silent, holding hands, enjoying each other's company. We reached a viewpoint where we could observe the city lights below in the distance.

The whole time I was thinking I wanted to say something, to confide, but I kept my silence. Instead I made small talk about the view and they responded with polite agreement. We walked back to the cabin where we were staying, and still I was silent.

When we got back to the cabin, I slept on the floor in the loft, and Joe and Linda stayed in the bedroom downstairs. It must have been about an hour later that I felt something was different. It was dark. I looked over the banister of the loft and saw Joe standing in the living room, looking up at me from the shadows. The light of the moon in the night sky shone through the windows.

Seeing him standing there startled me. He walked back and forth a couple times, looking up at me. I think he sensed I was feeling troubled. Finally, I said hi. He asked if everything was all right. I felt vulnerable and empty inside. I admired the effort of friendship at the moment to talk. I dared not say what I was feeling about Jeff and did not want to project myself onto him. That could start something that should not be permitted to happen on my part and embarrass myself. I thought about what was happening between Jeff and me. I did not want to start anything with Joe. I already felt like the male harlot in silence.

I reassured him. "I'm all right." There was a moment of silence as we both hesitated, and then he left, heading back to his room.

Joe does not recall this and denies any attractions or tensions ever happened between us, but this is the way I remember it.

I was frightened and ashamed of what I was thinking. I desperately wanted to be held and assured with an answer from On High, showing me why I was having these feelings. I prayed for strength and finally went to sleep. I concluded I could not trouble Joe with my dilemma and kept it to myself to work it out. I continued to love Joe and Linda as a brother and sister in Christ from a distance since it was safer for me and I acted kind towards them.

Joe and Linda were the second elder couple to leave after Bill and Stacy. As before, they just left, nothing was said by the elders. No formal ceremony was given, as though they never existed. We were given the impression not too ask, and we were afraid to ask – afraid to find the truth. We were worried because we did not want to be cursed or cast out. I wondered what they could have done or what had happened to make them leave.

It was a year later when I found out Joe and Linda had separated, and my heart sunk. Then I discovered even later that Joe had slipped into the gay lifestyle. This puzzled me, and my heart went out to him.

I was curious about Joe, and I became more determined to find him. I inquired at the post office to get his address, and I found out he lived not too far from my apartment.

One evening after work, I walked to his apartment but then hesitated. What was I doing? I had to find out for myself. I didn't know what to expect. I arrived apparently just when he got home from work, and he was surprised. I went into his apartment where he had his piano and a couple pictures of Linda on the wall.

We made light conversation. We did not talk about the ministry, about Linda, or about what he was doing. I know he felt very awkward, as I did. I wanted to say something that would touch him in some way and help him to open up, but that was not going to happen. I wanted to leave.

He talked a little about his job as a telephone bill collector, but the old chemistry wasn't there. The conversation was polite but strained. Then he told me he goes to work very early in the morning, and he needed to go to bed. He offered to take me home. Since I had walked, I accepted the offer. I got into his car and said very little. I said maybe we could get together and have dinner sometime. He smiled and said, "Yeah, sure." He seemed to be thinking, "What else am I going to say?"

That was the last time I saw him.

Pairing Off

Lisa G. started to come to Shekinah in late 1973 or early '74. She had been invited by her older brother, Kelly. The siblings looked very much alike, and she reminded me of a young Doris Day.

Lydia befriended Lisa, and so did other popular girls of the choir. Lisa had a pleasing personality and was well received by everyone. She also attended the Sunday morning church service at the Neighborhood Foursquare Church, often wearing a delightfully stylish "Doris Day hat," as I called it.

How could anyone not notice her. She was tall with long blonde hair, and she was one of the best dressed girls in the choir. She became one of the backup singers and eventually got her own solo spot, singing "Fairest Lord Jesus." Eventually she worked the testimony lines, acting as a spokes model on the stage. She held the microphone next to Brant during the testimonies during the healing service.

Lisa dated a number of guys while at the ministry. The first person she dated briefly was Bobby, a committed Christian who recently was released from prison. They dated for awhile and even were thinking of marriage, but soon they broke it off.

After Kyle was keeping his distance from Brant, Lisa and Kyle began dating each other for a while. That all changed when Brant showed interest in Lisa. Apparently, Brant convinced Kyle not to get further involved with Lisa.

Lisa would travel with the ministry to the outreach events as part of the choir. At times, even her attire would be the same color and material that Brant was wearing. It seemed to send a message that they belonged together. It was tough to decide who the better dresser was – they both looked so perfect, like Barbie and Ken.

Lisa got to know the rest of the Baker family very quickly, including Kevin and Jo Ellen, who was living in Palm Springs at the time. I believe Jo Ellen saw early on that Lisa was a great match for Brant, especially compared to the other women who were interested in her son. Jo Ellen maneuvered to hook up Lisa with Brant while Lisa kept her distance. In fact, Jo Ellen coached Lisa not to spend time with him, other than being on stage with him during the service or seeing him as part of a group. Finally, Kevin brought Lisa as a companion to Jo Ellen's place in Palm Springs when Brant was there. Whether it was planned that way, or it just worked out, I don't know.

During that August, when things were in the early courting stages, Brant wanted to take Claudia out for her birthday as friends and thought a double date would be best. He asked Eric to take Lisa G., and Eric agreed. Eric and Lisa knew each other back in high school – something I didn't know at the time.

Before the outing, Brant wanted me to get extra cash from Robbie at the Saturday service for the birthday celebration the following week. When the day arrived, I wore a coat and tie since I was driving the limo to pick up everyone. I drove them to a nice restaurant in Hollywood, everyone sitting in the back, dressed like celebrities. They were excited for a nice evening, one that would cost about hundred dollars a plate.

I dropped them off in front of the restaurant, and I was told to come back in a few hours. Not far from Beverly Hills, I parked the car down a side street and waited. It was several hours later when I picked them up. They were deeply engaged in conversation, laughing about the evening. Everyone at the restaurant kept gazing at them. It was as though they were celebrities, but the spectators could not figure out who they were.

Brant reprimanded me jokingly, saying I did not leave him enough cash to cover the tip and he was embarrassed. Claudia told him not to worry about it since it all worked out anyway.

I threw up my hands, broadly taking them off the wheel for a moment. "How could I know it would cost a hundred dollars a plate?" It was an outrageous fortune in those days.

They all laughed. Brant reached over and bonked me on the head with a church bulletin that was in the back seat. We all continued to laugh and had a good time as I drove everyone home.

In the time that followed, Claudia and Eric became close as a couple. Soon they were making plans for marriage. Claudia now realized she felt that the Lord was preparing her to get married again – to Eric.

Claudia had been removed from her position with Brant, yet once Eric came into the picture, she slowly worked her way back to Brant's side again. Apparently, she was on safer ground once she had a spouse on her side. I always thought it was ironic she was closest to Brant when she was romantically unavailable. I didn't see the handwriting on the wall then, though soon it would become clear.

Brant Comes Under Attack

Brant began showing signs of burnout from 1974 through 1975. It seemed he was getting more tired and sleeping longer. He would rest more and drink more coffee right before a service. Just as the service started, he would get the surge of energy he needed, but right afterwards his energy would crash.

Brant thought he was under spiritual attack, a comment he made while being escorted to the car after a service. He was feeling faint and said, "What a way to make a living. There has to be an easier way."

He noticed he was getting sores on his face, guessing it was a form of acne. He would just cover them up with the makeup. But he had other health problems too, and they manifested before a service or when he was under stress. Once when we were on the way to a service in San Diego, he had a coughing fit in the back seat of the limo. He started to cough and hack as though he was choking.

He said, "What is this?" wiping his nose.

I was concerned, glancing into the back seat while I drove. "Let me see."

"No, it's too gross," he said, realizing it was a clot of blood that came out of his nose. We both thought it was the devil attacking him.

Later Brant made an appointment to see a dermatologist in Long Beach to diagnose and treat the sores. I went with him, both for logistical reasons and to offer support. While we were waiting for the doctor in the waiting room, a patient recognized Brant. I overheard what he said about Brant being "that preacher on television." It was awkward, given the private nature of the circumstances.

I don't remember if Brant got a prescription to treat the sores. I do remember he didn't want to go back for a second appointment because of something the doctor said to him. Just as strangely as the sores showed up, they mysteriously disappeared. Despite the healing, Brant remained tired.

In between one of Brant's moves, Brant and I were living together in the downstairs duplex next door to the Shekinah House. This meant I was with him almost constantly, and I could observe his declining health up close.

Another Move

Brant remained in the duplex for another month then made the decision to move to Hollywood. I remained in the duplex but was soon sharing the apartment with Terry H. Steve, Teddi., along with his brother and his wife where upstairs.

Terry was a funny lovable deacon with bright red hair and freckles. He ushered and played the drums in the orchestra. Once Brant moved out, Terry lived with me for a short time. I got to know some of the other deacons fairly well since we all lived together. All of us in the main house seemed to get along. They were a great group and fun to live with. Their companionship offered a much-needed relief from the stress of serving Brant. I was helplessly watching him decline in front of my eyes. We all were.

I had to drive up to Hollywood several times during the week to run Brant's errands. We would end up talking briefly in his apartment while he got ready to go somewhere. He would tell me about the different people that he met in the apartment complex, and he would complain about not getting enough sleep. He said the tenants next door were always up late at night with their bed pounding against the wall of his bedroom while they had sex. I offered my condolences, but he joked that it made him jealous – they were having a better time than he was.

Besides this couple, Brant told me about the male bodybuilder down the hall who was also a painter. He invited Brant into his apartment, and Brant went there to be polite. "He is a good artist," Brant said then he rolled his eyes. I didn't understand, so he elaborated. "He paints nude men!"

I never would have thought of that. It made me curious to meet him for myself. I ran into Brant's neighbor a few times, passing him in the hallway, but I was too shy to say anything or spark up a conversation. As I dropped off Brant's dry cleaning, I saw him coming down the hall. Usually he was leaving to go to church. I later learned he was a parishioner at Church at the North Hollywood Assembly of God.

Even though things were friendly between us and I believed we were on good terms, I felt like my time as Brant's personal assistant was coming to an end. He was becoming more distant. He first separated himself from the church elders, and now it seemed that he was separating himself from everyone else from the ministry, including me. I wasn't the only one who noticed.

The excuse Brant gave for isolating himself from us was that he wanted to be closer to the North Hollywood Assembly of God Church. Some thought it was his way of avoiding responsibility for the problems he was facing with different people and the ministry.

While Brant was living in Hollywood, occupying his time in that neighborhood, I was running around in Long Beach, busy doing errands for him. More and more, I was feeling pushed out. It was clear Claudia and Eric had moved in and taken over much of what I was doing. Brant also delegated responsibilities to paid staff and the many volunteers who sacrificed their time and gave money to the church. All Brant had to do was pop in once a week and show up at outreach events in his sports car.

Once the limo was no longer needed, I started to feel shut out. I was getting rides to the outreaches with Eric and Claudia, as well as other elders. Brant relied on me less and less – not just for driving, but also for errands and administrative duties. Eric was a college graduate with sharp administrative skills, and increasingly he took over tasks that previously were mine. Intuitive, I knew I would be replaced. In time, my hunch would play out.

CHAPTER 13:
THE BEGINNING OF THE END

It was a Saturday in February 1975. I was in Brant's dressing room at the Foursquare Church, setting things up with help from Claudia and Eric. Brant came in, looking very upbeat, and he sat in his chair. Steve. came in and gave his usual business briefing. Kevin B. was also there.

During a break in the discussion, Brant took a deep breath, preparing to make an announcement. "I've talked it over with several people, and I have made a decision that will change my life." He pulled out a small ring box and opened it up. "I have decided to marry Lisa." He blushed, adding, "I am going to ask her tonight."

Everyone gasped, then the room exploded into excited chatter. After a moment, we decided I should get some long-stemmed roses for Lisa. Kevin said he would drive me. We rushed to the florist and ordered two dozen long-stemmed roses with a flowing ribbon attached.

When we got back to the church, the service was in progress. Brant had already made his entrance during the worship song. The music was winding down, ready for the next transition in the service. Kevin said he would take the roses to Brant, and he made his way toward the front.

I was in the sound booth at the back of the hall, waiting for the announcement as I observed below. Kevin was on the sidelines by the dressing room, ready for his cue to come in with the roses. Brant started to speak from the stage, saying the first words that would lead into his proposal to Lisa. As he continued speaking, the moment took on a strange tone. This was an announcement, not a proposal, and the offer of marriage was anything but intimate. It seemed more like a live show, announcing the winner of a beauty pageant.

Then the moment came. Brant extended his hand toward the risers where Lisa stood in the choir stunned, holding her cheeks. "I've decided to make Lisa my wife," he said with a sweeping gesture. "Lisa, will you be mine?"

All the girls around Lisa hugged her. Kevin came out to present the roses to her and she stepped down from the riser to approach Brant as he presented the ring to Lisa. Brant never asked her for her hand in marriage. He just slipped the ring onto her finger.

Brant was undeniably attractive, and he had his pick of women. So many of the other girls tried to win Brant's affection, and they were rejected. This was the first time I know of that Brant asked a woman to marry him. When Brant did ask Lisa for her hand, many girls were disappointed.

All the women were smiling in the choir, giddy with excitement. The congregation reacted with a long applause. Brant and Lisa were both smiling and blushing, holding hands. Lisa made her way back to the choir in a daze, the roses safely in Kevin's care. Brant continued on with church business, blushing while he finished making announcements. From there, he took up the offering as the choir began the next number. The emotional congregation was especially generous that week. Far from business as usual, their engagement marked a dramatic turn in the tide of events – especially for me.

I Am Let Go

The service continued on through the evening. Afterwards Brant and Lisa went off with Claudia, Eric, Kevin and a few others. I remained at the church to clean up, then went back to my apartment.

Later that evening, Eric and Claudia came to see me at home. I knew something was up from their looks on their faces. I was alone when they came in. We were all sitting down in the living room when they gave me a message from Brant. They said they all felt I did not seem focused on Brant's needs any longer, and they had decided to let me go. Just like that.

The decision must have been made that night when Claudia and Eric went out to celebrate with Brant. I felt confused. Eventually I accepted it as part of the Lord's plan for me.

The real reason was Claudia and Eric had stepped in and taken over my job. Eric was the educated person, and he was skilled in areas I wasn't. Kevin made sniping comments about me behind my back, and he gradually took over part of my job as well.

They said Brant wanted me to stay and my rent would be provided for as long as I remained on the Shekinah property. I would also continue to get my allowance of $15 a week. I found out later Brant didn't really want me to stay. He wanted me out as soon as possible, but Eric interceded for me, thinking dismissing me abruptly was too harsh. Because of Eric's intervention, Brant changed his mind.

My dismissal felt sudden and jarring at the time. Looking back, I could see the tension of the last several months had taken its toll. It was a relief to have it finally over with.

Eric asked for all the things I was holding for Brant. I gave him his ministry wardrobe, keys, and a jar I had been using to collect all of Brant's loose change. When I went to get the money jar, Claudia stopped me. She said she and Eric had talked it over and it was all right for me to keep the money jar. There was probably about fifty dollars in it. I didn't know whether to feel lucky or like a charity case. Overall, I was deeply humbled.

After they left, I was confused. What would I do now? Was my learning period over with Brant and the ministry? However, I felt my purpose was not fulfilled yet, it seemed the Lord had other designs for me.

I felt trapped. Moving back in with one of my parents was not an option. I had nowhere to go, and so I was forced to remain at the Shekinah house, unable to leave, unable to fit in.

Claudia called me the next day to see how I was doing. I don't remember what I said. I just accepted the fact that this is what the Lord wanted. I was hurt, crushed and strangely relieved.

Yes, I was relieved. I saw it as an answer to a prayer. It forced me to break free from my relationship with Jeff. My chance to see him was cut off since I no longer had a car. He would be better off – I was sure of it. I talked to him about a week later and told him I was let go and replaced with Eric and Claudia. He did not say much, just said he was sorry to hear that. There was much unspoken feeling between us, but it would have to wait until later if it ever was to be said at all.

I had the strange feeling I was not supposed to leave yet. Maybe I was just too scared to leave. I felt a quiet desperation building within me about my finances. I prayed about it, but it didn't really calm my uneasiness.

Claudia called me a few times that week to see how I was doing, and she encouraged me. It was like being dumped by a lover. Claudia herself had gone through this same experience with Brant, so she could relate to my pain. I knew the Lord was not done with me yet. I still had work to do with this ministry.

Starting Again

I didn't go to the service the following week. I still needed time. I ended up joining the choir within a couple weeks. Some thought it wasn't a good idea.

I got scornful looks from people, as if to say, "What are you doing here?" But nobody said anything to my face. On the outside, I carried on like nothing had happened. Inside I was quaking.

I really enjoyed being in the choir with Terry B. He was very good at what he did, directing the choir. Joe and Linda. were still with the ministry, and Joe played the piano for rehearsals.

A girl in the orchestra named Virginia worked at a convalescent hospital as a dishwasher and server. She told me her employer had another opening. I applied that week, and I was hired a few weeks later.

It was an early morning shift. I took the bus – I no longer had access to the church's cars. Each day when I arrived at work, I'd get the trays ready and pour the juice. After that I'd take the carts of food to each room and leave them for the nurse's aides to serve. I said hello and smiled at some of the patients in their rooms as I picked up their trays when they were done. I welcomed the interaction; it made me feel normal, like I fit in somewhere. Once I brought the carts of food back from the rooms, I started loading dishes in the dishwasher and cleaning the floor. That was the whole routine.

It was a menial job, and it was only part time work – but it was enough. It didn't interfere with the ministry schedule, and it covered the extras I needed.

Going to the Saturday services was hard. I'd see Brant rush by on the way to his dressing room, and I knew what was taking place in the back. He seemed more preoccupied with Lisa now, and he kept boasting about his engagement with her like a prize trophy. It was hard to sit in the choir since I was used to being on the move and getting things done in my role as Brant's assistant. It took some time to let that go. Meanwhile I continued to minister in the Word of Knowledge during the healing part of the service.

Time passed, gaining speed as I moved into the rhythm of my new life. Eventually I talked to my parents about what happened. I told them about getting another job, about the ministry, and just how unsure I was about what to do next. They both encouraged me.

My father offered to give me our old family car, the 1966 Mustang. My dad had gotten another car for himself, so I took him up on his offer. I was very thankful to have transportation again.

My mother suggested I look into going to school, and she made some other suggestions. She was well meaning, but I was not ready to leave Long Beach yet. I ended up taking a basic writing class at the community college, but it was very intimidating.

Since I no longer ate on the run with Brant, I started to take my meals next door with the other deacons. I paid for my portion of the food. It was Georgette A., Debbi and Carolyn who did the cooking. During the first month, I did not have enough to cover the cost. Georgette let me slide until I got paid. That was a blessing I will never forget.

At the end of the month, Steve. wanted to see me privately. I followed him upstairs, and then he asked me about my portion of the rent. I was stunned. How could he not know about my arrangement? I told him that Brant and Claudia said I did not have to pay rent as long as I did not move off the property and continued to get my weekly allowance. He seemed embarrassed, shuffling his feet and looking at the floor. "Nobody tells me anything," he said jokingly. I thanked him, still a little shaken. He told me not to worry about it, and we went back downstairs.

I moved back into the main house. I took Joe and Linda's old room off the living room. This left my old apartment free, so Kelly and Lilly moved back in. I think Lilly had had her first pregnancy in that apartment.

During a meeting at the Shekinah house in November of 1975, we got a phone call. Lilly had lost her baby. She'd gone to the doctor that day for her final prenatal checkup, but the doctor said her baby girl was dead. We were all upset and deeply concerned for her. We stopped our meeting and prayed for her.

Lilly went to the hospital the next day to deliver her stillborn child.

A Return to Momentum

Brant had a way of glossing things over and moving on, spinning his way out of tense dynamics leaving someone else to speak for him. His response to the personal tragedies that touched our group always seemed to fall short, somehow underwhelming. His next move was indeed a public spectacle.

It wasn't all that surprising to discover that Brant's and Lisa's engagement didn't last. They called it off at the end of the year. It was a combination of factors – a lack of time together coupled with Brant's grandmother dying. It was like watching a Hollywood couple on display, both living such active public lifestyles. Brant's very public proposal ended in a very public break up.

Brant felt that Lisa was not committed to the ministry. She didn't make it to every service, and she wanted to do other things after working at the church. Brant saw these choices as a lack of commitment on her part. It appeared the only time Lisa and Brant had time together was at the services. There was very little time for bonding outside of that environment.

The final straw came when Brant's grandmother died later that year. Her passing was devastating for Brant. It was his grandmother who had given him his first sign to experience a vision and of the Holy Spirit. She was in the hospital at the time, and her words of counsel had a lasting effect on him.

Brant always said he and his grandmother would live to experience the rapture and the return of Jesus. It was terribly upsetting for him when she didn't live out the promise. When his grandmother died, I think Brant took this as a sign that things were not going right with him.

True to his character, Brant didn't confront Lisa for the breakup. He ended his engagement with her by having Claudia deliver the news. Lisa was furious. Although she didn't make a public scene, she refused to give back the ring. Just like other gossip within the ministry, the news spread in hushed tones throughout the congregation, trickling through the aisles and down corridors like a mist. At one of the outreach services, Claudia finally coaxed the ring from Lisa and returned it to Brant. The buzz died down soon after that. Brant acted like nothing happened.

Ironically Lisa remained with the ministry and continued her involvement with the choir for another year. She sang in the choir and held the microphone during testimony time. People felt sorry for Lisa and all she had experienced.

The memorial service for Brant's grandmother was held at the Foursquare Church. Brant was upstairs in the sound both at the back of the church with Claudia. He was upset and crying the whole time. Billy Adams gave the service.

I still felt drawn to the church, and I did my best to be active in it. As well as singing in the choir, I ushered and was a catcher in the healing line during the service. I stopped attending the outreaches for awhile as I adjusted my work schedule. No one questioned me about what happened to my position with Brant. I was still given more or less free rein to wander the grounds. It felt strange to be apart, but I was grateful I hadn't been pushed all the way out.

A few months later, I was asked to assist Brant again for a Saturday service. Part of the core ministry was attending an outreach in Washington state, and Brant flew back to Long Beach for the Saturday service. He was glad to see me and said it was like old times. I have to admit it felt perfectly natural for me too. Though he said we should do it again, that was the last time I assisted him with any service.

I remained friends with Claudia and Eric. In fact, they asked me to be a member of their wedding that year, 1975. They were planning to get married after one of the Angeles Temple healing services. I felt honored and accepted their invitation.

Brant agreed to perform very few weddings, but theirs was one of those rare exceptions. In the ceremony, I was one of Eric's groomsmen. Since

I understood what it takes to cater to Brant, they teased me about it behind his back as we prepared for the wedding. The teasing continued at church services as well. To me, it was a sign that things were returning to normal and I was once again accepted within the church.

Later that year another area opened up for me to expand my ministry experience. In the summer of 1975, Elaine. approached me at an Angeles Temple meeting. She asked me if I wanted to get involved in a drama ministry that she was forming called ACTS. The first show she wanted to produce was based on Charlie Brown and the Peanuts characters, giving it a Christian theme. I told her I had a background in theater during high school, and I would love to get back into it.

Elaine was a very bright, zealous and articulate woman. I greatly admired her perception and wit. She was involved in the ministry from the beginning stages, but I had never really gotten to know her up to that point. We were involved in different areas of the ministry. Once I joined her drama group, we got to know each other fairly well. Elaine and I met often, talking and exchanging ideas for skits to do. She wrote them down, and we all worked on them together as an ensemble.

We met as a group every couple of weeks, talking about the material we wanted use and working on different skits. After some rehearsal, we did a couple of performances at a Wednesday night service. Brant loved it – he was laughing the whole time. We were off to a great start.

As a group we took a few field trips that included Universal Studios and attending a few professional plays. The trips inspired a lot of us, especially Elaine. She wanted to grow as an actress and writer herself, and she thought the ACTS group was her outlet.

Elaine decided to take some classes in Hollywood, and some of the elders in the ministry were supportive. I thought it was a great idea too, and I wanted to attend with her. She came across a series of workshops held at an experimental acting college, given by actors from the film industry. Elaine, a woman in our group named Pam, and I took a comedy workshop that turned out to be excellent. The instructors included beloved celebrities like Ed Asner, Lucille Ball and Lilly Tomlin.

This was an incredible six-week course, and we all got a great high from this workshop. Ed Asner taught one week, and Lilly Tomlin held her class after a live show of hers, and we all met in the audience. It was a thrill and extremely educational about the craft of comedy. Before class, Elaine, Pam and myself prayed for Lucy in the car.

Lucille Ball committed to teaching for four of the six weeks. It was a memorable experience to meet and be so close to Lucille Ball. It was great to watch her interact with all the young actors and openly share her story. Her coaching during that four-week period was invaluable. At the end of the last class Elaine gave Lucy one of Lilly's records as the whole class escorted her to her station wagon. Lucy sucked in the air and exhaled holding back tears. I could tell it was a great moment for her as well.

Word got around among the ministry that Elaine and I were mingling with Hollywood celebrities, and we became part of the church gossip. Brant even mentioned it a few times in his messages, dropping our names as if we were stars ourselves. I thought it was funny that Brant would mention my name in his messages like nothing had happened. The irony was that I was now coming into my own.

A New Singing Group

Towards the end of summer, as the drama troupe was being formed, I was asked to be part of a sixteen-voice singing group. Kelly and Lilly G. were in charge of it. Brant's idea was to have a smaller group that could travel when the full choir could not. We were called the Shekinah Singers.

When the group was being formed, Kelly, was matching us up in pairs, my first singing partner was a woman named, Madge. This pairing was inno-cent on Kelly's part, I'm sure, and he didn't know my connection with Madge went deep. I had once asked her to marry me.

Madge was the second woman I had romantic feelings for since my relationship with Brigid. She was a few years older than I, and she was a Godly woman in my eyes. At the time we were forming the new singing group, I still had romantic feelings for Madge. My heart skipped a beat when she showed up at our first rehearsal. Then when she and I were paired together in the group, I thought it was the work of the Lord.

Madge talked to Kelly about singing with me, and she made him aware of our past together. He assumed I would have a problem singing with her, though she did not. She worked in the Word of Knowledge part of the healing service, holding the microphone on stage with Brant during testimony time. She had a romantic history with Brant too, yet she managed to work with him in spite of it.

Madge had once approached Brant and asked him to marry her. This happened before he was engaged to Lisa. It happened in Palm Springs after a service at Jo Ellen's condo. I don't know how intimate they were at the time (it was more on her part to believe something was there but a total surprise to Brant.) There was enough feeling there for Madge to imagine herself spending the rest of her life with Brant. Instead, Brant publicly rebuked her and sent her off by herself, feeling embarrassed and confused. They were never close again after the way he treated her. She continued to hold the microphone after that incident, somehow keeping her dignity.

After Brant spurned Madge in Palm Springs, Claudia befriended her. A short time later, Claudia and Eric were married – clearly both women were over Brant. Their friendship gave me reason to hope, and I confided in Claudia about my feelings for Madge. I told her how much I felt for her and how our singing together in the choir might be a sign from the Lord. Claudia was sympathetic, and she said she would pray about it for me. She also planned for several of us to socialize outside of church as a group, and she included Madge.

I finally got the courage to approach Madge after a Saturday service at the Foursquare Church. I noticed she was talking to another guy, and I must admit to some pangs of jealousy. Steve C. was a deacon and played the bass guitar in the orchestra. I could see why she might be attracted to him. Besides being talented, he was beefy and had lots of energy. Seeing them together made me feel queasy, as if my golden opportunity was slipping away. I knew if I was going to have any kind of chance with her, I'd better do it soon.

Right there in the sanctuary, I opened up to Madge and shared my tender feelings. I told her how I thought the Lord was putting us together. She smiled and said, "Steve C. just came and told me the same thing." It threw me off balance. Then she told me straight out she had no intention of starting a relationship or get married. I was stunned.

I laughed out loud, embarrassed. "Boy, did I pick the right timing." She then laughed with me. There was no malice in her.

"Well, I guess that's my answer then," I said. We prayed together about God blessing each other. Then we parted, laughing. I felt like such a fool. After that, we got along fine. When we were paired off in the singing group, we laughed how ironic it was.

Getting involved with the singing group was a good experience. It offered a way to get to know people in a closer group than before. Before we formed the group, I did not have a chance to get to know people, other than in passing during services. For instance, Meg, and I connected again as friends. We had known each other through high school, but only from a distance. Singing together in this close-knit group pushed us to make a tighter bond. The same was true of all the members. There were fifteen of us in the original group – seven women and eight men. We all quickly connected, drawer closer together than ever before.

Kevin was part of this close-knit group, and he seemed really thrilled. This helped break down the barrier between him and me. At one time, he felt keen competition with me and suggested that I had come between him and Brant. Now it seemed we were more on an even plane again, and he no longer felt threatened.

When the Shekinah Singers was formed as a group, there was a rush to get ready to work on an album. We wanted to complete it within six or seven weeks. Although there were people already singing solos, the only time we could rehearse was after people got off work. We used music on tape to rehearse the songs we were learning – not the live band we would be recording with. There were going to be several solos on the album, requiring even more rehearsal. I thought this schedule was rushed, since it really takes a couple months to get voices in shape and trained.

Like everyone else, I worked hard to do my part for the good of the group. Still, I petitioned to get more time for rehearsal. My objections were overruled, and we proceeded with the album project on schedule.

When the time came to record the music, we were barely ready. All of us had a case of nerves – there's an intimidation factor that comes into play when the sound engineer tells you, "We're rolling." Though we were singing in a familiar surrounding – the Foursquare Church – the live microphones and reel-to-reel tape made our surroundings suddenly seem strange.

The choir only recorded one take for each song because of our skimpy budget. The soloist's performance was added during a separate recording session. We did not quite get the clean recording we wanted, but the engineers were able to work their magic and the album turned out fine. Our work was immortalized on 12" vinyl. The Shekinah Singers album cover featured a picture of the group taken at Griffith Park in Los Angeles. Though we were just a bunch of young locals, we felt like we'd hit the big time.

As a group we traveled to outreaches in the surrounding area. When it was not too far, the choir would come as well. The outreaches were mainly in Southern California and in the San Francisco Bay Area, but there were several out of state. We traveled as far as Washington, Arizona, Colorado and Nevada.

More than once, Brant was a guest on TBN with Paul and Jan Crouch. He brought a couple soloists, and the Shekinah Singers sung backup. We appeared on the show often enough we developed a routine. It varied slightly from the outreaches, but it was clear we were beginning to operate like a well-oiled machine.

We would arrive at the location and set up the sound equipment. Next, we warmed up our voices as a group with a couple songs. Then we prayed together and finished getting ourselves ready before the service. By the time we were dressed and warmed up, Brant arrived and sat in the back or on the side lines, watching us as his plan came together. We spent time with him before the show began, and we went on to sing our numbers in between the different guests on the show. It seemed we were on our way to the big time.

Our Act Hits the Road

Getting around to the various performances was a problem. Not all of us arrived on time, and there was a considerable amount of time that could be put to better use if we had a bus. Robbie. and Steve. were put in charge of getting us one.

Ben was a single man in his late thirties, and he worked as a power crane operator. Though it's a blue-collar job, this is work that pays extremely well. Ben was doing well for himself and had few responsibilities.

Ben first became aware of the ministry through the television programs, and started to come to the services in San Diego, then to Long Beach. He heard that the ministry was looking for a bus, and he offered to get one. He first approached Robbie and Steve about doing this and they did not take him seriously.

However, Ben was perfectly serious. He sold some real estate he owned so he could purchase a tour bus for us. When he showed up with it, we were dumbfounded. Ben had the Shekinah Fellowship logo painted on the bus. He even served as one of the drivers. This was a great blessing for all of us, and Ben's generosity was astonishing.

We used the bus to transport the church choir members and the Shekinah Singers. It was a great asset to the ministry. Traveling proved to be a great way to meet different people within the choir and get to know them. It brought our group closer together, travel as a unit. We often prayed before we started each trip and sang songs along the way.

When we went to outreaches in other states, members of the host churches provided us with lodging in their homes. We stayed at hotels as well, often doubling up and even sharing a bed with another singer or musician. Some members thought this seemed unfair since some of the elders got a hotel room of their own. I was not bothered by it. As for Brant, he often flew in at the last moment, and he stayed in a room by himself.

Besides lodging, we had to cover the cost for our transportation and meals. The ministry chiped in for Shekinah Singers who needed help, but when the choir toured, they were required to provide for their own expenses. The expense was part of the reason Brant wanted to scale down and travel with a smaller singing group. Besides projecting a more intimate feel, it made economic sense.

Over the course of time, the ministry stopped doing television studio productions. Instead we started taping the healing services and breaking them up to several half hour segments. They were edited to add announcements and soloists. This was a unique format, and the television audience got an idea what was taking place in the healing services. Kathryn Kuhlman never allowed her healing sessions to be televised and shown on her program. What we were doing with the TV program had never been done before.

When we went to other churches, I would pick up what was going on with them behind the scenes. I paid attention to how we were treated and observe comments the minister made. In the course of time, I noticed our group was beginning to have influence on the churches around us. One area where we especially had an effect on was the offering.

Our ministry never really pushed for offerings in the beginning. We asked for a certain amount when we went to a host church, but I never saw Brant just come out and ask for it straight up. This left others to do it for him. Some were more eager than others to ask for it on his behalf for the ministry. Sometimes – rarely – Brant would be part of a TBN telethon, and the Shekinah Singers were there as well.

Occasionally the minister from a host church we were visiting took up a separate offering to support our work. Some ministers were more adept at priming the congregation for a good offering, seeding the pot. The seed concept started to take off, and one minister talked about sowing a seed faith for God to bless them.

"How many people would give $1,000 right now for God to bless them. Let me see your hands." Ushers collected the cash. Then the minister would say, "How about $100? How many people would give $100 for God to bless them. Raise your hands now." Kevin would be on the sidelines, counting all the hands. Later he was the one counting all the money.

CHAPTER 14:

FOX WEST COAST THEATER

As the ministry was outgrowing the Foursquare Church, there was mounting tension between the Foursquare Church and Shekinah. This tension was fomented by Jo Ellen, and it was based on the fear of a conspiracy that the Foursquare was taking over the Shekinah ministry.

Pastor Adams intended to help relieve Brant and the ministry of some of the pressure. He wanted to insulate them, but somehow the whole thing got blown out of proportion. It resulted in a power struggle for leadership and direction.

It was Pastor Adams who opened the door to Angeles Temple and other outreaches with the Foursquare and Assembly of God churches. This was a threat for Jo Ellen and Brant. Jo Ellen felt she was the founder of the Shekinah ministry, and she manipulated Brant's steps like a stage mother, pulling strings behind the scenes. She fabricated a story that Pastor Adams was having a nervous breakdown, acting irrationally by trying to take over the ministry.

This was a favorite card that Jo Ellen and Brant often played when they wanted to break off relationships with key people who had helped build the ministry. They repeated the claim several times – there always seemed to be someone who wanted to take over the ministry and had some kind of nervous breakdown.

To remove Pastor Adams, they held an emergency meeting after a Saturday night service at the Shekinah house. They congregated upstairs in Steve's apartment. Pastor Adams, Steve and the other elders were there. Brant was not part of that meeting. I was in the living room in the main house and sensed something was going on, judging by the body language and facial expressions of my house mates. When I asked them directly, no one had details. The only information I got was that Pastor Adams was taking over the ministry and was having a nervous breakdown.

About an hour later, Pastor Adams came into the main house looking very distressed. He seemed like he was in shock, and he had a dazed look on his face. I offered him something to drink, but everyone else left him alone. He kept his head held down, looking very sad. After he finished a glass of water, he went back into the meeting, which continued late into the night. Finally, I overheard everyone leaving, but I could only glean snatches of chatter.

One thing that was clear after the meeting was that the ministry had to move from the Foursquare Church. Perhaps Pastor Adams had been hoping it was going to work out and some compromise could be reached with Brant. Whatever his hopes, there was no compromise.

This meant another building had to be located quickly, and the Shekinah ministry had to move. Claudia again was instrumental in locating a building. She and Eric were living downtown in the historic Lafayette Hotel, an Art Deco icon that had been converted to apartments. A few blocks from their apartment was the huge historic Fox Theater on Ocean Blvd., and it happened to be vacant. Claudia contacted the leasing office then spoke to Jo Ellen to work out the lease terms. Nothing was said to the congregation, but rumors spread quickly about plans to move as soon as possible. The word was that a building had been located.

The theater was in familiar territory for us. It was right across the street from the old site of the Long Beach Civic Auditorium where Shekinah had hosted the Easter-In Gathering a few years earlier. Since then, the auditorium had been torn down and replaced with a new building. This made the neighborhood seem gentrified. The irony was that Shekinah's new home was located directly in between two X-Rated theaters.

The Fox Theater had originally opened in July of 1925 as a combination Vaudeville and film venue. It got a makeover in the 1940's, modernizing it for sound and other movie technologies. The facility was huge with a seating capacity of 2,000. There was a full stage, orchestra pit, a trap door, dressing rooms underneath the stage, a full lighting system, and several back drops. The front of the building even had a large naked statue, a graceful replica of Venus. Looking from the stage into the main auditorium, the five-story ceiling was impressive, even overwhelming. I thought this would be a great place to do full drama productions.

I got a tour of the building with one of the deacons. When we entered through the back door, there was only one light on the stage area. The dim lighting made the place look spooky, and at first, we hesitated to go on. Walking below the stage through the narrow hallway into the dressing rooms gave me a creepy feeling. There was graffiti on the walls, including a satanic pentagram and a Nazi Swastika. It smelled musty, and there was old urine in some areas. It reminded me of being in the Roman catacombs, meandering through that twisted old maze, the ghosts of yesteryear echoing down the halls.

This move was a bold new direction for Brant and the ministry. I remember thinking this could be a sign for Brant. Kathryn Kuhlman had passed away in February of that that year, leaving a void in Evangelical leadership. I thought Brant would surely fill the vacancy. This historic building seemed exciting and mysterious, and I thought it would make a brilliant setting for his ascension.

Overall, the interior of the theater was in sad shape and needed a quick makeover. Before moving in, it needed painting and cleaning to make it presentable for the congregation. The front of the theater was much more open and brighter than backstage, but it still needed an overhaul. Retail shops in the front of the building could be converted to a nursery area with a bit of work. There were a number of offices that looked promising, and it had one large room that could be used for board meetings. There was a whole suite of offices on the second floor above the lobby area, but they needed cleaning and painting as well.

Many of us volunteered to scrub and clean, and even steam clean the upholstery seats while praying over them. New carpet was laid in high traffic areas and in the offices. Kevin went on a shopping spree, getting antiques for Brant's office, plus fixtures, furnishings, and chandeliers for the offices.

Cosmetic touches weren't the only changes that were needed. The plumbing in the main floor restrooms was leaking. The stage lighting needed rewiring to get it to work, and an entire sound system needed to be installed. On the stage, we added risers for the choir as well as a grand piano and an organ. People volunteered their time, and many worked around the clock to get the building ready for the move.

We had less than three weeks to move to the new location. The last push was done while Pastor Adams was away on a trip to Israel. Brant originally was scheduled to go with the Adams group, but he backed out.

Once Brant split with the Adams and Foursquare Church, Brant never even talked to Pastor Adams about the move to the Fox West Coast Theater. He just cut off all ties off with him and had Jo Ellen or Steve speak for him. Yet again, Brant could not face conflict of any kind, and this move was no exception.

Pastor Adams got back from Israel just in time for the last Saturday service at the Foursquare Church. That's when the announcement was made that the ministry would be moving to the Fox Theater. Flyers announcing the move were already inserted in the bulletins that were passed out among the congregation. At the close of the service, Brant was making the final announcement when Pastor Adams came on stage, taking the microphone. Brant looked stunned. Knowing he was trapped and could not intercept him; Brant stepped a few feet away from him. The moment was tense and awkward.

Pastor Adams could have taken the opportunity to admonish the ministry and expose what was going on, to air out his disappointment. Instead, he smiled and took the high road. He gave a brief history of the relationship that they had built with the ministry, and he talked about the family that had been formed. He added that the Foursquare never charged the ministry for the use of the building or the use of the electricity. He expressed his sadness to see the ministry leave and invited people to continue to come to the Sunday services. He closed in prayer by giving a blessing to Brant and the ministry.

Everyone applauded, and the organ struck a chord. Adams walked off the stage, not looking at Brant. Brant took the microphone and quickly went into a song. Afterward everyone was dismissed, and Brant quickly exited the stage.

Brant left the building to avoid any possible conflict with anyone. As soon as the congregation left, people went to work on removing what belonged to the ministry. Kevin worked like mad, tearing down everything in Brant's dressing room, and he even took the carpet.

It was awkward and sad as Pastor Adams, Terry B. and Mrs. Adams watched the parishioners leave in a huff like spoiled children. Pastor Adams made sarcastic remarks to Terry B. as they watched everything they helped build get stripped away. There were so many mixed emotions as everyone was in a rush to leave. The elders and volunteers just picked up and left without any thanks. It was horrible and sad for all of us, and Brant's lack of leadership soured those final hours even more.

The bitter mood didn't last. The following week at the new location, there was excitement and anticipation in the air. The main floor was full, and the congregation murmured with expectation before the service. It was business as usual for a Saturday service. The orchestra played, the choir sang, and Brant made his usual grand appearance, taking center stage and leading the worship songs. Kelly G., who was already the assistant choir director now replaced Terry. Lilly G. was now the full-time organist in place of Mrs. Adams. We had launched and were sailing full ahead under our own power.

Pastor Adams came to the service, quietly sitting in the back row under the balcony, looking sad and hurt. No one talked to him. He continued to come for several weeks, always sitting in the same location. He looked like a father who had lost his son, trying to reach out to him. I'm sure it broke his heart.

Brant was the son that Pastor Adams never had. For Brant to turn his back and not respond to him must have taken a toll. By this time, several elders had left Brant and the ministry. Now Brant cut off the man who had opened several doors for him – had helped him expand the ministry. He closed the door on their friendship.

Within a month, a television taping was scheduled combined with an official grand opening ceremony dedication combined with Paul & Jan Crouch having a TBN rally at the theater. The monthly Angeles Temple meetings continued for about another year after the move.

The ministry was given the opportunity to buy the property very inexpensively at the time along with the whole corner lot. This was a time when real estate was at a low and would have been a good investment. There was tremendous growth potential, but Brant's maturity was not there.

Coming Into My Own

I was with the Shekinah Singers for about two years when the structure of the ministry changed. During this time, Brant's health kept declining. Finally, he took a sabbatical for a year to recover from what amounted to a complete physical break down. His sickness cast a pall over the congregation. It was hard to say which was worse – dealing with his advancing illness or dealing with the void his leave of absence created. Just as with all other private news, the congregation was abuzz with gossip.

When the ministry started the Shekinah Christian Center based at the Fox Theater, I decided to make a change of my own. I broke away from the Shekinah Singers and got involved more with the drama group. I also figured it was time for me to make this change and move out of the Shekinah house.

Joel was in the choir and in the drama group. His apartment was in the downtown area not far from the Fox Theater, so I approached him about rooming together. He had a small one-bedroom apartment, and I proposed that I could sleep in the living room. Joel was hesitant at first, but he warmed up to the idea once he did the math. Later I found a larger one-bedroom apartment across the street, and we moved there together. Once again, Joel had the bedroom and I had the living room area.

Joel was a very committed Christian and very much starstruck with the ministry. He must have thought I was something since I'd held several positions in the ministry. He seemed especially impressed that I worked so closely with Brant as his assistant.

I lived with Joel for several months. To make ends meet, I temporarily hired on where he worked as a bus driver. Steve, the bass player in the orchestra, worked there too. My job as a bus driver lasted several months, through the summer and fall.

The bus trainer also attended the ministry, and he volunteered to drive the ministry bus at times. I did my share of driving for the ministry as well, doing tour routes through the summer.

I started to drive school routes in the early fall, but my driving career was abruptly cut short after I had a couple of minor accidents. Once I banged the side of the bus against a pole on a foggy morning. Another time, I backed the bus into a parked car. I was embarrassed and felt humiliated about the accidents. In hindsight, I'm sure it was all for the best that I did not pursue a career as a bus driver.

Soon after this, Joel told me he was going to move into his parent's house, save some money and go back to Bible school. He only came to the ministry a little while longer, then he moved

I always admired his dedication and his commitment to his faith.

When Joel moved in with his parents, I had to give up the apartment since I was temporarily out of work. I began to feel depressed. I ended up moving back to the Shekinah House. I shared the upstairs apartment where Steve and Teddi lived before. Now with me and three others – Ralph D., Bob L. and Jerry S. Ralph. Ralph and I were in the singing group and Bob L played in the orchestra. Jerry served as a counselor and did some graphic design for the ministry. We divided the rent among all of us.

I ended up getting a job at a company called Unitrex. The company distributed adding machines and the early models of digital watches. Some of the people from Shekinah also had jobs there. I worked with Steve A. on refurbishing adding machines for resale. It was steady work, and it taught me a skill. This period gave me a new kind of stability and independence. Even though I was still living in the Shekinah House, I felt myself coming into my own.

This feeling wasn't meant to last. Within a year, Jo Ellen decided to sell the Shekinah house property and we all had to move. We talked about finding another large house – we all liked living together and we'd become a family – but it did not work out.

It was not long afterwards that Unitrex went out of business and I had to find another job. I worked as a stock clerk and Ralph and I got an apartment in the same complex as Steve and Georgette A. Then Ralph decided to move back home to save money since he and Meg where making plans to get married. Finally, I had enough money to find an apartment for myself. It would be my first apartment on my own.

Brant's Breakdown

Before we made the move to the theater, the ministry changed its name from Shekinah Fellowship to Brant Baker Ministries. The ministry started bleeding money and had to file bankruptcy. The Shekinah Fellowship went under. It was a stunning blow, especially to those of us who had been involved from the start. Though the ministry reformed and changed its name, these developments took their toll on Brant – the drain that led to his physical breakdown. This is when he decided to take a year off.

After about six months, Brant started to come back for an occasional appearance. Once a month he would preach, and the other Saturday services were filled by other speakers.

His absence had an impact on the ministry financially, and a number of staff members had to be let go. Brant's health issues were a mystery to many of us. He was getting tired a lot and would get sick after the service. We were told he had a heart condition, though that didn't explain the aggregate of his symptoms – the sores, coughing up blood, and other plagues upon his health. The medications he was on made him look stoned at times.

I first became aware of Brant's physical condition while I worked closely with him during that period, over a year. Thinking back, I realize how much Brant was starting to feel the effects of his ill health. He had put his body through a great deal during the last ten years and was now catching up on him.

Brant's compulsive, addictive behavior led him on a wild ride in his teens, and his mother indulged him. He was always very passionate about what he started. As a result, he burned out, leaving his mother to clean up the aftermath. This pattern emerged more than once.

Jo Ellen wanted to see Brant succeed so she could save face. Her sisters had married well and became successful financially. Jo Ellen was always try-ing to keep up, to validate her own choices. She wanted to feel proud of her boys – Brant and Kevin – and boast about what a great job she did raising her sons.

At one point, after giving up on the Olympic Skater dream, Brant started doing some modeling. He was good at it. He was really good looking, and he showed promise. This led him to get involved in the Hollywood scene, working at a movie studio as a gopher. It was a low-level job, but it opened doors for him in a whole new way. He started going to parties, making connections with drug dealers and gays. During this time, Brant experimented in an alternative lifestyle. He even used another name, putting it on like a mask when he ran in the Hollywood circles. Soon the lifestyle consumed him.

For a young man with gorgeous good looks, Hollywood was a sea of glamour, and Brant was drowning in it. Being exposed to the Hollywood entertainment industry, he had become reckless, looking for love and acceptance in the wrong places. It left him feeling even more empty inside. His mother tried to intervene, but it would take a huge hook to pull him out of the quagmire he'd slipped into.

Both modeling and working at the movie studio exposed him to the creative field of fashion. Brant absorbed everything he could about fashion and style. This worked for him as an asset later on when he opened a clothing store.

His mother Jo Ellen made attempts to expose him to spiritual matters during this time. She had been looking for spiritual answers for herself, which lead her to Calvary Chapel. Teaching a study group at Jo Ellen's house helped Chuck get started in the ministry. By the time Calvary Chapel was getting off the ground, Jo Ellen was able to pique Brant's interest.

Little by little, Brant got hooked on religion. He saw the genuineness of the message, the spirit of something that was real. It made a stark contrast with what he was experiencing in the world of fashion and fantasy, sex and drugs. Jo Ellen's attempts to pull him out of Hollywood were finding some ground.

During this time, Brant opened a clothing store in Hollywood. He loved what he was doing, and he showed remarkable fashion sense as a style counsel. He coordinated clothes and accessories for his customers, and built a following. Unfortunately, it didn't last long.

Talented though he was, Brant's accounting was flawed. He mismanaged the finances of the business and had to close the store. It was a disappointment for Brant and source of shame for his social climbing mother. Though Brant was still searching for himself, his mother was undaunted.

Jo Ellen opened a second clothing store for him, listing the business in his name. The boutique was located in Newport Beach near Costa Mesa. Jo Ellen took a firmer hand with the finances this time, and the second store fared better than the first. She enlisted Kevin's help as a clerk to keep the shop open.

But Jo Ellen didn't have much skill with parental control of her boys. Both of them were hard to manage at times, and their sibling rivalry was a constant test of her nerves. It also created a tense atmosphere in the boutique, alienating customers and sparking rumors.

When he didn't get what he wanted, Kevin would throw fits in the store, tossing expensive merchandise around. Several times he knocked over displays. Brant would shriek in protest, appealing to his mother to take his side and punish Kevin. They acted more like kids than young men. It was clear that if time didn't mellow the brothers, the second store would soon go the way of the first one. Something had to change.

The change came when Brant converted to Christianity and got the call to join the ministry. Once again, his mother was his biggest backer. Given his personal history, it should have come as no surprise a few years later when the ministry started to unravel. But it was his health that became his final undoing.

Just how much Brant was really exposed to the Hollywood scene and homosexual lifestyle was always hazy for us in the Shekinah Fellowship. Brant had a tendency to dramatize and boast about the lifestyle he'd left behind. He was indeed a drama queen. Hyperbole was just his way. The degree of his turpitude changed with each telling of the story.

From what I recall, Brant never came out and said he was gay, but all the signs were there. His mannerisms, his love of fashion, his open appreciation of attractive men... his outward intimacy with Kyle – these were all clues to his inner life. His former wild ways added to a good conversion story about how he gave his life to Jesus. No one really questioned Brant's spiritual integrity when he talked about his Christian conversion. He had a love of Jesus and a sense of humility. That's what mattered back then.

Being raised in the '60s in the Hollywood area, Brant briefly became part of the underground culture of drug use and free love. By the time he was twenty, Brant was deep into the lifestyle with no fear of consequences – not that consequences of any kind seemed to bother him. Restraint and accountability were alien to him generally.

At the time I worked with the ministry, HIV and AIDS were unknown. Though the virus existed, there is an incubation period of five to seven years before any signs of illness begin showing up. The most common exposure to HIV was either from intravenous drug use or a gay lifestyle without using protection. Brant's conversion story fit the profile of someone at risk for AIDS. His wild history coincided with the disease's timeline, and Brant started to show signs of a physical breakdown soon after his rise to ecclesiastical stardom.

These signs started to show while I was working with him. When I was eighteen, Brant was twenty-five. On his twenty-six birthday, complained to me about how tired he was after the services. He drank more coffee before the services, and he constantly felt tired.

I thought since he was so young, he shouldn't be tired all the time. At first it was hard for me to take his complaints seriously – maybe he was just being overly dramatic, as he was with so many things. Everyone around him just smiled and encouraged him to keep going. We all said he just needed rest. After all, who wouldn't be tired after standing on their feet for several hours?

Preaching and praying for several hundred people in the healing line did have its cost. He often got a burst of energy just before he went on the stage. The Holy Spirit gave him a rush. It was like a different entity took over his body and he became a different personality, using his body as a conduit of the Holy Spirit. Afterwards, his energy crashed, and he felt completely drained.

Looking back, his diet was not the best for supporting the amount of energy he was putting out. When I first worked with him, he had started to gain weight. It all went to his stomach, and he felt self-conscience about it. This made for more than one awkward situation, especially since I was the one who helped him with his wardrobe.

The time I was Brant's assistant one time we traveled to Bakersfield for an outreach, and we were sharing a hotel room. When I woke up the next morning, he threw a towel at me. "Do you know you talk in your sleep?"

I was puzzled and felt embarrassed. "You spoke in tongues in your sleep," he said, "and then you told me I was too fat,"

I started to laugh, and he added, "You're lucky you said it while you were sleeping. I took it as a word from the Lord."

I couldn't deny saying it. He caught me judging him in my private thoughts. All we could do was laugh.

After that, Brant was determined to lose weight, and he even asked me to help him. He cut back on his food intake, ate fewer calories and did not eat any bread. He was only eating one meal a day or just nibbling on food. He drank very little water and preferred coffee before the service. He would leave a cup of orange juice next to the podium. After a service, he had a beef patty, a baked potato and salad. He would do some sit ups every day, and he also took kelp supplements he heard about from Claudia.

Brant used to be heavy when he was a young teenager, and it gave him a complex. He was sensitive about being overweight. He talked about this in some of his early sermons, about how it made him feel low. Eventually he lost weight as he became older and grew taller.

Some models he met in Hollywood told him about their "trick" of throwing up after eating. Though he didn't realize they were describing the eating disorder known as bulimia, he decided not to follow their lead. Instead he focused on his meal planning. What he did eat was skimpy portions that were nutritionally incomplete. I was concerned because it seemed like he was eating so little food during that time. Brant would be tempted by desserts, and he told me to take them away when we went out. Sometimes he would take just a bite and give me the rest.

Once we were invited to dinner at a pastor's home after a service in Bakersfield. The hostess served a great home cooked meal, and she sliced up some homemade pie for dessert. It looked really good, and as the guest of honor, she served Brant first. Before he could dive in, I snatched the pie away from him. Everyone just looked at me. Brant was shocked, his eyes big as saucers. "How could you do that to me?"

It was a rude thing to do, and I knew it. Looking back, it was also insulting to the hostess who had made the pie for him.

"I thought you wanted me to help you," I said defensively. He was still stunned that I embarrassed him, and I felt awkward. He reached over and cut the piece in half, scooping some up for himself and giving me the rest. Everyone at the table started to laugh. Brant kept teasing me until I apologized.

"Are you enjoying the pie?" He gave me a sulky look, trying to make me feel guilty.

"Oh, yes, it is very good," I said with my mouth full. Everyone laughed some more as Brant and I hammed it up. Though the moment took a comedic turn, there was an underlying pathos. If any of us could have seen the future, I doubt we would be laughing.

Brant was experiencing burnout by pushing himself so hard for several years. "I don't know if I can do this any longer," he often confided while getting dressed before the service. "Isn't that terrible?"

Over and over again, Brant said in his messages he wanted to "burn out for Jesus since he is coming so soon." That is just what happened to him at an early age. His declaration was a self-fulfilling prophecy.

We were all young at the time, and we had the energy and drive to work all day and night. Then we'd drive to an outreach, getting back home late at night. We'd get little or no sleep, and off we'd go again the next day. This kind of drive is what Brant wanted to see, and he pushed himself just as hard as the rest of us.

In time his passion turned morbid. At first, he just wanted to take a break. He said he wanted to go to the mountains and work on pottery. He started to see and talked about other evangelists who self-destructed – names like "AA Allen," the Pentecostal evangelist who died from alcoholism at 59. Brant said he understood why he drank because of the pressure of the ministry. He also said he understood how Aimee Semple McPherson could have accidentally overdosed on medication.

Even after I stopped working as his personal assistant, he dropped hints in is messages about his own burnout. After Kathryn Kuhlman died of heart failure, he said she exhausted herself serving the Lord. It sounded like he was putting this on himself as a death wish. His words were not exactly a cry for help – more like a soft whisper, portending tragedy yet to come.

Sister Edith Lends A Hand

Sister Edith Kabish was a woman in her sixties. Her blonde hair was piled high on her head, and her horn-rimmed glasses evoked the spirit of a 19th century librarian. Her wardrobe was equally anachronistic, mostly ankle-length dresses with angel wing sleeves. She had a charming rural accent with a twist of a drawl, something she picked up while living in a small town in Oregon.

Sister Edith had a warm, down home country charm that seemed oddly appropriate on the island our ministry occupied amid the surrounding urban sprawl. She was a force for good.

Before joining the Shekinah Fellowship, Sister Edith had ministered for years with Kathryn Kuhlman's healing services. She served as a Word of Knowledge helper, and she also worked in the healing lines, screening witnesses before they went up onstage to testify. I don't know if she was paid or volunteered, but she approached her work like a professional.

She was a caring person, always with a smile that welcomed you. She was quick to offer some pie, tea or coffee. She had the wisdom of years of experience working one-on-one with people on a personal level. Before that, she was in the ministry for many years and worked as a bookkeeper.

Sister Edith held her own Bible Study group and had a small following. They met in coffee houses in back rooms, even though she was a tea drinker. She also had three assistants, women she was mentoring – Joanne, Michelle and Marti. I came to know them well.

Sister Edith had a unique prophetic gift, much like a Kathryn Kuhlman did. She taught Bible Study, and toward the end of her class, she would call out to different people in the room to come forward. She said that she saw a glowing mist over them. One of her assistants would lead the person from their seat up to the front, and they lined up in a row.

Sister Edith went down the line and, one by one, talked about the parishioners standing in front of her. She talked about their background, their talents or their jobs and gave a prophetic word of encouragement to each person, something unique to them. I was called out by her a number of times, and her messages were always apt and encouraging.

Sometimes during her teaching or while counseling someone in a prayer line, she had a difficult time standing up, and she acted like she was drunk. This often happened because the Holy Spirit had come into her, and it was hard for her to keep her balance. I have seen this phenomenon among others who ministered in the gifts of prophecy and healing. It often looks showy when done in large gatherings, but I can see how this happened since I have experienced it as well.

With Sister Edith, one of her assistants stood by her to keep her stabilized. When she talked to the person, she often did not see their face because of the glowing fog over them. Once the prophetic word was given, the fog lifted from them.

She had a favorite phrase when she gave an inspiring teaching or a prophetic word from the Lord. If she liked the message, she would say, "Me too, Lord!" Soon others in the congregation would also say "Me too, Lord!" when they liked what they heard.

Sister Edith came to the Saturday services at the Foursquare Church with her assistants in tow. She would come to see Brant and witness the young people he preached with. She liked it that they patterned the service after Kathryn Kuhlman's ministry.

I believe it was Jo Ellen who introduced Sister Edith to Brant. She attended the Shekinah ministry every couple of weeks. Soon she was holding Bible studies for those who worked in the Saturday night healing services and Word of Knowledge. She had a genuine interest in helping the ministry, and she gave it her all.

Her support was a positive thing for the ministry, given her experience with Kathryn Kuhlman. She never appeared to be close to Brant, and she remained politely professional with him. At the same time, she had a motherly love for the young men and women in the congregation. She poured out love wherever she went, and she was a joy to be around.

One of my favorite teaching stories Sister Edith told in her weekly studies was about one of her experiences with Kathryn Kuhlman. Elaine wrote a summary of it:

I attended her weekly Bible Study and learned a great deal that has stayed with me. One of my favorite stories of Sister Edith›s was when she was working with the great healer icon, Kathryn Kuhlman. She was one of Kuhlman›s stage workers and told of this one fellow who came up to get saved, and he was cussing like a Bandit into the microphone, «Jesus Christ! Holy Shit, Goddamn!» in exclamation of the experience of the Holy Spirit that he was having.

Sister Edith said she was mortified and the thousands in the audience gasped in horror. Kuhlman grabbed the man's hand and turned to the audience and said:

"Beloved, it is not your business how this man expresses himself. Don't be blocked from seeing the human being because of what you think about the words he uses, those are just his words, what he is use to. Your judgements will stop you from rejoicing with this man in what is actually happening here. No colorful words can stop what God has planned for his life, but they can stop you from being useful if you allow it. Beloved, reach out your hand to this man just as he is. God wants us to come to him just as we are. That's the grace of Jesus. That's the message we're here to learn."

Sister Edith said that it changed her life and freed her up to be fearless with anyone. I'll never forget that Bible Study.

Sister Edith and her assistants worked in the Saturday healing services when the ministry moved to the Fox West Coast Theater. When the split happened between the Foursquare Church and Brant's ministry, she stayed out of ministry politics and just offered assistance. She figured the Lord would take care of settling the score between the dueling factions.

It was mostly her assistants – Joanne, Michelle, and Marti – who came to the Saturday services, and Sister Edith attended a couple times a month. Sometimes she worked in the service, while other times she was just part of the congregation. Her assistants often attended the outreach services as well.

It was always good to see Sister Edith. She gave a feeling of stability and support, especially after Pastor Adams and his wife were no longer connected with the ministry. Sister Edith was a true inspiration to many, including me. But like many aspects of Brant's ministry, Sister Edith's involvement wasn't meant to last.

Brant took a tour group to Israel, and Sister Edith went along. It seemed like an amazing dream – members of our congregation walking through the same streets and hilltops where Jesus did. Since I was on my own financially, I couldn't afford to go.

From the reports I got about the way the trip went, it's probably best I stayed home. It wasn't one incident or anything that anyone could name... but it was clear there was a divide between Brant and Sister Edith. Some told me it put a damper on the whole trip.

It was not too long after they returned home from the Israel tour that Brant cut back his schedule. His health was deteriorating rapidly and had something of a physical breakdown. He became more distant from those of us in the Long Beach group, including Sister Edith.

Jo Ellen and Bob took on more of the administrative duties at this time, and they made changes and cutbacks to the ministry. Sister Edith continued to remain supportive of the ministry while the changes where taking place. But it was clearer to her than to any of the rest of us that the ministry was collapsing in slow motion. At some point between the disappointing trip to Israel and Brant's physical breakdown, Sister Edith decided to leave.

At this point, Brant was already doing the Saturday services only once a month. He was slowly beginning to recover but still couldn't carry the full weight of the ministry. Sister Edith had filled in for Brant for a couple Saturday services. I wondered at the time what she may have been thinking about her role there. I thought she might be reminded of her role in Kathryn Kuhlman's services. Maybe there was something unpleasant in the past that would not be put to rest. I couldn't say but only pondered it.

Before Sister Edith left, I talked with her privately about my ideas – my vision for the ministry. I was strongly feeling led to step up and help Brant and Shekinah. I paid a visit to Sister Edith and outlined my plans to her, hoping for some support and guidance.

When I saw Sister Edith, she was aware of my former position with Brant and the different roles I had played in the ministry. She also had given me a number of prophetic words of encouragement during some of the Bible studies she led. I felt we had a connection.

I showed up early for one of her Bible studies at the Fox Theater. I asked her assistant Joanne if I could meet with her. Joanne told me she was in the boardroom upstairs, and she cheerfully led the way. When I got there, Sister Edith was delighted to see me. She was having some tea at the large conference table, a life size portrait of Kathryn Kuhlman hanging behind her.

I gave her a summary of what I felt led to do. I told her I was looking for any words of advice and a further confirmation. She paused and looked at me for a moment, surprised by what I'd said. She told me, "If you feel you must do this, then do what you must do with the Lord's blessing." She gave me a big hug. Moments later, I left the room.

Shekinah Christian Center

Sister Edith supported the ministry when the elders decided to form Shekinah Christian Center at the Fox Theater. The ministry booked guest Evangelist ministers for the weekly Saturday services while Brant was away. Shekinah Christian Center was a home base to provide Sunday and weekday services. The Center also served as an alternative for those who could not accompany the ministry when Brant traveled to the outreaches.

The elders needed to locate a minister to fill the role of a pastor for Shekinah Christian Center. A person named Jim M took the position. He worked as a TV production assistant and announcer with the TBN Ministry under Paul & Jan Crouch. He also had his own game show for kids and oversaw the Saturday morning Kids PTL (Praise The Lord) show.

Jim M already knew Brant by reputation and eventually conducted several interviews with him. Brant appeared on Jim M show a number of times, bringing soloists and the Shekinah Singers with him.

Elaine also knew Jim M, and our drama group was on the show several times. The show was live, and we'd honed our improvisation skills. Sometimes while the cameras were rolling, we made mistakes with our lines and would have to cover them impromptu.

Jim M was in his early thirties, a little overweight but energetic. His most prominent trait was that he really cared about people, and it showed. Jim M came from a Baptist background and at one time was a Baptist minister, though before working with TBN, he became a Charismatic Christian. When he worked for TBN, his doctrine complied with their bylaws associated with the Assembly of God denomination.

Jim M was married for a number of years but fell in love with someone else. Their love began in secret, and in the course of time, he divorced his wife and married his new love. Eventually he had to resign from the TBN ministry because their bylaws didn't recognize or support divorce. Because of that, Jim M had to leave TBN.

Brant and the elders offered Jim M the pastor position for Shekinah Christian Center. He was excited he was going to be of service to the Lord in this way, and we were excited to have a new pastor.

Jim M held church on Sunday mornings and on Wednesdays. One of his first initiatives involved starting a Sunday school. There were a number of young children who attended church, and they flocked to the new program. I decided I wanted to be a part of it.

Jim M thought about staging a children's drama production. He heard I had done some theater, and he asked me to collaborate with him on an original play. I was thrilled he asked me – his idea was a good one. I took his concept and tailored it to fit the group we had.

It was the first time I put a production together from beginning to end and coordinated all the cast and crew we needed. There were a lot of challenges I hadn't counted on, from script rewrites to costume choices. I needed a hand. One of the cast members, Kristy, wanted to assist me, and I welcomed her help. In time, we grew close, but first we had to endure some real-life drama.

It was during this time Jo Ellen and Bob became more deeply involved in the operations of the ministry. They mostly worked behind the scenes, overseeing the administrative decisions. I don't think Jim M was aware it was Jo Ellen who was making the major decisions and overseeing the course of the elders.

While Brant was gone, Jim M filled in during one of the Saturday services, along with other Evangelical ministers who came from outside our church. Jim M had mentioned to Brant he admired his puffy sleeve shirts he used to wear. Brant had Claudia give Jim M one of his puffy sleeved shirts. It was meant as a joke, but Jim M didn't take it that way. He put it on, and strangely, it looked right on him.

For the Saturday service, everyone knew their place and cue like a well-oiled machine. The service went on without Brant, just as before. The only difference was Brant was not center stage singing "Great is Thy Faithfulness." Jim M took the mic in stride and sang the hymn with the help of the choir leader.

It was strange to watch Jim M take center stage. It was like nothing changed. Only the main character, Brant, was missing, replaced with a stand-in. For Jim M, conducting the service was a great honor and an emotional high. His face was transcendent.

Jim M stepped into the role of leadership almost seamlessly. Besides leading the services, he kept us together and steered us on the path during times of transition. I appreciated his strong hand on the church's rudder. However, it didn't go over well with others.

Kelly and Lilly were a solid, genuine Christian couple. They had a strong relationship and marriage, and they were dedicated servants of the Lord. Therefore, it surprised me when I learned they decided to leave the ministry. Their story was they wanted to branch out on their own and form a Christian music ministry. In hindsight, I'm sure they must have seen the handwriting on the wall and did not agree with the direction Brant was taking the ministry. They figured it was time to leave.

I think they did not want to cause any waves or create a confrontation. For them, it was easier to bow out gracefully. Lilly had already produced a couple of albums on her own. She was attempting to break into the Christian music market by getting more bookings. Lilly was also pregnant again, and everyone was excited for her. It made sense for her to move on, and that meant it would have been awkward for Kelly to stay.

Unlike the other elders who seemed to just disappear, Kelly and Lilly made a public announcement they felt led in another direction. All of us in the congregation were sad. At least we knew where Kelly and Lilly were going. It didn't make their leaving any easier, though. We decided to give them a festive send-off.

The going away celebration was held at Shekinah Christian Center on a Wednesday during service. Jim M hosted the ceremony and gave a rousing speech. Everyone ate cake and gave the couple presents. Someone made a patchwork quilt for them from old choir dresses. Brant came to their going away celebration, though he was too weak to lead it. It was hard for him to watch them go. In fact, everyone felt keenly disappointed.

I was especially saddened by Kelly and Lilly leaving. I thought my heart would break. I thought about it and reviewed my relationship with Kelly over the past couple of years. The couple was a real role model for the rest of us. I think Kelly really tried his best to be a good elder and spiritual leader. More than any of these things, I'd desperately fallen in love with Kelly. It was not meant to be.

Kelly was a few years older than me. He was slender with an athletic built, over six feet tall. He had blond hair and a great singing and speaking voice. He was very articulate like Joe. and he took his time to express his thoughts, which made him come across as intelligent. His voice was not deep like Joe's but a little lighter and distinguished. Maybe he spoke that way because he was a spiritual leader and wanted to model the rest of his peer elders.

At the start, I really looked up to Kelly and loved him as a solid, safe Christian brother. I thought after my affair and falling out with Jeff, Kelly would be safe territory to develop a Christian male friendship with if I made the effort. It scared me that I had deep feelings towards him and was attracted to him but didn't really understand why I felt that way.

Kelly's kindness toward me made me melt inside. He was kind to everyone, and that was part of his charm. Because his natural grace was overpowering to me, I kept my guard up emotionally to protect myself and him. I respected his position too much to make my feelings known, especially after what I experienced with Jeff.

Jeff and Ann were gone, and Joe and Linda left mysteriously, leaving a void for me. I hoped Kelly would fill that void in a way that would be emotionally nontoxic. My thinking was I had to prove something to myself that I could have a male friendship without turning it into something sexual. The guilt I felt ate me up emotionally. I felt ashamed to even think these thoughts, but I had to prove it to myself.

I think he knew I was hurting inside after Brant dismissed me, and Kelly was extra kind to me. I was honored when he prayed for me and flattered when I was invited to be in the Shekinah Singers. I really wanted Kelly's approval and did not want to disappoint him or let him and Lilly down. I had so many bottled up emotions, wanting to have approval and be loved by one of my male peers. I needed to express it somehow. I needed to feel clean and wholesome inside.

My friendship with Kelly slowly developed as I made an extra effort to engage in small talk with him. Soon I started dropping in on Kelly and Lilly at home to hang out and asked if they needed anything. Sometimes we played cards or a board game. The visits were always pleasant, and I would go home feeling a glow inside.

In time I managed to build up the courage to tell Kelly how I felt about him, how I loved him as a Christian brother. He saw my earnestness and responded with equal sincerity. "It sounds like you just gave your heart to me. I don't know what to do with it." That was all I needed to know for the time being.

Now I made myself vulnerable to him and had to prove to both of us that I would be a good friend without being needy. In the privacy of my own mind, it sounded so heroic and hollow. I felt stupid.

A New Low

At times I was possessive of Kelly, the way I had been with Jeff. I felt rejected if I did not get the attention and response, I was looking for from him. Silently I would beat myself up. "Why do I feel this way? I shouldn't feel this way." But I did.

I was confused and even got angry I allowed myself to get worked up about these perceived slights, yet I continued to put myself through the same hell over and over again.

I was slowly beginning to realize this cycle was not healthy. It was harming me. Yet I could not stop myself from feeling this way. I felt alone inside and thought, "Does God really understand?" These feelings seemed inescapable. I couldn't understand why God would give me these emotions without giving me a way to express them.

I started to get angry. Something just snapped inside me. I felt trapped in a role I didn't ask for. The direction of the ministry and the trials of this relationship were causing me incredible stress. My heart was broken, and I didn't know how I could go on living. My inner conflict was a tremendous burden, and the events going on around me were pulling me in several directions. Something was about to break – I could feel it.

Things came to a head one night over a simple misunderstanding. Kelly came to my home to deliver a package. Kelly and Lilly had become home distributors for Shaklee products, and I'd placed an order with them for some vitamins. But when the order arrived, Kelly didn't have time for a visit. He was in a hurry – just dropped them off and left.

After he left, I realized nothing more was ever going to go on between us beyond just friendship. This was certainly not going to be like Jeff and me. In the beginning, I thought I would be fine with that. In fact, that's the way I'd wanted it at first. It was ridiculous to even think something more would happen between us.

I tried to prove to myself I wasn't attracted to men by developing a brotherly Christian friendship with Kelly. But that's not the way things really worked out. I was deeply in love. I thought I could bear it if he felt the same way I did. Nothing could be further from the truth.

When Kelly left that day, I was crushed and felt completely rejected. He would never love me – not the way I wanted him. He was straight, and he was married. He couldn't have been farther away from me if he were on the moon. I got so upset and angry, I smashed the bottle of vitamins on the kitchen floor. The little green Shaklee vitamin pills and shards of glass went everywhere, a blurry kaleidoscope through my angry tears.

I felt sick to my stomach. I thought I was going to throw up. I started to pick up the vitamins off the floor and swept up the glass, wiping the shards off the pills. I continued to cry. I felt like I had just split in two, with one part of myself rational and mechanical, picking up the pills and putting them into another container, watching my other self-howl with rage at life's incredible injustice. I wanted to kill myself. I simply wanted to die.

I finished cleaning up the mess, and my mother called. She knew something was wrong. I wanted to reach out to her and tell her what I was going through, but I didn't think she'd understand. How was I going to explain the complicated emotional mess I'd gotten myself into? This was a friendship with a man. How could I tell her about the searing pain I felt?

I told my mother I was feeling really low, like I'd just hit a new bottom. I even told her I was thinking about suicide. There was silence on the phone for a moment. She was calm and asked if she could come over. I said yes.

My mother lived about two hours away in Laguna Beach. She called my sister Meredith and told her what was going on. Meredith called me and talked to me while my mother was on the way. She said she loved me and did not want me to do anything to hurt myself – it was not worth it, whatever the problem. She said she was coming over with mom. The rest of the conversation was a blur.

I don't remember the next couple of hours, other than taking a walk-in night air. I rambled through the neighborhood, rehearsing what I was going to say. When my mom and Meredith got to my place, it was late at night. I didn't know where to begin to explain. It all seemed so shameful and embarrassing.

We talked very little since we were all exhausted by then. It was enough that they came. They both spent the night and left early the next morning. I thanked them from coming. We hugged, and they left.

The whole episode scared me. It felt sordid to begin with, and now I was ashamed that I'd caused my mother and Meredith so much grief. Still, I was grateful they came to support me when I'd felt so desperate.

In time I learned to accept the reality of the situation. I came to realize this was just a friendship with Kelly, and I was seeking approval from someone I deeply admired. I did my best to let it go and work through the web of feelings that remained within me.

When Kelly and Lilly left the ministry, we kept in touch. My apartment was not that far from theirs, which made it easy to say hello from time to time.

After they left, they appeared to be struggling financially. They were not getting many bookings, and with Lilly pregnant it got harder for her to land gigs. I didn't ask if Kelly was looking for any other type of work. I assumed it would have been difficult in her condition.

I committed myself to friendship with both of them and did what I could to support them. I wanted to prove I could be a good friend and do what a friend should do in helping and serving them. In time their friendship became a true blessing.

Greg Directs the Choir

About a year earlier, Kelly had located a single man, Greg, to replace him as a choir leader. They met when Greg started to attend the services of the Angeles Temple. As they got to know each other, it became clear to Kelly that Greg was the candidate he'd been looking for.

I don't know if Kelly realized that Greg was gay. If he did know, he must have thought Greg had quit the gay lifestyle when he became a Christian. I think Kelly just thought of Greg as a talented musician – that he was just the right person to replace Kelly as choir director.

Greg moved into the shared housing where several folks from the ministry lived, including Kevin, Bob, and Jo Ellen. Jo Ellen had been living off and on with Brant in Hollywood while Brant was recovering.

At the same time that Greg appeared, a married couple named Dennis and Geri B. also filled in the gap in the music ministry that Kelly and Lilly had left. Dennis was a talented organist who replaced Lilly, and his wife Geri was a soloist. She also joined the Shekinah Singers, the group I was part of.

During this period, Brigid came back with her husband Rick to get involved in the ministry again. Bob L. convinced her to lead the Shekinah singers' group. The new people infused fresh energy into the ministry, and for a time things were looking up. But it wasn't meant to last.

Even though Greg's mannerisms fit the stereotype of a gay man, few in the ministry figured out that Greg was actively gay. They were blinded by his dazzling talent – at least temporarily. They figured it out later when rumors spread about him.

Greg had been kind to me the whole time I knew him. The times we had short conversations; he would often act in a teasing way. It made me think he wanted something more from me. I shrugged it off with a smile on my face and thought little of it.

During a service at Angeles Temple, Greg told me I was the topic of gossip among the gay followers who came to the meetings. They felt sorry for me since they knew I used to be "Brant's number one boy" but he kicked me out.

I felt embarrassed. Greg implied I had a sexual relationship with Brant – and that everyone knew it. I smiled and laughed it off. I knew the truth – that's not what really happened. Still, it meant my reputation was tarnished.

While Greg was working on a couple of the musical presentations for the choir to perform, he asked me to decorate some of the back drops to display behind the choir. I came up with a couple of designs that he liked. I was given the money to buy the supplies and went to work.

I don't know what was going on with Kevin, Greg and Dennis B, but they were flirting with each other constantly. During the service, Greg and Dennis would often exchange sexual innuendos from backstage, and Kevin would pick up the cue and play along. Don't other people see what's going on? I wondered.

Greg flirted with me several times. I don't know if he was teasing me or testing me. I responded with a laugh to cover the fact he made me nervous inside. I did not know how to take it, just continued to laugh it off and tried to ignore it.

Soon after this, Kelly and Lilly left. A short while later, Greg was fired. I don't know who actually gave him notice, but I do know that he was let go because of his "flamboyant behavior." It could no longer be ignored.

It was Jim M. who made a public announcement to the congregation that Greg had been let go. He said Greg's behavior was inappropriate – not scriptural or appropriate for a minister in a leadership position. When Jim M announced that Brigid would take over the position as choir leader, the transition was complete.

The Firings Continue

Not long after Greg was fired, Dennis the organ player stopped showing up. Rumor had it that Dennis now fully embraced the gay lifestyle. His wife Geri continued to be involved in the church, and she even dated someone from the ministry. I felt bad for Geri since she had a daughter, and now she was a single parent. Others in the ministry showed sympathy toward her too. Bit by bit, Shekinah was evolving into a completely different organization than the one I'd first joined.

I'd always been reserved about discussing my own romantic preferences. Still, I couldn't help wondering where I stood with the ministry now. Were they judging me as harshly? Did they think I was flamboyant or inappropriate? Would I be let go too?

Even though Jim M worked with enthusiasm to get the center off the ground, he was fired within a few months. I didn't understand why. I thought his efforts were starting to sow good results. Jo Ellen disagreed. She's the one who had him fired.

It appeared to Jo Ellen and Brant that Jim M was trying to turn the Shekinah Center into a Baptist Church – especially after Jim M ordered a baptism tank and put it in the front of the theater. Baptist hymnals were now used for the Sunday service too.

Several people in the congregation were shocked that Jim M was fired, but no one was more surprised than Jim M. Kristy told me what happened. She was there when he was let go. Kristy had walked in on Jim M when he was packing up his office, crying.

I talked to Jim M on the phone later, and he briefly told me what happened. He said he had upset Jo Ellen with his choices, and she did not like the changes. I wondered why she did not speak to him or have Robbie talk to him. They could have made some adjustments and kept some continuity for the ministry. But change seemed to be the only constant.

It was autumn now, and it looked like the Christmas production was off. Then Jim M told me he wanted me to go ahead with the production, despite his leaving. He reasoned that everything else would continue until they found a replacement for him.

I was sad for Jim M and confused, but I was also excited about the challenge to continue with the production. I thought Jim M was a good organizer. He'd laid a good foundation because he had people willing to continue on with the work and help the center grow. Among other events, he'd arranged for the Sunday School staff to attend a special training seminar.

This was an exciting event that offered the chance to meet various vendors who were promoting their Sunday School Material. Since Kristy and I were a team, we attended the various workshops and looked over the different exhibits together. The event gave us a common bond. Besides boosting our skills, it brought Kristy and me closer together. In time, we would discover a bond that surpassed any other.

The same week Jim M got fired, Robbie W. replaced him with another minister, Mike. Ironically, Robbie himself was fired shortly after hiring Mike. Robbie turned out to be yet another elder who just disappeared. Nothing was said by anyone in the administration to acknowledge his departure.

Mike was a man in his early thirties. His wife Judy was a nurse, and they had two young children, a boy and girl. Both Mike and Judy were very caring people.

Mike was an imposing figure, well over six feet tall, but he was a gentle person with a laid-back personality. He was quiet, a contrast compared to Jim M excitable nervous energy. I worked more closely with Mike than I had Jim M. I even babysat their kids one time when he and Judy went to a private event. I started to feel a real fellowship with him.

Mike was already a supporter of the ministry when Robbie hired him. He was a Brethren minister before, and he had been coming to the Shekinah services at the Foursquare Church. Unfortunately, Mike had to leave the Brethren Church since he had an addiction to pornography. It seemed like a dark time for him. Later Mikeecame involved with the charismatic movement and got the help he needed to overcome his addiction.

A short time later, Mikeecame an independent minister. He started his own congregation, conducting seminars and producing a radio show on overcoming sexual addictions. The show went well, and it launched his career in a new direction.

He was excited when he got the offer to work with the Shekinah Ministry. He must have been just as excited as Jim M was at the start, in the days before Jim M started to see what was really going on behind the scenes with the Baker family.

Like Jim M, I think Mike was clueless about what was really taking place behind the scenes. He saw the position as an opportunity to be part of this great ministry and to help his Christian brother Brant during a difficult time. Mike made progress working with the ministry staff, and he bypassed Jo Ellen. He continued the Sunday services and Sunday school program, and he started a series of relationship and marriage counseling workshops. He was fully committed to the ministry.

My New Leadership Role

Mike gave me free rein to continue with the Christmas production. Jim M had given me the chance to expand my horizons and grow with a new project. Mike gave me the chance to carry on with the project and prove myself. It was an opportunity to grow, taking on more responsibility with the drama production and Sunday School.

I was energized by this challenge, and I got deeply involved. My first job was to rewrite the play to incorporate the Sunday School. Then, as director, I auditioned the rest of the cast, and I organized a crew. I even took on a role myself as part of the cast. Kristy was my production assistant, and I cast her in the role of the angel who tells Mary she will have a child. There were costumes to be made, a set to be built, and rehearsals to schedule. It was exciting to see it all come together.

The Sunday School department helped tell the Christmas story, centered around a classroom environment. During the play, the classroom made several different scene changes to tell the story.

When it came to the night of the performance, all the right people were there to see it. The theater was not packed, but it was over half full. Brant came along with the rest of the Baker family. Claudia and Eric were there, along with Sister Edith and her entourage, and the rest of my peers in the singing group.

I hoped Elaine would come, making the trip from Hollywood. Her inspiration and example gave me the faith and encouragement to be a drama director. Although Brant had seen me perform before in the other drama productions I did with Elaine, this was different. I was the one in charge. I wanted approval from Brant and the others, and I was ready for my next level of growth. By showing up, I felt they would see I was capable to do more then what I have done before.

The night of the performance, I peeked at the audience from the wing's backstage. I could see them all there in the audience, just beyond the stage lights. It was the culmination of months of hard work for something we were all passionate about, and I was excited and proud.

I was no longer part of the Shekinah Singers group at this point, though I missed their camaraderie and singing with them. I incorporated the group into the production, singing several pieces along with performing some of the action in the drama. It turned out to be a nice touch that added richness to the show.

As high as my hopes were, unfortunately we didn't get all the technical bugs worked out. There were some lighting changes and backdrop cues that came in late. Someone forgot to place the doll we used as the baby Jesus in the manager. The cradle was empty! Just as the curtain came up, one of the stage crew tossed the doll to Mary and Joseph. The doll came flying across the stage. Mary caught the doll like a football and immediately bundled up the baby Jesus like nothing had happened.

In between scenes, I had a couple of quick costume changes backstage that Kristy helped me with. Kevin showed up backstage and decided he was going to help me with a quick change. I don't know why he did that, but it turned out to be a good thing. I needed his help. The timing for the costume change was tight.

I told Kevin, "I used to help your brother change, and now you're helping me." We both laughed as he helped me slip on my belt while Kristy straightened my tie. The performance ended with Mike giving a salvation message and inviting the audience to attend church. I was backstage where many of us were listening to the message and praying. When it was over, Kevin came up to me and gave me a compliment.

He said Brant was pleased and impressed with what I had done. It was the encouragement I had been waiting for. It felt important to hear that. Kristy gave me a card and a small present from the rest of the cast and crew. The night was a big moment for me.

It appeared the Shekinah Center was growing and coming together in the period following the Christmas production. Brant continued to conduct the services once a month, and guest speakers appeared in between. The ministry had stopped the television broadcasts because of funding. Even so, the Center continued its forward motion.

Mike seemed to be getting settled in his position. Since Judy was working full time, he hired Kristy to be a nanny for his kids, and he moved his family closer to Long Beach. But right in the middle of his move, Mike was fired.

Jo Ellen had seen Mike as some kind of threat to her authority. She conjured up a scandal and accused him of taking funds from the ministry. He went home upset. Judy got home a short while later, and Kristy was still there watching their kids.

Mike told Kristy and Judy what happened. He started to cry, then Judy did too. When I got home from work that day, Kristy called me to tell me what happened. I did not understand the reason he was fired. It was upsetting and confusing for those of us who had seen this before. Jo Ellen had pulled this same stunt twice within the year.

Publicly, the church elders told us the ministry was losing money because Brant was not there to conduct weekly services. They said Shekinah Christian Center was not bringing in enough funds to support Mike. It was demoralizing to go through this upheaval one more time. At least Mike lasted longer than Jim M had. In the wake of his departure, the congregation was dispirited, united only by our confusion and grief.

CHAPTER 15:

SHUFFLING THE BOARD

In the course of time, Eric and Claudia became the ambassadors for Brant's directives. They put out fires as they ignited. They acted in Brant's place to discipline elders and volunteers. Eric supervised the men, and Claudia worked with the women. Eric was put in the awkward position of firing any remaining elders who had not already left on their own. Some of the elders simply left before Eric had a chance to fire them, and nothing was said about it to the congregation.

I wondered about the reasons they left and whatever became of them. To many, it was as if they'd never existed. All of us felt too awkward to talk about their departures – there were so many of them. Shekinah Christian Center was supposed to be a community of joy and worship. It had rapidly devolved into a soap opera.

To replace the elders who left, Jo Ellen formed her own Board of Directors. They were made up of professional older men and women who attended the ministry and had money. They cared about both the ministry and Brant, but I wondered how much Jo Ellen felt for the flock.

Jo Ellen systematically fired each minister from Shekinah Christian Center and blamed it on financial problems. I think she was paranoid, thinking those ministers were in conflict with Brant's vision and her need to be in control.

To further cut costs, Bob told Eric to fire Steve. In Jo Ellen's way, she was doing her best to keep the ministry afloat, but her manipulative tactics were unsavory. All these changes started to cause concern among the core group and deacons. The core group that was left still seemed to be in the dark, baffled by the turn of events.

Rick P. was the minister who followed after Mike's ouster. Rick was a young Italian newlywed. Before he agreed to become part of Shekinah Christian Center, he was just as clueless as the others before him. He didn't know what was really taking place behind the scenes of the ministry.

Rick had just graduated with a Bible degree from Melodyland Christian Center in Anaheim. His stepsister, Michelle, was part of the entourage who worked with Sister Edith. Her mother – Rick's stepmother – was named JoAnne.

The Bakers Take Over

All the changes made for a dizzying tide of events – ministers being replaced, elders leaving, and the Bakers taking over the administrative roles. The maelstrom caused mixed emotions among many of the core people who remained. Nothing was being done to stem the purge.

Many of the elders and volunteers were talking privately among themselves about what was going on, whispering to each other backstage or in private quarters. I was invited to join a secret prayer and discussion meeting at Jack & Terri's place. The group included Steve & Georgette A., Danny & Debbie R., Rick P. with his new wife, Jim and Carol R. and a few others. Ironically it was held at my former apartment. Revisiting my old place reinforced for me just how many changes I personally had gone through in the course of my service to the Lord and to the Bakers.

Steve and Rick led the meeting. Everyone got a chance to air out their feelings. Brant was gone, all the original elders were gone, and the Center itself seemed to be adrift without a rudder. We were all so young and wondered just what was happening in our church. Our leader and shepherd Brant was mostly absent, and those left in charge were making counterproductive decisions. It was the first time a core group of us gathered, questioning the leadership of the Bakers and what had taken place so far.

The consensus was that we did not like what the Bakers were doing. Rumors were circulating that Jo Ellen wanted Kevin to fill in for Brant while he was recovering, which did not go well with the group. We agreed that a temporary shepherd was needed since two pastors were already fired from Jo Ellen. We went around the room and each of us shared what we felt the Lord put on our hearts. Many just said they wanted to continue to minister and felt lost and displaced without Brant there. We agreed that the Holy Spirit was still moving through us and our ministry, despite the shakeup.

During this period of change, I already felt God was talking to me, inspiring me to help Brant with his recovery. I believe my heart was in the right place, but the approach I was thinking about was radical. Maybe it was a trap to ensnare me and inflate my ego.

What made me want to come in and rescue Brant, either as a friend or as part of the ministry? Whatever it was, I felt I had to follow through with it. It could not have been any worse than seeing Kevin's attempts to get the attention he craved. He was motivated by his inflated ego to follow in his brother's footsteps and take over the services. My motives were far less self-serving.

I thought the Lord wanted me to help Brant recover by putting him on a special program of diet, exercise and some kind of creative recreation. Maybe even a part-time job would do him good if it had little pressure.

It made sense to me for the elders to choose a temporary leader to conduct the services and oversee some administrative tasks while Brant recuperated. The elders had already accepted two other ministers from the outside – and then they fired them. Why not promote from within? A small voice began whispering to me. Perhaps I could serve as that mediator between Brant and the ministry.

It made sense. I was with the ministry from its early stages, and I'd worked with Brant hand in glove. I had been Brant's personal servant, following in his shadow day and night. The years I spent working and observing Brant trained me well. Who better to relay his message and spread his vision?

I decided to offer to conduct the healing services myself. The thought made me quake a little inside. Would the ministering body accept me as a leader, even if only temporarily? Wouldn't I stand a better chance of succeeding than the others had?

I thought this could be my purpose and calling – this time in the ministry. Was this some kind of test of obedience to see if I was willing to go through this?

Over the next several weeks, I wrote several pages I felt were inspired by the Holy Spirit. I poured out my ideas about how to get each department in the ministry back on track. But then I hung back, afraid to overstep my place in the ministry. The vision was too grandiose, too radical, for me to step in to do this.

I thought of Joseph in the Old Testament. He came on the scene to rescue Egypt from famine, and he ended up second in command. I thought God would use one of the younger people within the group of the ministry. It only made sense.

I know many were looking to Steve A. because he was a tall, humble guy. He was charismatic, and he appeared to have wisdom. Then the secret meeting was called, and we all were pressed for our input.

We went around the room and shared our heart. No one offered any solutions other than just that we needed to pray. My heart was beating fast as I wondered if I was supposed to say something now. At last I opened my mouth and started to explain my thoughts about what I felt the Lord was leading me to do.

Once I finished sharing, the room fell quiet as a tomb. Many at the table were stunned by what I said. They smiled politely, wondering if I was some kind of self-proclaimed prophet. My message hadn't gone over well.

Rick P. spoke first. He was new in the group, and his words were humble. "I do not have the history of being in this ministry like many of you here." That was all he said. Though he served to break the silence, he offered nothing of substance. He certainly wasn't supportive. I felt stupid and utterly humiliated.

Then Danny R. spoke up with the deepest cut of all. "Some of it makes sense. I want a shepherd, but I don't want to follow Jud."

That stung me. I don't blame him for saying it. I told the group what I thought because we had all agreed to share what was in our hearts and minds. I trusted in their support. I didn't get it – not for my ideas, not for my offer of interim leadership.

Nothing further was said in that meeting about the ideas I'd offered, and the subject never came up again once the meeting was over. Still, I pondered them in my heart for some time.

We concluded our meeting by deciding to address our concerns before Jo Ellen and the

Board. The next Board meeting was to take place the following night. We agreed that Steve and Rick would be the two spokespersons for the group, and they'd address our concerns before the Board.

At the time, Robbie W. and Dottie were the most recent elders to leave. Jack. got in touch with Robbie to ask his advice about the ministry's direction. Robbie warned him that Jo Ellen would try to manipulate the people in the meeting and attempt to wrest control from them. This notion came as no surprise to any of us.

The Board Meeting

The following night, everyone who was in the secret youth meeting gathered downstairs in the theater. Once we were all assembled, we went upstairs into the Board room unannounced.

When we entered, I immediately noticed that Jo Ellen had a look of surprise on her face. I also saw that Eric, Claudia and Kevin Baker were there. We were welcomed by the others on the Board. It was clear they were all surprised we showed up, and they seemed concerned. They wanted to give us the floor to speak.

All the members Jo Ellen placed on the Board were willing to hear what we, the youth in the ministry, had to say. They agreed the ministry must come from the youth.

Steve A was the spokesperson for us. He shared in a humble tone what was in our minds and hearts. There was no finger pointing, only our perspective about what was missing since Brant was gone. He used spiritual jargon, hinting at who was more or less responsible. Jo Ellen picked up on it and stirred her tea nervously. Kevin was silent.

Once Steve A was finished, Rick spoke up. All the Board members listened to him with concerned ears and empathy. One Board member agreed the people who should be running the Board are the youth. Jo Ellen spoke up and suggested the blame was on Robbie, the last elder to leave. She also blamed the last two ministers who led Shekinah Christian Center. Rick chimed in, speaking humbly but offering only spiritual fluff.

The Board asked us what we thought needed to be done. Jo Ellen said, "You need a shepherd while Brant is gone." That seemed to be the answer people were looking for. Steve

A and Rick agreed. The rest of the Board signaled approval, nodding their heads and making small comments. Jo Ellen concluded since Rick had just graduated from Bible College, it made sense he should be appointed.

Rick was stunned and remained silent. He was not expecting that answer. He told me later it made more sense it would be someone who had been a part of it for awhile. He was new to the ministry.

Jo Ellen continued to play her cards, trying to make people feel good. "We need to come together and all of us share since we are family. It is the youth that made me come to Shekinah and get involved. I love you all. Let's go around the room and each of us share what is on our heart and what the Lord is speaking to you."

What Jo Ellen was really doing was sending out her radar to determine whom she could trust and whom to screen out. One by one, each person in the room shared. They all gave safe answers, trying to come up with a solution. Some, like Eric, gave long winded while others offered short contributions. It was something like a cozy campfire meeting, exchanging fuzzy feelings. They all agreed Shekinah played an important part in their lives and wanted to continue ministering for the Lord since that was the only world they knew. Then it was getting late and the group started to become restless.

I was getting nervous about whether to share what I felt God was leading me to do. It was contrary to what others were saying. I already knew from the meeting the other night it might not be accepted. Yet I felt I still needed to say what was in my heart and mind. I decided I had to go ahead.

My heart was beating rapidly as I prepared to speak. For a moment time slowed down. I felt in my mind I was sending out waves of energy to the group, as though I was pronouncing a prophetic event that was going to take place. I found my courage and cleared my throat.

And then the worst possible thing happened – Jo Ellen began to close the meeting. My heart sank.

It was as if something unholy had intervened. I felt we were being deceived. Suddenly I envisioned an earthquake in the room. In my mind's eye, I saw the walls and floor shake. There was a deep rumbling sound, and the chandelier over the Board table come crashing down. The building was coming apart around us. I saw the Brant Baker Ministry and the Baker family would come to an end, and the people in the congregation would be scattered.

Then the vision parted, and the meeting was over. I was left confused. Was this vision caused by my feelings? Was it the result of repressed anger and disappointment? I still had one more chance.

Jo Ellen Confides In Me

I followed Jo Ellen to her car and asked to speak to her. Her response was terse. "Make it quick. I need to go."

We sat in her car, and immediately Jo Ellen started to cry. I was stunned to see this powerful woman reduced to tears. It was not like her. I had never seen her vulnerable before, not to anyone. Then she opened up, defensive.

She said she was doing her best to keep the ministry afloat, but it was difficult. Brant was sick. He was no longer a guest on TBN, and the ministry television shows had been discontinued. Attendance at the Center was falling off, and money was getting tight. She blamed Robbie for ruining the TV ministry. She blamed the two other ministers who were fired for the falling attendance, among other things.

I did not learn the real reason Robbie and Steve left until years later. All I knew was the ministry was suffering financially because Brant was suffering physically. He simply had to recover, or the Center would fail. And here was his smothering mother crying to me in the front seat of her car.

"I paid them good money and they ruined it," she sobbed.

I felt sorry for her and put my hand on hers. Her tears gave me courage to boldly speak my mind. "I did not get a chance to share what was in my heart during the meeting. I feel the Lord has shown me a way to bring back the ministry and help Brant."

She was stunned for a moment. I could scarcely believe what I was saying myself. She stammered, "What is it?" Then she was breaking down and shaking. "I have to go," she said.

I stumbled over my words, confused. "We need to get together."

Jo Ellen acted like she did not hear me, and she started the car. "I love all of you and just don't know what to do."

I reassured her, told her it would all work out. Then I blurted what I'd been holding back. "I wrote down a plan." She just looked at me for a moment. I realized I spoke too soon. Suddenly I felt uneasy. I knew I could not trust her with what I had to share.

There was a brief silence, then she changed her tone and expression. She became very cold and businesslike. "I need to go," she said. Then I got out of the car.

It was years later when I learned what was really going on. While Brant was both attending and ministering at the North Hollywood Assembly of God, he befriended the head pastor, Pastor Sanders. The ministry had already done a number of healing services at the church, and Brant would attend their weekly prayer service on his own while he lived in Hollywood.

Brant asked Sanders in confidence for counseling because he was struggling with homosexuality. What Sanders did at this point appeared to be selfishly motivated. He was not acting as a minister who cared about a wounded member of his flock asking for help. It appeared he made a political move to make himself look good at his church. The result was a profound betrayal.

Once Sanders heard Brant's plea for help, Sanders held an emergency board meeting informing them they would no longer have Brant ministering at his church. He also contacted Paul and Jan at TBN and told them about Brant engaging in homosexuality. Paul immediately cut off any ties with Brant and the television tapings to be aired. At the time, I was not aware that Paul perhaps did not want anything pointed back to him that had to do with homosexuality to jeopardize TBN ministry. A number of years later it was found out he was secretly dealing with his own same sex attractions.

Had Sanders seen Brant as a young man asking for a pastor's help in private, Brant might have gone in a different direction in life. He could have had some type of self-discovery and made vastly different choices than he did – full commitment to celibacy, heterosexuality, or even choosing to fully and opening embrace the gay lifestyle. The duality he was living might have ended.

He might have come out of the closet about being gay, quit the ministry altogether, bailed out and started new. Or he could have gotten the counseling he was seeking at the time and overcome his behavior. If so, he would have been accepted among Christian evangelicals and continued on with his healing ministry. This would have had a huge effect on his congregation and his television audiences.

Instead, Sanders betrayed Brant and took a wrecking ball to his career and his calling. Jo Ellen felt she had to cover up for her son, shifting the blame onto the elders of the ministry. Brant tried to carry on, balancing two worlds. Those who accepted his homosexuality formed a close-knit group that he trusted and got support from – in secret.

Brant continued the healing services as a minister because he wanted to. I think he felt it gave his life a Christian purpose. He did not want to disappoint himself or his dwindling followers who believed in the Jesus he preached about.

All of this was going on when I was with Jo Ellen in the car after the board meeting. Had I known the reality of the situation; I don't know whether I would have understood where Brant was coming from. I was still quite young. I doubt I would have continued to my attempt to help Brant and the ministry. I might have seriously considered a different path myself. At this point I was still feeling shame about my own sexual identity. I was trying to live a victorious Christian heterosexual lifestyle and overcome my own homosexuality.

As time went on, I kept Elaine in the loop about what was going on in the ministry since she could not make the earlier youth meeting. She knew Jo Ellen could not be trusted. Jo Ellen was consistent - she was paranoid that others were trying to take over the ministry. If you tried to talk to her about the problems of the ministry, she was sure to lash out, act out, and eventually find her revenge.

Jo Ellen must have realized she was close to a mutiny among the group of us who came into the Board meeting. If we were more organized, we might have taken over the ministry from the Bakers. It is hard to know what type of split would have happened if Brant had found out about our solidarity. In light of his situation, Jo Ellen's behavior toward me in the car is understandable, though I have never condoned the actions she took afterward.

Sister Edith Takes Her Leave

A week later, Rick became the third ordained minister of Shekinah Christian Center. He was not aware of the incidents that had taken place with the two previous ministers. He was also unaware of the traps Jo Ellen and Kevin consistently laid. Rick was sucked up like a fish fresh out of water. It was his first assignment right out of Bible school, and he fit in. He had an innocent Shepherd's heart, and he took the time to listen to the followers of the ministry.

I befriended Rick and his wife right away. I would talk to Rick in between the services, and he would listen. He knew who I was and that I'd held several positions in the ministry over the course of several years. I filled him in about what had taken place over the last couple years, especially the last year with the other ministers. He said he felt the Lord wanted him here for now, but he felt suspicious of Jo Ellen and Kevin. He knew they were watching him closely. He felt something was going on, and he started to see what was taking place. Rick agreed to stay on only for a few months.

Sister Edith was still involved with the ministry. That was the time period I decided to approach Sister Edith privately about what I wanted to do to help Brant and the ministry. We had a talk in the Board room, and I outlined my ministry inspirations to her. Though her words were encouraging, it was hard for me to read her true response. She was politely neutral.

Her answer came a few weeks later: Sister Edith had decided to leave. She made the announcement during her midweek service as she was training a group to work in the healing services. My friend Kristy was at this meeting and heard her announcement. I was not there that evening, as if a guardian angel lent a hand to spare me from the drama. Everyone there that night was caught completely off guard. The reaction to her calmly professional announcement was horrifying.

Sister Edith addressed the group calmly but firmly. She said the Lord had told her that her work here was done, and it was time for her to leave. She encouraged us to continue to do what the Lord was having us do. She also told the group she tried to give the news to Brant personally several times, but regretfully she was unable to contact him.

Jo Ellen looked on from the side of the stage. She knew about Sister Edith's plans to leave since Sister Edith had tried to reach Brant several times to give notice. Jo Ellen had taken the messages from her. For some reason, it seems the messages never got to Brant.

Brant was there in the hall that evening, signing some letters in his office upstairs and listening to Sister Edith on the intercom. When he heard her announcement, Brant came unglued.

He burst out of his office with Eric following close behind him. He raced down the hallway, downstairs through the narrow passageway to the second level of the balcony, down the stairs to the first floor, down the front aisle and up to the foot of the stage. He bolted past his mother, up the steps, and confronted Sister Edith, shouting, "How can you leave? How can you leave?!"

Anyone who had come to the church that night for solace was surely shocked and disappointed. The Shepherd was in a panic, attacking his trusted servant.

Sister Edith remained calm and looked blankly at Brant. "Now, dear, you are a hard man to reach. I tried to contact you several times."

"No you didn't!" Brant accused.

Again, Sister Edith faced Brant, unblinking. "It's time for me to leave."

"We treated you like a queen!" Brant's face was beet red.

Sister Edith met his gaze squarely as the congregation looked on in amazement. You could hear a pin drop. Sister Edith told Brant she'd never expected to be treated as a queen – that she was only a servant. The contrast between them was telling, and clearly Brant could see he was helpless and outclassed.

Brant stormed off the stage past his mother, and Eric followed. Sister Edith gave a short blessing to those at the service. Her two assistants swept her up, helping her off the stage and out the door.

Jo Ellen stepped in, gave a short prayer and dismissed the group. Everyone was in shock from what had just taken place. No one milled around afterward. They all went home.

The following Saturday service, Joanne and Michelle showed up and worked in the healing service as before. Marti and Sister Edith didn't attend.

The following Wednesday, Jo Ellen gave a brief talk on the stage before the service. I was there, and I remember Jo Ellen making disparaging remarks to the group about Sister Edith. Jo Ellen told the congregation that Sister Edith was no one until she came to Shekinah – just a woman who held small Bible study meetings in the back of a coffee shop. I'll never forget the looks on people's faces that day. Many were in shock that Jo Ellen would say something so harsh and petty, so patently untrue about Sister Edith.

After the meeting was over, Jo Ellen did a bit more housekeeping, weeding out personnel. She combed through the staff who helped with that meeting as well as volunteers for the Word of Knowledge group. In time, Jo Ellen dominated the decision making in the ministry.

My friend Kristy was one of the volunteers Jo Ellen weeded out. Sister Edith had picked her to work with the Word of Knowledge in the healing services. At the time, Kristy didn't understand why Jo Ellen let her go. She didn't see it was political, and she felt confused and hurt by what appeared to be an arbitrary dismissal. Kristy remained in the choir despite being upset about the slight.

Two of Sister Edith's assistants, Joanne and Michelle, continued to come to the services, and I found out later that they'd had some kind of disagreement with Sister Edith. They ended up leaving Sister Edith and got more involved in the Shekinah ministry. But Jo Ellen became suspicious of them too and kept a cautious eye on Sister Edith's former assistants.

I couldn't believe the harsh turn of events I was witnessing. Sister Edith was wise and mature. She made a solid contribution to the ministry, offering some stability in direction and spiritual support. She simply knew it was time for her to move on, so she left. To be publicly harassed and disparaged on her way out the door was shameful. It was sad to see her maligned by the very people she gave so much support. Sister Edith continued to minister in small groups for some time, and she seemed to get along just fine without Jo Ellen and Shekinah.

Joanne and her daughter Michelle remained after Sister Edith left. They worked with Jo Ellen to keep the center running, though there was clearly a sense that the organization's energy was declining. Joanne and Michelle shared the task of giving messages on Wednesdays to dwindling membership. The Sunday school stopped offering services altogether.

I felt sad and a bit nostalgic to see this house of God fall to such a state of decay. I remembered the hope and energy that had once united us all in spirit – the sense of expectation for the coming rapture, and the kinship we'd all felt around the healing services.

It was clear that Love was a faded memory in this place. I still had hope of resurrecting it. I decided to make one last play to bring Shekinah back to its former glory. I knew it was a risk. Looking back, it's hard to know if my naivete worked against me or proved to be a blessing in disguise. What happened next was not what I expected.

As Far As I Could Go

Everyone in the ministry was reeling from Sister Edith's departure. There was a general feeling of depression among the congregation, even despair. Attendance numbers were dwindled rapidly along with the ministry's finances.

I couldn't help feeling that, having served Brant directly, I had a unique ability to help make the situation better. There must be something I could do. After a great deal of thought, I came up with a strategy to put my plan into action and help save the ministry from terminal disaster.

Up to this point, no one had been receptive to the plan I'd felt divinely inspired to create. Despite my best efforts, no one else was getting excited about it. Sister Edith had been neutral at best, and then she left. Jo Ellen had flatly refused to listen to me. How could I help Brant get well, corral the energies of the remaining elders, and move the ministry back into a positive direction?

I decided to gather up my courage and bypass Jo Ellen. I'd approach Brant directly when I had the chance, and I'd share my ideas with him. I pondered what Brant kept saying over the pulpit. "Anyone can do what I do." I took him at his word, and I believed I could do this.

In my mind, I reviewed my history with Brant like a movie montage. I felt like a prophet in training – like Elisha was to Elijah. Was this the time and the hour to step up? Should I take the risk and help the ministry through this difficulty while Shekinah's true Shepherd was recovering? I thought surely, I would have Brant's support. We would carry on despite the challenges, like Joseph when he was second in command of Egypt during a time of crises.

The challenge seemed insurmountable. To approach Brant, I had to wait for just the right moment. I did not even know where he lived at the time. That was a secret for only his family, Eric, Claudia and a few others. He was well protected, but I knew I could have access to him if I wanted to. The people who protected him also knew I was not a threat. I would have to approach him during a service or whenever he showed up. My heart fluttered to think about overcoming these obstacles, but I felt strongly I had been called by the Lord to do this.

The opportunity came when Brant showed up at the Center midweek for a birthday party the ministry put on for him. It was held on the second-floor lobby area. I think Jo Ellen talked him into coming. She knew it was important for him to show up whenever he could during this time. So much still depended on him and his personal charisma.

Before Brant arrived, Jo Ellen warned everyone to give him some room when he arrived. We were not supposed to touch him. He was still not feeling well, and he was quite thin. It was strange to stay seated in our folding chairs and behave like obedient children – so different from the days of hugs and Brant's supportive arms around us all.

Brant soon arrived with a couple men I did not recognize. He was so thin then and looked incredibly pale, even though his makeup tried to cover it.

After a short speech and a few presents, the cake was served. Jo Ellen and Kevin left the area. Brant was just standing there alone. Nobody talked to him. For a moment, I felt deeply sad for him, a shadow of his former self. Then I realized this was my chance to approach him.

I took him by the hand and led him to a private corner of the room to talk. He was stunned that I approached him, but he was willing to go with me. I knew my time was likely going to be brief, so I just came out and told him what was on my mind. I told him I felt the Lord had showed me how to help the ministry.

His curiosity was aroused, but still he seemed skeptical. "What is it?"

I said we would have to get together to talk at length since he was leaving, and I did not have my plans with me. I felt nervous to share this with him, and he had a blank puzzled stare.

What am I doing? I thought. But I'd started the wheels in motion, and there was no going back. He agreed to meet with me, and he would get a hold of me through Eric or Claudia within the week. He must have wondered about my plan after I left him – his former servant, one who knew him so intimately, inspired by the Lord to deliver a message and save the church he'd started.

My intentions were pure, but in reality, I was in way over my head. Besides Brant's own misgivings, Jo Ellen and the rest of the Baker family would never let it happen. My message was doomed to be delivered stillborn.

I did not hear from Brant the following week. His promise to contact me was clearly a deflection in an uncomfortable moment. Still I felt I needed to follow through and talk to him. He was starting to show up more often at the Center, maybe once or twice a week. I was sure I could find an opportunity.

Brant came to do a Saturday service, and he appeared as frail as an old man. Eric and his bodyguards ushered him into his dressing room to get prepared. An older man named Forrest also joined them.

Forrest was a nice guy, shorter than me, in his late forties. He was a former body builder who owned a gym with his wife Barbra, and he had a mail order business selling martial arts equipment. He would come into Brant's room and give him a massage before and after the services to help him relax.

When Brant first arrived that Saturday, he was followed by his entourage to the dressing-room. Then he went back upstairs to give his usual pep talk to the choir and other ministers. His handlers then ushered him back downstairs through the stage door into his dressing room again.

I followed the group that surrounded him. I talked to his bodyguard, Rocky, who was blocking the dressing room door. Rocky was a member of the Shekinah Singers, and I knew him. We exchanged smiles, and I told Rocky I wanted to talk to Brant. He said he would check and be right back. A moment later, I was then ushered into the room. Brant was on the floor, getting a massage from Forrest.

Jo Ellen left the room as soon as I arrived. Kevin, Eric, and Claudia stayed – a constant presence now. I knew I had to be careful with my words. I was friendly and made small talk, and then I asked why he did not get in touch with me. He said he thought it over and brushed me off.

"Whatever message you felt you have for me; I would have gotten it." I told him I thought he needed someone who would help him get his health back. He needed someone to assist him with getting exercise, food, and recreation while he recovered.

He was glib, almost flippant. "I was already thinking about that myself."

I did not respond for a moment. Kevin looked in our direction, eavesdropping on our conversation. Brant added that Kevin was helping him. I continued to press the point, adding that there were some other things we needed to discuss.

Brant paused a moment. "I will get in touch with you," he said.

I saw an opening and reminded him that I had been a student in this ministry. I felt a season had come for me to help him again, like a flower that re-blooms.

I went on with a parable, hoping to give him a clue that he was being misled by his family. I spoke of a king that was trapped in a tower by his family and they only let him out once in awhile to give a speech to the people. The king needed to break away from them for a season, free himself and get control of his kingdom again.

Brant paused, clearly interested. "Do I have your number?"

Kevin spoke up. "I have it." He met my eyes briefly, a challenge for control.

I left the room, knowing I was in dangerous territory. Still, I believed that I was protected. Brant seemed to connect with the meaning in my story, though he needed clarity. Kevin felt threatened, suspicious that I was moving in on his territory.

I went upstairs in the front of the theater and headed to the upper mezzanine. On the way, I saw Jo Ellen coming out of the office door and headed downstairs. She was the last person I wanted to talk to at that moment. I turned around to avoid her.

Jo Ellen called out to me. I ignored her, and she called out again. I swallowed hard and turned around to face her. It took a lot of nerve for me to confront her.

"What did you tell Brant?!" She had a stern look on her face. She asked me again, this time in a threatening voice. "What did you talk to Brant about? If you said anything to upset him..." Her chin was quivering with anger.

"I said nothing threatening." I stayed calm. "What I told Brant is between him and me, and if he chooses to tell you, it is up to him."

Jo Ellen said nothing and walked on past me. I knew I was marked at this point, a fresh name on her personal hit list. She would get rid of me as soon as she could. Unless...

Again, I waited for Brant to get in touch with me. Still no word.

A month went by before I attempted to reach him one more time. I found Eric in the Board room one Saturday before Brant arrived. Eric was placing a stack of cards for Brant to sign. I asked if Brant had said anything to him about meeting with me.

"No, but he kept trying to figure out the meaning of your story. It bothered him."

"I am only trying to help him, "I said.

Eric gave me an understanding look. "We are all trying to serve the Lord in our own way."

I asked Eric if I could talk to Brant. Eric agreed. "I'll see what I can do. Come back in about ten minutes."

I left and walked down the long hallway. Jo Ellen came out of an office, and we passed each other. I did not look at her, only kept smiling as though I was heading a different direction.

Eric saw me and directed me to enter the Board room from the hallway. I stood there, waiting. Rocky was nearby, guarding the door. I told him, "I'm waiting for Eric." Rocky smiled. There was a brief pause.

Eric opened the door and let me into the Board room. Brant was busy signing cards. For the moment, we were alone.

Brant looked up at me. He got up from the long table and spoke firmly. "I thought about what you said, and I don't need the help. If you think you are blossoming, then the Lord will direct you, and whatever words you have for me, I don't need to know."

He seemed scared and lost, trying to draw from a well of strength that had run dry. He was giving me the brush off without even hearing what I had to say. How could he be so threatened when I only wanted to help? I felt sorry for him and hurt. Clearly his mother and brother had gotten to him and influenced his thinking. They'd tainted him with their fear and negativity. They'd lost faith – all of them.

I told him he was trapped like the character in the story I'd told him. He was alone in his tower, and he needed help to be freed. "You only come out to say a few words and bless the people with your smile. Meanwhile you've allowed others to trap you inside. You need to be set free."

He did not respond, only sat down and continued to sign the cards.

Others entered the room, coming and going as though I was never there. It was as though time had stopped for a moment, preventing others from entering the room until I was done with what I had to say. Once our conversation stopped, time continued again.

I had a strange feeling. I left confused and upset. I was angered by the deception – the hypocrisy and the waste of opportunity.

Was I done? For now, I had gone as far as I could go. I believed I did my part, and now it was time to start thinking of moving on. But where? Little did I know that time would give me my answer and provide me with a willing partner.

CHAPTER 16:

WHAT TO DO ABOUT THE MINISTRY

While Elaine had been producing the drama performances at the ministry over the past several years, I became good friends with her. Early on, we only made small talk. In time she started to share her concerns about what she'd observed with the ministry.

We talked about the rumors being spread about different people, and we speculated about how true they were. Sometimes one of us had privileged information to offer, but there was always a point of discretion. She was hesitant about how much to tell me, and I did not push the issue.

Elaine had remained friends with Steve and Teddi through the years. After Steve was fired, Elaine remained in contact with both. They proved to be good friends to her. Even so, Steve was careful at this point about how much he could confide in Elaine.

Elaine had recently moved to Hollywood to get her foot in the door of the acting business. Her new home was more centrally located to her work. She was starting to network with people in the film industry, taking acting classes and volunteering with theater groups. Her move to Hollywood was her way of breaking away from the ministry, getting a new start for herself, and finding her voice among new Christian groups involved in the film industry.

Whenever Elaine came to the Long Beach services, she and I would often get together. She would tell me what she was observing at the Center, and she'd often question what was taking place in the ministry.

Elaine had a hard time justifying how some people were treated after they left the ministry, how favoritism was being played out for different people. She questioned how the money was being spent, what it was spent on, what the ministry had evolved into, along with the prescription drugs he was on that seemed to alter his behavior.

A secretary at Shekinah named Kathy B. was also involved in our drama group. She had drama experience from her college days and had her sights on a career in the entertainment industry. She was my second singing partner in the Shekinah Singers after Madge decided to step down from the choir. Kathy had shared Elaine's interest in moving to Hollywood, and eventually they became roommates. After the move, Kathy ended up working as a secretary at Disney Studios.

By the time the others and I confronted the Board members that night and attempted to clear the air, Elaine and Kathy had already moved to Hollywood. Elaine was more direct with me about what was taking place in the organization. She had a special kind of insight and was able to get to the heart of the matter.

One by one, more people were starting to leave. While other people were questioning what was happening in the ministry, Kathy wanted to remain neutral. She did not want to say anything critical about Brant and the ministry. She agreed with what was being said about them but did not want to add fuel to the fire.

After Elaine moved to Hollywood, she continued coming to the Saturday services but had less contact with others. She was forging new relationships in Hollywood and trying to get her career going.

Most of the problems centered around the Baker family – Bob, Jo Ellen, and Kevin. Either Brant did not know what was going on, or he knew about it and just ignored what was taking place. His declining health was a major distraction for him, and it seemed to open the door for others to take advantage of his inattention. Perhaps because of their own conduct, the Bakers were suspicious of many people, thinking they were going to try to take over their ministry.

Besides the financial piece and possible misappropriation of funds, another issue for the ministry was the prevalence of gay tendencies in the organization. I don't know how much Elaine knew about Brant's homosexuality, if anything at all. She did know about Kevin engaging in homosexuality behind the scenes. We knew Greg, the choir director, was gay, and that led to his being fired.

It left me confused and scared inside. My mind flashed back to the relationship I had with Jeff. I was keeping it secret, and I still felt the pain and shame of it. I often wondered what would happen to me if it ever got around that I had a gay past, one that continued even after my very public healing from such attractions. I shuddered to think about it.

Before Greg was fired, Brant asked Elaine to talk to Greg. Brant wanted her to ask Greg to tone down his effeminate mannerisms. He said people were starting to talk behind Greg's back, and it would not look good for the ministry to have a gay choir director. I thought that was strange since Brant had the same traits. He was not as overt as Greg was in public, but Brant still projected an effeminate aura. Nonetheless, Elaine agreed and had the awkward conversation with Greg.

During this era, the words gay or homosexual were not generally used in conversation. Elaine alluded to their mannerisms and behavior, saying that things were not adding up or that they seemed ungodly. I think she wanted to spare me in some way about what she knew. I understood what she was implying – that she suspected as much about me.

Despite her observations, I believe Elaine's focus was on how the ministry's money was being spent through the years. She questioned the decisions that were made as the ministry progressed and questioned how people were put into leadership positions. There were inconsistencies at every step.

I was still somewhat naive and protective of Brant. I saw him as a friend and as a victim of circumstance who needed to be rescued from his own family and the church elders. I had been accepting what was being said about the rest of the Baker family and some of the others, but I still did not see Brant as accountable.

As the months rolled on, Elaine and I would talk for hours about what was happening to Shekinah. The decline was steady, but we felt unempowered to do anything that would correct the course.

Elaine painted a different picture of Brant. Finally, she showed me a side of him that I was forced to see. She connected the dots in a way that showed me how responsible Brant was for these inconsistencies within the ministry.

Suddenly I knew she was right. My eyes were opened, putting the connections together. As she spoke, it became clear that I could no longer make excuses for Brant. The realization hit me like a thunderbolt, a powerful and agonizing pain as I recognized the truth of what Elaine laid out. Brant was deeply involved.

He was not the victim of someone else's deception or misdeeds. He was at the bottom of it, the energy that drove it all. He was the leader of a movement, and everything he did – every choice he made – drove the activity within the ministry. And his energy was on a path to self-destruction. The choices Brant made all added up to fiscal decline and moral decay for Shekinah Christian Center. Thanks to Elaine, suddenly it all became clear to me. He needed intervention.

The question was, what were we going to do about it?

I sincerely thought at the time that I could come to the rescue and help Brant and the ministry get back on a moral standing. I told Elaine about my thoughts, and I suggested a plan to help the ministry. I kept her updated about what I knew and what I was doing.

Elaine was supportive but skeptical. She never really put me down for my bold ideas, but she made me really think things over. She challenged me to examine my own motives and be clear about why I wanted to do this. I took her words to heart. Ultimately, I told her I had to follow through what God was leading me to do.

It was pure fantasy on my part. I did not realize the ramifications of what I was asking for. I'd been involved with Brant's ministry for almost six years, and I'd worked with Brant personally. I thought I could help. In reality, I was blind to Brant's destiny, and I was spared any foreknowledge of the consequences for the ministry.

A New (Girl) Friend

My friendship with Kristy deepened while we continued to be involved with Shekinah Christian Center. Not only had she been involved with the choir and Sunday school, she also came during the week to volunteer time as a part-time receptionist. She answered phone calls and helped with the printing. She helped the custodian with cleaning the theater and offices in the building. Shekinah was a major part of her life.

Along with her many volunteer positions in the ministry, Shekinah offered her a way of escape from her own personal home life. This was true for many of us teens during the early stages of the ministry. Later on, Kristy became the nanny for Mike. while he was the pastor for Shekinah Christian Center.

Like many of us, Kristy felt a calling. She had visions of how God would use her talents in some great way before Jesus's return. Even though none of us really had any plans for what to do next in our lives, Kristy and I both knew that Shekinah was our training ground. At some point we needed to make the choice to remain or venture out on our own. Early on, Kristy received training with Sister Edith to be one of the Word of Knowledge workers in the Saturday services.

As Kristy and I got to know each other more, we shared confidences about our personal backgrounds. We confided in each other about our hopes for the future of the ministry. We talked about what was going wrong with it and what was right. I shared with her my darkest fears for Brant and told her I hoped I could make a difference.

Kristy agreed that Brant needed help. She said what I was doing made sense, especially since I'd been with the ministry so long and had worked with Brant personally. She encouraged me to continue to do what I felt led to do. She was a good listener, and she offered to pray for me, so I could follow through with my inspired plans.

At the same time, Kristy said she too felt nervous for the future of Shekinah. There were signs that the path of the ministry was on shaky ground. She saw Brant at Shekinah Center during the week, and increasingly he did not look good. His health clearly was failing.

As part of her janitorial duties, Kristy cleaned the restroom in Brant's dressing room. It frequently smelled like vomit. When she would empty his wastebasket, she often saw a wad of Kleenex full of snot and puke. It made her feel disgusted, and I myself felt queasy when she told me about it. Privately I wondered if I had been removed from my post as his personal aide to spare me from some unfortunate circumstance. It was a passing thought, but it left a trail of doubt.

I let Kristy know what was going on with me – my vision for leadership – and I trusted her with my boldest ideas. I filled her in on how I felt led to help Brant and the ministry, and updated her about what I was working on toward that end. She always received my ideas with genuine support, and I started to become fond of her and her gentle ways.

Kristy always looked rather angelic with her curly strawberry blond hair and soft voice. I didn't really pay any attention to her until she volunteered to work with me in the Sunday school. Then I started to notice her more and more. When she sang in the choir, she wore long flowing choir dress, looking like she'd stepped out of a classical painting. All that was missing was her halo. Later, when she wanted to help with the drama production, my casting her in the role of an angel seemed like an obvious choice.

We had become friends by then, spending more and more time together. Once we got to know each other better, she confided her romantic feelings for me. I felt close to her, and I encouraged her to speak her heart. She took a deep breath and smiled that angelic smile of hers, trembling slightly but holding her chin high.

Kristy told me at first, she knew who I was because of the different positions I'd held in the ministry. She had been watching me from a distance. Then the Lord directed her attention to me more fully when I had a small part in a drama production we were doing with the choir. There were other girls in the choir who admired me too, she said, and that gave her further encouragement.

Not long after rehearsals started, she grew deeply attached to me. She told me how the Lord had directed her on the path to our relationship. She had been patient, waiting for the right opportunity for the door to open once I had befriended her. At first, she was not sure a romance with me would work out or could happen at all. Then the Lord gave her a sign to hold onto the promise that she and I would be together. She said scripture had pointed the way.

I was overwhelmed. I resisted getting romantically involved with Kristy because I just didn't know how it would work out. I had already bombed with several other girls, and I cared too much about Kristy to set up our relationship for failure.

I paused and considered, staring into her porcelain face under that crown of curls. "Let's be friends for now," I told her, "and let the Lord work on the rest."

Kristy Confides

After Sister Edith left, Jo Ellen terminated a number of Sister Edith's trainees in a very firm and cold way. Kristy was one of them. Jo Ellen confronted her and sharply told her she would no longer be part of this area of the ministry.

Kristy took it personally. She thought Jo Ellen only let the pretty girls work the Word of Knowledge part of the service. Despite bruised feelings, Kristy continued to come to the Center. She remained involved in the other areas of the ministry, but she kept her distance from Jo Ellen. I was supportive, of course, and Jo Ellen's harsh treatment only served to bring Kristy and me closer together. I wasn't prepared for what happened next.

Kristy called me at my apartment after work one day and said she wanted to tell me something. She asked to meet with me. I agreed, a little more than curious about what she wanted to say. In light of her earlier advances toward me, I felt a bit nervous about what was on her mind.

We got together that week, and the most convenient place we could think of was the theater. We went upstairs to one of the offices and closed the door. She was silent for a moment, and I remember the second hand on the office clock ticking loudly in the room. Finally, Kristy took a deep breath and broke the stillness in the room.

She began by telling me again she had something important to say to me. I nodded, encouraging her to go on. She felt it was important in light of our studies with Mike. We were learning about basic counseling techniques. If she was going to counsel others, she needed to break her silence about something.

It made sense she wanted to confide something to me. Our friendship was deepening, and we felt close to each other. Also, with the counseling techniques we were learning, she knew I would listen to her deeply and keep anything she said confidential.

Even with the training from the classes, I made some assumptions about what she was trying to share with me. I thought she was going to tell me she had sex before with another guy and needed to tell me about it. I was way off base.

Kristy spoke a little about her home life, opening up about her childhood and the way she was raised. Then she mentioned her father. She stopped, hesitant and trembling. She opened her mouth to speak, but the words seemed to stick in her throat. Her face was flush, and her eyes filled with tears, choking back the shame of a long-held secret. Finally, her confession tumbled out of her mouth.

Kristy had had an incestuous relationship with her father when she was a little girl. He sexually abused her several times. She told me about the period when it happened but spared me the details. She shuddered when she said how hard it was to still live with her parents.

Kristy looked down at her hands, locking her fingers together, fidgeting. "I never told that to anyone before. You are the first because I know I can trust you."

I was silent for a moment, trying to take in what she told me. I could hardly envision what she was saying. This was so foreign to me, and I felt stunned by the depth of her family's betrayal. I wondered how this could happen to anyone, let alone someone I cared about.

Kristy was nervously fidgeting and bouncing her leg. I could tell she was waiting for some kind of response from me. I was still for a moment and collected my thoughts. I knew I'd never get another chance to get this right.

"I'm sorry that happened to you. This is the past, Kristy, and you are a new person in Christ."

"I never told anyone before," she said again. Clearly her mind was caught in a loop.

I wanted to say something to make her feel better about herself. I wanted her to feel safe and know that everything was going to be okay. By confiding in me, she risked creating an imbalance in our relationship. I didn't want that.

"As long as we are confessing," I said, "I'll tell you something I've never told anyone. I believe I can trust you."

I opened up to her about my healing from homosexuality a few years before at Shekinah. I told her how I was tested and struggled with my attraction to certain other men. I confessed to her that I'd had an affair with Jeff. Though I never had sex with him, the relationship was deep and lasted for some time.

At first, I thought it was brotherly love, but the feelings were so strong and full of passion. I confessed to Kristy that the situation left me deeply confused, and I couldn't understand why God would bring two people so close together if it was wrong. I told her I still cared about Jeff as a person, and our parting was really painful for me.

Somehow Kristy understood. She did not seem bothered by what I said and in fact she was just as supportive of me as I'd been to her. We both seemed to feel better after confiding in each other. We said a prayer together asking God to continue to lead us, guide us and heal us.

Neither Kristy nor I really understood the long-term psychological effects of what we had experienced and kept hidden inside. For my part, I certainly did not understand the complications that a victim of incest experienced. I didn't realize what the aftereffects can do to your psyche. I didn't know it required a long-term recovery.

Besides this, I also did not understand why I had experienced sexual and romantic feelings toward another man. It was hard to even verbalize what I was feeling, much less confess to Kristy what I had been holding inside for so long. Certainly Kristy tried to understand, and she seemed very compassionate. I felt compassion for her too.

I think we were both looking for some understanding and acceptance from each other about our own secrets that we'd held inside. All we had to go on were a few short Bible scriptures and a handful of classroom hours. The Christian answer to our deepest torment was that God would take care of it over time. We held tightly to that conviction like a lifeline in a stormy sea. The two of us found solace by gathering in His name.

Our friendship continued to deepen after that. I think we both felt empathetic about each other's tribulations and found a new appreciation of our friendship.

I Meet the Folks

Kristy lived in a rough neighborhood in Wilmington, a city that is centered around heavy industry and an oil field. Wilmington is next to Long Beach and east of San Pedro. The demographic is low income working class, mostly Latino. Kristy's street was sandwiched in between the Harbor Freeway and an oil refinery plant. The air was a mixture of the fresh salt air mixed with exhaust from the smokestacks at the refinery.

From Kristy's place, I could see the Palos Verdes Peninsula in the distance beyond the refinery. Every time I looked in that direction, I would remember visiting my mother's relatives there. I'd think of the pretty drive through the hills and along the coast when I was a child.

I started to pick up Kristy at her home, so we could spend more time together. As I drove down Pacific Coast Highway into the heart of Wilmington, I noticed it was very different from the surrounding area. It was like being in a Third World country, with store signs written in Spanish and rough characters in shabby clothes standing on street corners. It made me feel unsafe, and I wanted to get to Kristy's place as soon as possible.

When I got to her house, though, she would not let me inside. I would knock on the door, but she'd slip out and shut the door quickly, so I couldn't see inside. I was curious to meet her family, privately wondering what kind of parents would abuse their child. I also wondered what secret she was keeping from me behind the hastily closed door. I asked Kristy why she wouldn't let me in.

"You don't want to come into my house," she said. "My mother is just not a good housekeeper."

I told her that didn't matter and pressed her a bit more. Then she said she was embarrassed by her parents' housekeeping. "Besides," she added, "my parents really don't talk to each other." She was afraid I would judge her because of her parents. Kristy seemed really afraid of them.

Kristy had tried to move out several times before, but every time she started to work at a job, she ended up giving most of her paycheck to her mother. This left very little for her personal needs and church activities. Moving out became something of a pipe dream.

Finally, Kristy invited me to her house for dinner. My first impression when I entered her home was that it was small inside. Even though she had spent a great deal of time cleaning house, there was little room to move around. The furniture was ragged, and there were piles of papers on every surface.

Kristy said that her mother had cooked a real meal for us, which I took as a gracious gesture. She led me into the living room, where her parents were both watching television. Kristy introduced me to them.

"Mom, Dad... this is Jud." I smiled and made small talk, but they did not respond much. The TV was all-consuming and sucked all conversation out of the room.

Kristy's parents were not what I envisioned. I thought they would be mean looking parents that abused their only child. Instead, her father looked kind of handsome. He was a soft-spoken man with reddish blond hair that was a little wavy. He had the same smooth skin as Kristy's. She took more after her father's facial features. He didn't get up to introduce himself. I think he just said, "Hello" while he continued to watch TV.

Then Kristy's mother got up and greeted me with a smile. "Hello." She was a tall woman in her forties with short curly dark hair. She stooped over a little and wore a white neck brace. I thought the neck brace was strange, but she acted very nice and said little.

To avoid any further conversation with her parents, Kristy gave me a short tour of the small house. She took me into the tiny kitchen. The cabinet doors had all been removed, showing the food and mismatched dishes. The counter tops were covered with various dishes and groceries still in bags. The stove was an older green and white gas model from the 1920's. There was very little space to work on the counters.

Then Kristy took me into the backyard where there was a large shade tree. The garden area was overgrown with weeds and the grass was just a collection clumps strewn about the yard. There was a dog chain around the tree and a dog dish, remnants of a family pet that had died.

Off to one side, there was a detached garage that opened onto an alley. Kristy showed me inside the garage, which was packed with various broken pieces of furniture and boxes. It was the most clean and organized part of the entire house.

Dinner was served indoors on a picnic table that only had enough room for Kristy and me. The rest of the table was piled with old mail and bags of clutter. The air was heavy with cooking smells and the funk of neglect. I said little, just kept a humble attitude. I was grateful to be Kristy's guest, and I really was honored that Kristy's mother had prepared a meal for us.

Dinner was a new experience for me though, and I found myself struggling to get through it. Kristy's mother served us boiled cow tongue, mashed potatoes, beans, and overcooked vegetables. I'd never had tongue before, and all I saw was this big cooked organ, lolling on the plate in front of me.

The tongue was tough and chewy. I tried to eat it but ended up stashing it in my paper napkin, trying to hide it. If the dog had still been alive, he would have had a feast from my plate. Instead I just ate the mashed potatoes, beans and a few vegetables. I tried to be polite, smiling with my mouth full while chewing.

Kristy's mother told me, "You don't have to eat it if you don't want to – if you're not use to it, I mean." Kristy echoed her mother. I smiled and continued to eat, silently thankful for my daily bread. It was one of the worst meals of my life, but I grinned all through it. This adventure was my first real date with Kristy. It was far from my last.

One Wild Ride After Another

That summer, one of our more notable dates happened when Kristy and I went with my high school friend Sue O. to Disneyland. Disneyland was not far from where we lived, and even as young adults, everyone loved to go. They were having a special event, and Sue was able to get some discount tickets.

The plan was that Kristy was going to drive to my apartment, then we were going to meet Sue at Disneyland. Just as I was getting ready to go, I got a phone call at my apartment. It was Kristy. She sounded distressed, and she was crying. She said she had been in a car accident, and she needed to be picked up. She gave me the location in Wilmington off of Pacific Coast Highway.

I hurried to the scene. The police were there already along with several people involved in the accident. There were four cars involved in a fender bender, all of them simmering in the summer heat. Kristy was at the back end of the collision, looking lovely but obviously distressed. She wore a crisp summer dress and a red flower comb in her hair. Her fresh look was quite a contrast with her parent's car – the front end was crunched like an accordion.

We went inside a fast food place nearby to finish the report. The officer filling out the accident report was a model of sincerity. He asked Kristy several questions, but she cracked jokes in a flippant, sarcastic tone. Eventually we got through the paperwork, and we were free to go.

Kristy told me she was upset because her parents were out of town on vacation and she was afraid of what they would do to her because of the wreck. She was too upset to drive her parent's car, so I let her drive my white Mustang back to her place. Her parent's car was still drive-able, so I told her I would follow her there.

When I drove back to Kristy's house, I parked at the curb and waited for her on the front lawn. Sitting there on the grass, I noticed the radiator was leaking and a puddle was forming on the street. I waited quite awhile for her and wondered why it was taking so long.

A moment later, I saw her running up to the house out of breath, shouting to me. "I hitchhiked. I had to hitchhike!" Her hair was a mess. The flower comb was dangling down, and her makeup was smudged.

I was confused. "What happened?"

Kristy told me, "My car would not start because the ignition cylinder came out." She panicked, and she managed to beg a Latino man for a ride in his truck. He agreed to drive her home. She was scared because he kept looking her over. She had him drop her off a couple blocks from her house, though, because she did not want to let him know where she lived. She ran the rest of the way home, smearing her makeup and tousling her hair in the process.

I asked Kristy where the car was. She told me, and again she said the ignition had come out. It sounded very strange to me, and I couldn't figure out what would have gone wrong. We'd have to check it and see. First, I pointed out the leaking radiator on her parent's car. With her help, I added water from the garden hose. Then we went off in search of my own distressed vehicle.

We got back to my car. I climbed in and discovered that, not only would my key not fit into the ignition, the whole mechanism had come out, just as she said. I looked around and realized this was not even my car. It was a different white Mustang. It looked like my car, but the interior was different.

I climbed out of the car and noticed another white Mustang a few cars ahead, parked at the curb. That Mustang was mine. All that drama was for nothing. I started my car, and we drove back to Kristy's house where she went inside to freshen up. After another momentary delay, we drove on to Disneyland.

When we got to Disneyland, we met up with my friend, Sue O. I was glad to see her, and we embraced. The pain of jealousy immediately started to settle on Kristy. She did not say much about it, just kept silent and put on a good face.

I didn't realize it then, but the whole time we were at Disneyland, there was a private tug of war going on between Sue and Kristy. I wondered why it seemed there was a competition between them for seats on the rides. They would take turns sitting with me, but there was an undercurrent of tension the whole time. The reason for it only came out later on.

In the days following our trip to Disneyland, Kristy was really sore and could barely move. The auto accident combined with the carnival rides really worked over her body. She had a full-blown case of whiplash. She went to the doctor the following day, and he gave her some pain medication. It took her several weeks to recover.

While Elaine and I were putting our thoughts together about what we should do about the ministry, Kristy served as my sounding board. She had a hard time believing what I was telling her. Although she was aware of what was taking place behind the scenes, she would have preferred to just ignore it, afraid to look at it. The ministry was her second family and the friendships she had formed, it meant everything to her.

Elaine and I began to realize our roles in the ministry and even our lives were starting to change. Elaine had already made her move to Hollywood, but I still needed to make the break. I tried to follow my heart, but I had such mixed feelings about the people involved and their actions.

Like many others in the congregation, Kristy and I were in a state of confusion about what to do with the things we knew. I was afraid to lose something that was so familiar, such a big part of me. I didn't want to move on and walk away. There had to be some clear path out of the murky situation we found ourselves in, mired in the rough treatment and developing scandals rooted in the hypocrisy. But how?

As Elaine and I found more perspective through time and distance, a plan started to take shape. We just needed to write it down and put it into action. We prayed for guidance, and our prayers found a willing ear – just not in the way we'd expected.

A Plan to Restore Brant

Elaine was sharing more with me about what was taking place within the ministry and compared notes. She had the strong need to release her feelings and find some kind of solution that meant Brant could get help and be held accountable and restored to his place at the helm. She was concerned about the prescription drugs he was on given by his doctor. I agreed with her. We had known he was given medications. His eyes would be glassy and appeared spacey more than his usual self. His bodyguards had to walk closer to him to keep him stable. He seemed to snap out of it while conducting the healing service then he went right back into his stupor state.

I was a sounding board for Elaine while we expressed our concerns. We had many long conversations about what was taking place with the ministry.

Being so young and questing, the leadership and management of the ministry was a daring challenge for us. We had been conditioned not to question "God's anointed and His prophets." We had to balance our youthful enthusiasm with our relative inexperience as leaders. Time would tell, how well we managed to keep this balance.

Even though Elaine had moved up in the Hollywood area, she could not just let go and move on from the previous Shekinah ministry. One of her main concerns was how the money was being used to justify various salaries in the ministry. She was also concerned about some of the behaviors that were allowed to continue. She seemed to wrestle with the hypocrisy of these actions.

As a group, we came out of the simple lifestyle of Calvary Chapel Jesus People. The congregations were a core group of volunteers, a mixture of teenagers and young adults living together like struggling bohemians. We provided the bulk of the labor for the ministry. Any increase in lifestyle among the leadership would have been noticed by the congregation at large.

Despite this, Brant lived lavishly like a spoiled prince. His wardrobe, his gourmet tastes, his limousine all smacked of pleasures of the flesh, placing him in a higher standing than those around him. His tie collection alone was enough for ten ordinary men and raised eyebrows among the general volunteer staff. His attitude also had gone from happy to haughty. He had become more snappish and arrogant as he isolated himself further and further from the rest of us.

Elaine was starting to go the Vineyard in Sherman Oaks where Ken G. was now teaching. He had been a minister at Calvary Chapel under Chuck Smith. During one service, he shared a message about a minister who needed to be restored after falling into sin. The message got Elaine's attention. She wondered if Ken was speaking directly about Brant.

Elaine told me about the message. She wanted to make an appointment with Ken for us both to go to him and share what we knew about Brant. Ken was aware of Brant's background since they knew each other from Calvary Chapel. I thought back to his early messages, how Brant often referred to Ken's love for Jesus and talked about his own respect for Ken. I agreed with Elaine and told her a meeting with Ken would be a good idea. Elaine made the appointment.

Prior to meeting with Ken, I talked on the phone with Steve., seeking his advice about how to help Brant. I knew I could trust Steve with what I had to say, and he would be helpful. Still I felt nervous about telling him since I did not communicate with him all that much since he left Shekinah.

Steve was polite and listened intently. He asked if I could stand up to the Baker family and take the backlash, I was sure to get once I'd spoken my piece. I did not respond to his question out loud, taking in the full weight of what he'd said.

I pictured Steve with one of his firm gazes as he spoke quietly. "Just let the ministry die, Jud." He paused thoughtfully, then added, "Once the dust settles, then you can pick up the pieces and start again if you still feel led to do so."

It was hard to hear. Since he was one of the founders who had built the ministry, he must have felt hurt by what had happened to him. I could see why he would want to let it go. "I understand what you mean," I said, "but I still feel I need to try."

When the day arrived, Elaine picked me up in Long Beach and drove us to Ken's office at the church. On the way, I filled Elaine in about my conversation with Steve.

I remembered Ken from Calvary Chapel. Back then, he was instantly likable. It seemed little had changed. He stood out as a leader among leaders, both in his polished looks and his demeanor. Ken had clear blue eyes and a smooth complexion that conveyed a quality of clean living. His blond hair and rosy cheeks hinted at his Norwegian background, suggesting an even keel and a questing spirit. Unlike the dynamic speaking style of most ministers, Ken was soft spoken and humble. It was nice to see him after several years.

Ken greeted us warmly and opened up in our conversation. Elaine got to the point quickly, summarizing her position and the events of the ministry. From time to time, Ken interjected questions about Brant and the ministry. She answered as best she could and expressed her concerns about where Shekinah was heading. She expressed her concerns of his overall health, the medications he was on and how he had to take a leave of absence as other guest ministers came to fill in for Saturday services.

When Elaine finished, Ken asked me about my role and background. I summarized my history with Shekinah and the role I played in Brant's work up to this point. I further talked about what I had attempted to do to help restore Brant to health and leadership within the ministry. I explained that I'd approached Jo Ellen first, then Sister Edith, and finally Brant with the plans I thought were from the Lord. All of them were neutral at first, then negative except Sister Edith.

Ken smiled and listened patiently. He did not judge what I had to say, and he seemed to understand my motives and objectives. Rather than being negative, Ken opened up to us with a surprising perspective.

Ken told us he had always felt concerned about Brant. He felt Brant was too unstable to handle a leadership position, especially at such an early age. Knowing Brant's character and background, Ken believed Brant had built his house upon the sand. Now Brant found his ministry sinking into it, and it would only be a matter of time before the ministry's total collapse. Elaine and I looked at each other in surprise.

Ken added that he felt the Lord had directed him the ministry to restore ministers. He gave an example of what he had already done with a well-known teaching minister who was having marriage issues at the time.

Ken's beliefs were founded on the scriptural approach to restore a brother as put forward in Matthew 18:15-17. This scripture would have great significance for us later on. The passage talks about approaching a brother who has sinned, and the steps involved in restoring him.

If your brother does not acknowledge his fault to you in private, then you are to bring in other witnesses to address him and urge him to mend his ways. If he still refuses to listen, then you must tell it to the church.

Ken revealed to Elaine and me that the process had already begun. Before our meeting, Ken was well aware of some of the issues we discussed with him. Others from the congregation had talked to Ken personally about them and asked him to become involved. Ken and the others were seeking amends from Brant.

My approaching Brant had further prompted this action. For example, Ken said Brant would have to go back and apologize to those ministers he had placed in position and let go. Even with these actions, there was more work ahead.

Ken told us we would have to craft a scripturally sound document listing the issues we challenged and the changes we expected from Brant. We would need to demand that Brant get counseling and abide by the conditions we set forth for the good of the ministry. If Brant didn't make the required changes for himself and ministry, he would receive a warning. If he still did not comply, then he'd face expulsion.

Ken assured us he would help us with the process. He would guide us in drafting the document and review it before Elaine and I approached Brant.

It was such a comfort to hear these words from Ken. At last, we had a path and some hope. We weren't alone anymore. We had some guidance and a concrete plan of action. The three of us closed the meeting with prayer. Elaine and I thanked Ken for his time, and then we left. We had overcome a large hurdle. What a relief!

Now we faced another challenge – getting organized to write the document. We worked together to come up with the substance of what we wanted to say. Between the two of us, Elaine was the better writer. She took the lead on putting that part of the project together.

The next step was to find out where Brant lived. Only a few people in the ministry knew. I volunteered to do some investigating and locate his address. I felt I could get the information from Eric if I approached him the right way.

Elaine had also been in contact with Steve about what was taking place, and she voiced our concerns. Steve was helping by guiding her and acting as a sounding board for her. She had already established a relationship with Steve and his wife Teddi when they were employed by the ministry.

Elaine often told me how she trusted Steve, voicing her frustrations with the ministry. He had a way of putting people at ease, and Elaine was grateful to have him on our side. Steve chose not to give Elaine and me further details about the ministry's corruption. Instead he merely confirmed our own discoveries and suspicions and gave counsel and suggestions about what we should do.

At this time, Steve was still feeling the sting of being fired from his position. He felt betrayed by Brant as a friend and minister. He was still going through the hurt, reeling from being fired from an executive seat in the ministry. I am sure he was doing a lot of self-examination at that time. I sensed the bitter undertone when he spoke, yet he was helpful to us and seemed to trust Elaine and me with our mission.

Steve felt Elaine and I were in a perfect position to follow through with this mission. We could maneuver without others suspecting what we were up to. He knew we had to help Brant, even if it meant exposing deception and corruption to the congregation. Our plan was now taking on a life of its own, and we had backers. Next came the hard work of committing our position to paper.

Drafting the Grievance Letter

While Elaine worked on drafting the letter, I went to work on tracking down Brant's home address. I knew Eric would have it. On a Saturday service I found him in Brant's office in the Board room upstairs at the Fox Theater. He was busy making coffee and getting ready for Brant to arrive. Brant was about to meet Eric and sign some letters before getting ready in his dressing room in the basement under the stage.

By now Eric knew about my first attempts to talk to Brant to share my thoughts to help restore the ministry. Eric was supportive, but he kept his distance.

Since I was no longer in the loop about where Brant lived in the Hollywood area, Eric suggested that perhaps I should come by the following Saturday. "Maybe you will find an empty envelope with Brant's address on my worktable... right here." He pointed in the direction Brant's office. I nodded and exited the room before Jo Ellen and the others arrived.

The following week I entered Brant's office again. Claudia and Eric were busy as usual with their routine, getting ready before the service and Brant's arrival. We exchanged some small talk, and Claudia left the room. I stood there a moment. "Do you have it?"

Eric said nothing, merely pointed toward his desk. He looked at me meaningfully and said, "I'll be back."

He left the room without another word. I walked over to the small antique secretary desk where Eric worked. I saw part of an empty torn envelope with Brant's address on it. I looked at it for a moment then took it as Eric walked back in. He puttered around in the room. I said thank you, and I left.

Later that week, I called Elaine and told her I got the address. I told her what I had to do to get it, and we laughed about it. She said it was like something out of a spy novel. I wondered if there was a hidden camera somewhere in his office.

Elaine had been working on a first draft of the letter. When she got done, she and I went over it together, scrutinizing it for tone and substance. Next, we asked Ken K. and Steve to review it for any changes. Ken suggested some minor changes but otherwise said it was fine. Steve. and another person felt the document was not harsh enough. A couple other trusted parishioners read it too, and we got mixed reviews about whether it was strong enough.

Elaine and I made a few changes, then Kathy B. typed a final copy. Ken reviewed the letter one more time for grammar with one last check of the content. It was then ready to go.

Elaine and I decided on the delivery date. It was to take place the following Monday, knowing for sure he would be at home. First, we would scout the area where Brant lived to verify the location – it was in Brentwood.

I went to Elaine and Kathy's apartment that weekend to finalize our plans. We drove by Brant's apartment that Friday evening and parked on the side street. We walked down the sidewalk when suddenly I saw someone who looked like Brant. He was walking a dog, idly strolling toward us.

"Oh God, it's Brant!" I blurted.

"Let's act casual, like we were just in the neighborhood visiting a friend," she said. It sounded like a good idea to me. The man drew closer with the dog leading the way. Then he walked right by us, and we discovered it was not Brant at all. Elaine and I gave a sigh of relief.

We kept walking and located Brant's apartment complex. We hid in the corridors for a moment, then Elaine said she wanted to go up to the second floor to further confirm the location. I followed close behind her. She peeked into a window by the front door and thought she saw someone. We quickly left, running downstairs, out to the sidewalk, and into the car. We took off, breathing heavily and laughing nervously and mocking ourselves. What kind of spies were we anyway?

That Saturday, I talked with Kristy on the phone and told her what Elaine and I did to verify Brant's location. Kristy was feeling nervous about the whole thing, but she seemed to understand. She said she would be going to the service that night to sing in the choir.

Elaine and I went to the Vineyard on Sunday and spoke to Ken G. briefly after the service. He asked how our progress was. I told him we would be seeing Brant on Monday now that we verified where he lived. Ken nodded sagely and asked us to keep him informed.

Elaine and I did not have a backup plan. We didn't think about what we would do if Brant cut us off and asked us to leave. We did not know what to expect by meeting him face to face privately. We were hoping to spend some time with him beyond just handing him the letter and leaving. If nothing else, we could at least get the letter in his hand. Hopefully he would respond by calling Ken.

An Astonishing Meeting with Brant

That Monday, we went to Brant's apartment around 10:00 am. It ended up being the wrong apartment. He didn't live in the place we spied on the previous Friday evening. Flustered for a moment, we realized he lived in the apartment next door.

Elaine knocked on the door then turned to me and said, "I'll do the talking." I agreed since she was a better communicator than I was. Our hearts were beating fast, and I was feeling a little faint. It was difficult for me to confront him this way. I knew I had to stay strong, even though it was Elaine who would speak for us. Moments ticked by silently, waiting, then his dog started barking behind the door.

Brant came to the window and spoke through the screen. "Yes? Who is it?"

"It's me," Elaine replied. "Could we come in to talk to you?"

Brant was irritated. "No," he said flatly.

"It is important," Elaine insisted. She added that it had something to do with the ministry.

Brant was clearly disturbed. "Well, okay. I'll be there in a moment." He shut the window. A moment later, he came to the door holding his Pomeranian. He was in his robe, and he had not shaved yet. "How did you know where I was?"

We ignored the question and walked past him through the narrow entry into the living room. Elaine and I sat on the couch. Brant sat in a chair across from us. He was still holding his dog, then he put her on the floor. The dog jumped onto the couch then back to Brant. Between the dog and Brant's tension, the atmosphere was tinged with a note of chaos.

Elaine took a moment and focused. She opened the conversation by talking about our concern for him and the ministry. Brant looked puzzled then asked again, "How did you find me?"

Not wanting to reveal our source, Elaine looked straight into Brant's eyes. "We followed you."

Brant rolled his eyes, disturbed. "Oh, really."

Elaine continued with her tack. She reminded Brant how we both were friends to him and told him we were concerned about him and the ministry. She briefly reviewed the history of our involvement with him and the ministry. All the while, Brant said nothing.

Elaine told Brant she had contacted Ken at the Vineyard, and Ken had expressed his concern for Brant. She disclosed that she and I had a meeting with Ken first on the issues that concerned us relating to the Shekinah ministry. Brant seemed surprised that we talked to Ken. He leaned in closer for a moment and gave a brief smile, as though the memory of Ken pleased him.

Elaine continued talking, bringing up issues that needed to be addressed. "What issues?" Brant asked.

Elaine brought up the time when she was following up on some of the healings, gathering data. She had a hard time getting any confirmations from doctors to use to document that the ministry was effective. She was gathering testimonies of healings to put into a book similar to Kathryn Kuhlman's "I Believe In Miracles." That book had a number of testimonies from people who were touched and healed at her services. Brant said nothing.

Then Elaine eased into another topic, saying how he would never confront people on his own. When it came to issues and he had to confront someone on a personal basis, he would always have someone else do it for him.

This was one of Brant's character issues as a leader. As the ministry grew, he could break off a relationship or fire a person on his staff. He thought the message he wanted to convey would come out too harsh if he had to do it himself. In reality, he was a coward. He had to leave it up to someone else to do this work for him.

This is how it was done in the business world all the time. When someone in an executive position had to fire someone, the task fell to a lower ranking manager to carry out the wishes of their boss. But I thought the role of a minister should be different. Why did he not have the courage of his convictions? It took me the longest time to understand this about him since he was a man of God.

Well I was wrong, and it was hard to understand at the time. Brant always gave the appearance of openness. Those who worked around him stood by and allowed this to happen. They remained silent. Jo Ellen would often say, "I am the only one who knows what Brant wants."

Brant always seemed to have someone else carry out his wishes and express his thoughts for him. We just grew to accept it. The only person that I recall Brant breaking off a relationship with was Kyle. Brant and he knew their relationship was not healthy for either of them since Brant had such strong feelings for him.

I could understand how painful that must have been for both for them at the time. I believe this was one of the major turning points for Brant when it came to relationships with other men. I understood those same feelings, thinking of my relationship with Jeff when I knew I needed to break it off with him.

Elaine was finishing up her message. Up to this point, I had been quiet and resisted saying anything. Now I felt some things needed to be said for my part and get them out in the open. I asked Brant about the time he let me go. "Why did you not talk to me about the issue? Why didn't you give me a chance to talk it over and clear the air?" I felt myself choking on the words as I said them.

Brant paused, then said, "I thought it would be better coming from someone else instead of me. It would be less painful."

That was it then. He had made up his mind and never considered that there were two sides to every story. He dismissed me with a single sentence, as if my opinion was too insignificant to make a difference.

My face flushed, and harsh words tried to form. Instead my courage failed me, and I backed off. "You're right." I could see there was no way to change the past. If he was going to grow beyond his interpersonal failings, it was clear he wouldn't be learning the lesson from me.

A disturbed look crossed his face, as if to say, "See? I told you so."

Elaine took back the lead in the conversation. She was leading up to reading the letter to him, but fate intervened. The dog ran to the front door. It opened, and Jo Ellen walked in. I could see her from the corner of my eye in the kitchen area listening in. Fear gripped me.

Elaine and I looked at each other for a moment, stung, wondering what was going to happen next. Heat went through me like a bolt of lightning. I thought Jo Ellen was going to charge in at any moment, shrieking and trying to protect her son. Then I realize she would not cut Brant off like that in front of others.

I could hear her in the kitchen putting away some groceries while trying to be very quiet so as not to miss a word. Brant seized the moment to ask if we wanted any water. This broke some of the tension. Elaine and I said yes and made some small talk, while petting the dog. Brant motioned to his mother, and Jo Ellen came into the living room. She put water on the table and left, saying nothing. She went back to the kitchen to listen in on our conversation.

Elaine started to get the letter out of her purse, explaining that Ken had given us some instructions on how to address the issues that concerned us in the ministry. It looked like Elaine was just going to leave the letter unread, putting it on the table. But a moment later, she unfolded it and she started to read it out loud.

She read the introduction in a gentle, articulate, deliberate fashion, as though she were presenting a case before a panel or a jury. She paused and took a sip of water. We didn't know how far she would get. An understanding passed between Elaine and me that either Brant or Jo Ellen would soon start to protest and ask us to leave. Still Elaine kept reading in her gentle, well-modulated voice. The air was thick with tension.

Elaine continued reading the statement of issues. When it came to the part about the Baker family not acting from pure motives, Elaine reworded the paragraph. She did not mention their names, knowing that Jo Ellen was listening in on the conversation. If Joe Ellen had heard her name, who knows what she would have done at this point to stop the meeting?

The words Elaine read so calmly are printed here.

Mr. Brant Baker

Shekinah Fellowship

Long Beach, California 90801

25 September 1978

Brant,

We have made these statements in prayer, knowledge, and forethought. We believe that scripture dictates the basic structure and organization of church bodies, including the qualifications and duties of pastors, elders, deacons and lay congregation. (I Timothy 3:1-16; Titus 1:5-16, 2:1-15). We also believe that a church that does not follow these standards is a misrepresentation of Christ and His teachings. Therefore, such a church is wrong and without scriptural foundation to continue.

The personal observations listed below have been agreed upon by all of us and seen continually increasing within the last four years of Shekinah's organization. We believe that you are directly responsible for allowing them to happen, and we confront you in the authority of the scriptures according to Matthew 18:16-19. There have been numerous attempts to confront the issues on a personal basis as well as group confrontation at the board meetings, but every encounter has fallen on deaf ears. We now take the next step the scripture tells us to take, and we come to you in twos and threes so that every word will be established.

The following are not the total reasons alone for our concern but only samples of the permissive and unscriptural manner with which the ministry has been run.

For not establishing and running the church with the leadership that scripture dictates, i.e. with elders, deacons, and personal attention to problems, giving a loving example for others to follow, even after repeated requests by numerous members of the body for spiritual leadership and counsel.

For knowingly allowing repeated irrational, unloving, and prejudicial judgments to be made, in all areas of the ministry, by Jo Ellen, Kevin and Bob B., and other individuals who are not sound in character or pure in motive by scriptural definition.

For financially living grossly out of proportion to the others employed by the ministry and the yearly income gained in whole by the ministry. This includes:

Using funds sent in for evangelical purposes at will for your own personal desires.

Telling the rest of us that it was what God wanted, i.e., expensive gifts to the elders, your family, or guests.

Numerous trips

Living expenses, such as unlimited use of church credit cards for clothes, dinners and amusement in the extreme.

For continually separating yourself in spirit and in body from everybody else in the church, including congregation, as well as previous other leadership. Sister Edith, Mike., pastor Adams, Steve., etc.

For being "untouchable and inaccessible" by your own design because of your "personality and frailty."

For refusing to take scriptural or practical counsel from anyone when it opposes what you have already set in your mind to do, whether that counsel is from "eldership", general members or the advisory board.

For lording over the church in a spirit of intimidation and fear instead of love and service to the body.

For propagating and encouraging, by actions and words, feelings of obligation and sacrifice to Brant's Ministry, especially where money is concerned. (I Peter 5:2-4).

For willingly practicing uninvolvement in individuals lives, thereby never having to exhibit self-sacrifice for someone else on a continual personal and pictorial basis.

For refusing to listen to the needs of the people and willfully evading issues that pertain to spiritual, emotional and physical wellbeing in the body.

For the continual suggestion, implication and literal labeling of other pastors and other bodies of believers as inferior or lacking in comparison to Shekinah's "high" standards.

For promoting a judgmental attitude in the church that others outside of our "spirituality and maturity" are second class Christians.

For manifesting the emotional and mental inability to communicate in a healthy exchange with other people over a long period of time. Conducting yourself and making decisions in an irrational and emotionally unbalanced manner in consecutive instances, under varying circumstances.

We believe that God is using you. The gifts and calling of God are given without repentance. We believe in the potential of ministry that you have. We love and support you – Brant the person – and we want to see God use you in a great way. But we realize that unless there are these changes in your continual pattern of attitude and conduct, we can no longer silently watch you destroy yourself and those around you.

We believe that God is able to heal and restore your mental, emotional, spiritual and physical health and bring you into the fullness He has for you, but only after a positive separation from deceptive and unscriptural family influences and from the working organization of Brant's Ministry.

We love you, Brant, but we can no longer support and condone the character and practices of Shekinah.

Because of the direction given to us in Matthew 18, unless there is action on your part to tear down the old foundation and begin to build a new one, we are forced to fulfill our obligation to the scriptures and expose these wrongs to the church bodies.

Judson H.

Elaine.

Elaine paused, and Brant said nothing. Jo Ellen in the kitchen said nothing. Then Elaine reiterated our offer. "Ken wants to help you. He agreed to meet with you to discuss this with you to get your side of the issue. He is expecting your call within in a short time."

Brant remained quiet, pensive. He stared at his clasped hands, unmoving.

"You do understand," I added, "that if you do not agree to meet with Ken on an ongoing basis and showing some changes, we will have to follow through with Mathew 18. We'll have to bring this to the rest of the church body."

Brant said nothing, merely nodded his head yes, his eyes wide open and jaw slack. What was going through his head – how hard he was taking the information – I don't know. At this point, it seemed he was taken by surprise. He couldn't have expected that Elaine and I would show up at his place and present a case like this to him. Surely our visit and our words would have some effect.

Elaine stood up and prepared to go. She left Ken's card and our letter on the table. We both hugged him, and he looked so frail and lost. That was the last time I hugged him and saw him in person. I felt I lost a friend I had come to know and the person I respected. Brant walked us to the door and managed to say a feeble, "God bless." Then we all said goodbye.

Elaine and I said nothing until we reached the car. We got in and let out a loud sigh of relief, wondering if this really just happened. We laughed a little out of nervousness then started to review the meeting, going over each step.

We both had felt lost when Jo Ellen walked into the apartment. Neither one of us knew what was going to happen, and both of our hearts raced. Elaine told me that at first, she was just going to read the introduction of the letter. Soon she realized this could be her last chance to make sure Brant understood the seriousness of these issues. She decided to read the entire letter, even with the risk of Jo Ellen being there.

We discussed the part about Brant not confronting others himself when he needed to, and we talked about what I'd said in the conversation. Elaine felt I should not have backed down in confronting him. Brant needed to know that, in certain areas, it was his responsibility to talk to the individuals involved.

"I know," I told her. "I guess I just chickened out. He can be so intimidating."

"Yeah, no kidding!" she laughed.

Whatever the experience had yielded, now it was over. We both felt drained and relieved at the same time. We drove back to Elaine and Kathy's apartment, still going over the events of the meeting and reliving the confrontation.

Back at her place, Elaine made a couple phone calls to let Ken know the meeting actually took place. Then she called Steve. and reviewed the results with him. Steve sounded pleased, and he commented on how shocked Brant must have been. He also found it uncharacteristic that Jo Ellen had not stepped in, but perhaps she was being careful about how she conducted herself in front of Brant. Her shrewish behavior was fine around others, but even she was intimidated by her charismatic son.

Elaine said she needed to retrieve a rocking chair that she had loaned the church as one of the drama props. It was downstairs in the basement. I told her I'd take the chance and get it for her during a weekday morning. That would offer the least chance of running into Jo Ellen.

I called Kristy to let her know what had happened at the meeting. She was hesitant to return to the church for the Saturday service or the outreach that Sunday in San Diego. The news about our confrontation left her feeling torn and upset. She felt that helping the ministry was part of her calling. She was conflicted about distancing herself from it or the friends she had gotten to know.

Yet Kristy knew she had to decide, because I could no longer be connected with Shekinah. I could not return to the Fellowship and be welcomed at this point. Jo Ellen would make sure I would be ostracized or even banned in order to keep me away from Brant. Kristy was in love with me, and her loyalties were being tested. It was confusing for her.

I told Kristy I understood, and I would support her, whatever she decided. There was a brief silence, a heartfelt connection, then we ended the call.

Meanwhile Elaine and I were both exhausted. We rested part of the day, and I stayed one more night. For now, we'd played our hand. All we could do was wait.

CHAPTER 17:

THE AFTERMATH

The following week, I called Eric. By then he knew about our meeting at Brant's apartment. I told him I hoped our discussion would be helpful for Brant. Eric agreed but said little more than that. The conversation was brief but meaningful. I asked him about going into the Fox Theater to get Elaine's rocking chair.

"You might possibly be stopped and not welcomed," he said. "Your best chance is to go in the morning. The higher-ups will not be there."

I chose a Saturday morning to go into the theater, hoping the backstage door was unlocked. I lucked out – it was open. I entered the building and started to go downstairs when Jim R. saw me. He was doing his usual cleaning.

He gave me a sideways look as if he wondered why I was there. I don't know what he'd been told about me. I just wanted to go in, get the chair, and out of there as fast as I could. I told Jim I'd talked to Eric about picking up a drama prop that was Elaine's. Jim R said it should be all right.

I went right downstairs and he followed me, watching me. I located the prop while glancing at the many props I'd built. I felt a tug of longing and said goodbye to them all under my breath. It was my first real dawning that I was leaving Shekinah for good. A pageant of performances flashed in front of my eyes, years of comradeship and spiritual awakening. It had been a rich period of my life, but clearly it was time to move on. It seemed God now had another plan for me.

Jim R helped me get the rocking chair out of the room. I carried it up the narrow staircase and put it down on the stage floor. I walked out to the dimly lit stage, looking out to the auditorium. Jim R was in the wings, watching me. I paused for a moment to reminisce about everything that had taken place over the last several years. I gave my goodbyes again for the last time.

Looking out from the stage, I felt deeply sad. I did not know what would take place next in my phase of life. I told Jim R goodbye. He slammed the heavy metal backstage door behind me for the last time. I picked up the rocking chair and carried it back to my car down the narrow alleyway.

Kristy was still contemplating her decision, whether to leave or stay with the ministry. She went to one last Saturday service to sing in the choir. Everything was fine as usual that evening, but she felt uneasy throughout the service. She was afraid she would be approached by Jo Ellen. Kristy was sure Jo Ellen was going to question her about her involvement with me. She was afraid Jo Ellen would force her to make a choice between staying with the ministry and seeing me, thinking I was a bad influence. But Kristy's fears were unfounded, and she felt relieved there were no issues during that service.

The next day, Sunday, there was an outreach service in Escondido. Kristy had already made the decision to go ahead and sing in the choir. She got a ride from the theater in Long Beach and took the church bus that took the choir and wanted to be part of the group one more time since it was always fun to be among her church friends that she sang with. She felt fulfilled to be part of the ministry and a real sense of purpose.

After the bus arrived in Escondido, the choir went into the church to go warm up and review the songs to be sung that evening. A woman named Shirley approached Kristy during the rehearsal. Shirley was one of Jo Ellen's assistants, and she also was in the choir. "Do you know anything about a letter that Jud gave to Brant?" she asked.

Kristy was stung but played coy. "No, I don't know anything about that."

"Jo Ellen wants to talk to you. She said you have a choice to make."

"What kind of a choice?" Kristy started to feel queasy.

"You're going to have to decide if you want to stay in the choir and ministry," Shirley said. "Jo Ellen told me if you want to stay, you will have to stop seeing Jud."

Kristy was scared. Not only was a religious authority pressuring her about her personal life, Kristy was hearing about it second hand. As it was, Kristy did not want to have anything to do with Jo Ellen. She already had a run in with Jo Ellen over her dismissal from the Word of Knowledge group.

Kristy felt stuck and hurt inside. She had taken the ministry bus to the outreach, and now she had no other way to get home. She felt panic creeping in. Kristy knew right then she had to make a choice between her love for me and the ministry.

This was not a good situation, and now with the choir's performance still ahead of her that evening, Kristy was cornered. She was sure to run into Jo Ellen if she wasn't careful. She waited for the opportunity to leave the auditorium and went outside to avoid another confrontation with Jo Ellen. She waited until the service started and then slipped back into the choir when it came time to sing.

Her chance came soon enough. When the choir made the transition during the service, some of the members left to help in the healing service. Kristy slipped outside and climbed onto the bus. As she sat down in the back, she saw Jo Ellen coming out of the building right toward the bus. Kristy ducked down into her seat. She heard Jo Ellen step into the bus for a quick look and then leave. Kristy sat there in silence, wanting to leave and wondering if she could get home without any further confrontation.

A short time later the bus driver came onto the bus and saw Kristy. Her face was tense, and she was fighting back tears. The driver asked her what was wrong. Kristy told him she was avoiding Jo Ellen and she needed to get home. He was confused and didn't understand what she was talking about. Still he was kind, and he let her know he would not say anything to Jo Ellen or anyone else.

Kristy waited there on the bus for the rest of the evening, avoiding Shirley and Jo Ellen. The bus got back to the Fox Theater in Long Beach. Kristy trudged to her car, knowing that would be the last time she ever went to the ministry or the theater again.

Kristy called me the next day and filled me in about what had happened. It was a hard conversation to have with her. She was hurt since she knew she could not return to the ministry she loved. For my part, it was hard to hear confirmation that I'd been pushed out. It hurt to see that Kristy was suffering because of it.

Now a new life was to begin for Kristy and me. We could not go back. We could only move forward. If Brant followed through and met with Ken, things would look very different. As it was, it looked like the dye was cast. We could only wait and see.

Don't Look Back

I had some vacation time saved up at my job. I decided to take a couple weeks to help Kelly and his young family move cross country. We drove in a truck loaded with their household goods, and we stayed in hotels as we made our way to their new home in Georgia.

Our drive was fairly uneventful except for one nerve wracking incident at the beginning of our trip when we almost got stuck on a country road. We were towing Kelly's car with the truck, and we had trouble turning around for a few tense moments as we were trying to get back onto the highway. We got stuck on a narrow stretch of road, misjudging the length of the truck with the car behind it. With a ditch on one side of the road and a hill on the other, there was nowhere to navigate.

We ended up disconnecting the towing trailer from the truck, maneuvering each vehicle separately and blocking traffic all the while. A local person ended up helping us. In the end, we managed to pull the truck forward and make the turnaround without damaging either vehicle. It was touch and go, but we put our heads together and got through it. The incident served as a reminder of the rapport between Kelly and me, and I was glad to have him as my brother in Christ.

Along the rest of the trip, I filled Kelly in on our efforts to call Brant on his actions. I told him how Elaine and I had met with Brant, how Jo Ellen showed up in the middle of our meeting unannounced, and how difficult that confrontation had been. I filled him in on the rest of the issues and incidents. I also told Kelly about the letter having to go out to the congregation if things didn't change.

He listened attentively, commenting at each new point and asking questions. Kelly was astounded by the whole story and completely supportive. It was a relief to have someone to confide in about it and to get a few things off my chest. Our conversation was lively, and before I knew it, we were rolling across the George state line.

Once in Georgia, Lilly greeted us there with the baby. I met their new pastor, and I attended a couple of meetings that they held in the basement of their home. It was a new start for them, and Kelly looked really happy.

Kelly was hoping for a fresh start with a new ministry. Though the camaraderie was there between us, for my part the feeling was merely about friendship. I believe he felt the same. Kelly and Lilly got a new break – just what they were looking for when they left the Long Beach area of Southern California.

I was happy for them, and it was good to see them start a family. It forced me to turn my thoughts to my own future. In a sense, it gave me permission to pursue a new direction and find my own happiness. The trip had been good for me in that sense.

Soon it was time for me to fly back to California. When I got to the airport terminal, we hugged each other and said goodbye. "Don't look back," Kelly told me. I knew it would be different after that for him with his young family. I also felt I had grown and could find satisfaction with my own path.

When I got home, I continued to work at my job as a stock clerk, hoping for a change myself. The direction for Kristy and me was unclear. We were both unsure if we were going to be involved with another church or ministry. We knew that we would continue to minister someplace... but where?

I talked about going back to school with Kristy, but I did not know how to go about it yet. I had to work, and I was making just enough to support myself. Clearly change was in the wind, but I didn't know what direction it was going to blow. A few days later, Kristy called me after work and suggested that I move in with her at her parents' place. That way I could go to school at the community college up their street and get another job close by. As an alternative, I could work for her uncle, who was a contractor. All of this meant I could save up some money.

I thought about it, but I was hesitant. The dynamics of her family life were a bit strained, and the place was a mess. Her parents had a small three-bedroom house with one bathroom. There would be sacrifices. Still, the offer had a certain appeal.

Kristy's mother told me as long as I paid for my own food there was no reason to pay anything towards rent. Her father didn't seem to have an opinion one way or another. Kristy managed to convince me that this would be a way I could go to school. Besides the financial benefits, it would give us a way to be together more.

After a lot of deliberation, we decided to go ahead with the plan. I was to store most of my things in Kristy's parents' garage, and I would have my bedroom. Our relationship was chaste.

Initially I stayed on at my job as a stock clerk in Long Beach for a month. In the meantime, I worked it out with Kristy's uncle to work as an apprentice as a roofer. The job only lasted a few weeks since the weather was changing, and the winter rains were coming. Just as I started to settle in, the work was cut short. There were no roofing jobs in wintertime, even in Southern California.

Kristy told me about a government work program called the Comprehensive Employment & Training Act (CETA). I looked into it and discovered a six-month program that was closest to us in San Pedro. Its focused building basic clerical skills to get you into the work force and you got paid while you remained in the program. I signed up and was building my skills in no time. I really enjoyed going every day, knowing I was going to have a better job shortly. My new office skills would open doors for me – not to mention that they'd keep me out of the elements and off of roofs.

Things were starting to look up. Despite my holding pattern, waiting to hear about Brant, for the first time in months I felt like I could let my guard down. A short time later, I was in for a surprise. We all were.

Wait and See

A month after we met with Brant, he was interviewed on a weekly TV program called "Two on the Town." The moderator was a young reporter named Connie Chung, who later became quite famous as a journalist. At the time, she was around Brant's age and, like Brant, she was pretty talented and compelling.

The interview was done at the Fox Theater. The news program featured clips of Brant preaching at a Saturday service while Connie Chung spoke over the edited footage. She said Brant lived with his parents and almost looked too young to shave. She also commented that Brant looked like a young Donny Osmond, and she saw the miracle service as a well-oiled performance.

After the service she did a one-on-one interview in the boardroom upstairs where Brant had his office. During the interview, Brant was seated in front of large five-foot picture of Kathryn Kuhlman that hung on the wall.

Ms. Chung never referenced the picture behind Brant or asked who that was. It seemed strange she would not know who Kathryn Kuhlman was, especially because of the similarities between Kathryn and Brant – both in terms of their respective characters and their ministries. The connection was strikingly clear to anyone familiar with our religious sect.

But Connie Chung said nothing about it in the interview. She also said nothing during the interview to give credit to others in the ministry. It was the young people who provided the bulk of the labor for the ministry and supported Brant, making it possible for him to be in the spotlight as a minister. Connie Chung glossed over the fact the ministry was only possible because of the contributions of the team.

Despite these omissions, many saw the interview favorably and said it promoted the ministry. Still, many others did not think so. They believed Brant was stealing their thunder, and he came off as unappreciative. It was one more incident that divided Brant from the members of church.

A few weeks after we met with Brant, Ken called Elaine to follow up. By now, it was October 1978. I overheard their conversation. Ken was taking Brant's position, accepting his excuses and justifications for his behavior.

Ken went on to ask Elaine about our background with the ministry and question our motives. He appeared suspicious of us, when in reality we had come to Ken for help to improve the situation. After speaking with Brant, this was lost on Ken and he believed our report was not actually true. This left Elaine and me in an awkward position.

We wrote to Ken expressing our concerns and recapped the situation to date. This prompted a flurry of phone calls between Ken and Elaine, but we made little progress with our mission. It was only after a number of weeks went by that Ken began to realize our report to him had merit. Brant was not showing any signs of following through with Ken. Brant kept giving him excuses to reschedule the meetings he had originally agreed to, and he did little or nothing to cooperate with our efforts.

In January of 1979, Ken checked in with Elaine again about our position. He told her that Brant had ample time to respond, but he'd consistently put Ken off. While he didn't condone Brant's actions, he was hesitant to take any action that might be divisive for the congregation. Nonetheless, he wrote to Brant in early February. It was one final shot across the bow.

Mr. Brant Baker

Shekinah Fellowship

Long Beach, California 90811

2 February 1979

Dear Brant,

We receive material from your group from time to time to publicize the meetings coming up. I have to let you know that we cannot in good conscience before the Lord give out any of the material or recommend your work to the Body.

When we got together, I made it pretty clear that I felt there were some major problems in the ministry, and especially in your life. I accepted your explanation about many things and was looking forward to continuing in fellowship so that other areas could be helped. But you then broke the first and second scheduled meetings, indicating to me you actually had no interest in dealing with what I consider to be major problems.

We'll continue to pray for you, will always love you, but just want you to know that because of what I consider to be major unresolved problems, we cannot let our people attend your services.

Agape,

Ken G.

Ken also encouraged us to pray for guidance and take whatever action we felt guided to take. He wrote a letter to us to memorialize his perspective.

After receiving Ken's final decision and his view of the situation, we respected what he had to say.

It had further become clear to us by now that Brant was not going to go any further meeting with Ken since Ken went ahead and put the ball of the final decision back into our court. We followed Ken's suggestion, and we both continued to pray for help and guidance. Do we bow out and walk away and say nothing further and just bare the knowledge and pain in silence? Or do we dare take the next step to go forward?

It became clear to me we needed to go forward. We felt more strongly than ever that we had to be the ones to act. Because of this, I told Elaine I felt it was time to follow through and take things to the next level. It was time to pursue the measures outlined in Mathew 18. She and I agreed to circulate the information in the letter that we had given to Brant back in September. We had to take it to the congregation.

In forming the letter to send out to the ministry, Kristy and I got a mailing list from the choir director Brigid. We were planning to use the list to send out our wedding announcement, and this served as a convenient excuse to gathering the list of names. Elaine and I compiled a list of ministers involved with Shekinah, so we could send letters to them as well.

Compiling these lists and preparing the letter was a scary thing for us to do. We did not know if this would help Brant get the message to help himself. Only time would tell. This was such a hard thing to do. We were two of Brant's friends, once part of his privileged inner circle, but we were compelled to do this out of love and concern. Elaine and I knew we had to follow through with what we started. We couldn't ignore the situation and just walk away. It was truly an intervention.

Once the deed was done, many of the friends we had acquired through the years would distance themselves from us, and we would become outsiders. This was the direction we felt was required. We were guided by counsel from scripture and by elders we respected in the ministry.

We drafted the letters and sent them out on February 20, 1979. We felt both relieved and petrified at the same time. It seemed our hearts pounded relentlessly until at last we got a response. It came from an unexpected place.

Our Meeting with Chuck Smith

Elaine and I spent a day putting the letters together over a hundred copies once we gathered all the materials. Kathy B. had access to a folding machine at Disney Studio where she worked and had them folded for us.

Elaine and I compiled the addresses that we got hold of. Elaine got most of her list from Kathy since Kathy had her personal address list when she worked for the ministry. I got the choir list from Brigit, telling her I was going to use it to send out wedding invitations. I felt guilty about that but felt justified – what I told her was true. I simply omitted part of the story.

We compared our lists and selected those we felt would be key people. We sent the letters to key members of the ministry, past members, choir and ministers of the various outreaches that the ministry traveled to. We were nervously excited, and we discussed what the outcome might be. Now we just waited for any backlash in the form of phone calls or letters that might possibly come in.

Elaine, Kristy and I had already felt withdrawn from the ministry during the course of the past several months since our meeting with Brant. At the time, we did not realize what kind of effect the situation was having on us.

We were experiencing some kind of post-traumatic stress from a highly toxic situation. We didn't even know what the word was for with what we were experiencing. We just ignored the signs, too busy trying to find a new life for ourselves. The ministry was the only life we knew, starting in our late teens and early twenties. Now we had burned our bridges, and it felt like we had no way home. Sending the letters out would be our way to help others and release us from our burdens as well.

We wondered just what the ripple effect would be on the emotions among the ministry. What would their reaction be? Would people just ignore the letter or see it as an attack from Satan? Would they be shocked that we dared attack God's anointed one? Would they think we were only trying to cause discord among the congregation, trying to end God's work?

Since we'd never experienced anything like this before, all we could do was wait for the results. We tried to go on with our lives as normally as possible, coping with the waves of emotion that buffeted us.

There was silence at first, then different reports started coming in from various sources. Kristy gave me a report from a mutual friend of ours that Kevin was outraged and possibly seeking revenge. He felt this was an attack from Satan. Another report said Brant spoke to the choir, informing them that he had spoken to Ken G. and that Chuck Smith knew about the teachings of the ministry and that they met with them on the issues.

Soon a rumor circulated that I'd met with Brant, Ken and Chuck to discuss the situation. It was an obvious attempt to cover up the truth and try to patch over the allegations of the letter and issues.

Fearing a possible counterattack from Kevin, I decided to call Chuck Smith at home. Calling him directly was like calling father Abraham – he had given birth to so many Calvary Chapel churches, and he was at the root of Shekinah. Chuck was sometimes known as Big Daddy or, as we used to call him, Papa Chuck.

Kristy was with me when I called him in the early morning. To my surprise, he answered the phone right away.

I introduced myself, anxious and talking fast. To refresh his memory, I mentioned I was the friend of Sue O., who lived next door to him. I told him that I used to live in his neighborhood a number of years before with my parents.

Chuck said he remembered me, and I started to loosen up. I continued talking, telling him about my relationship with Brant and the ministry. I told him about the meeting we'd had with Ken. I said it was my understanding that he and Ken had already talked about the letter Elaine and I sent out.

Chuck asked if we could meet in his office that morning. He wanted to talk over the situation with Elaine and me to clear things up. We agreed on a time, and I hung up the phone. I was shaking inside, perspiring.

I called Elaine at her North Hollywood home right away. My call woke her up since she worked the night shift. I briefed her about my call to Chuck Smith and told her that he wanted to see us that morning. She agreed to meet me in Costa Mesa at Calvary Chapel. Kristy wanted to come with me, and she quickly got ready. We made the drive from Wilmington to Costa Mesa in a daze, my thoughts swirling. I didn't know what to expect and stayed quiet.

Kristy and I found Elaine waiting in the reception area of Chuck's office. He had not arrived yet. One of the receptionists was a young woman we knew named Carol B. She was involved with the Shekinah Singers as well as being part of Chuck's ministry.

While we waited, Carol B mentioned to Elaine that she got wind of the letters we sent out about Brant. Carol B was not in a position to talk about it because of her role at Calvary Chapel and her involvement with Brant's ministry. She had to remain neutral about the ministry, but her tone clearly showed concern.

Chuck soon arrived, and we were ushered into his office. He asked Carol B to get Ken on the phone to see if we could conference him in on the speaker phone. Chuck spent several minutes quietly reviewing all the letters at the center of this controversy. Then Carol B broke the silence, calling Chuck on the intercom. Apparently, some journalist had misrepresented Chuck's religious message, and there was some need for clarification.

"I never told him I was a hell-fire preacher. I don't know where he got that idea."

Chuck gave us a wink and a confident smirk, almost laughing. He hung up the phone and continued to read one of the letters, asking us a few short questions as he read. Elaine and I responded as briefly as possible, respecting his need for focus. Once he got done reading, he opened the conversation with some further questions.

Chuck wanted to review our roles and our involvement with the ministry. He wanted perspective on what was taking place, including the size of the congregation and other details. I responded with answers about the meetings and the size of the crowds that showed up. Then I gave him a brief history of my involvement with the ministry and serving Brant.

Elaine offered more answers to Chuck's questions, particularly about our interactions with Ken and our meeting with Brant at his home. We told Chuck how the Baker family had taken over the ministry and Jo Ellen's role in leading that effort. She was pushing Kevin to assume leadership of Shekinah and start conducting the healing services as well.

Chuck's response was unexpectedly emotional. It was the first time he deviated from his calm, collected state. "Kevin Baker!" he spat, the high pitch of his voice projecting his surprise. He shook his head, stunned for the moment.

Chuck looked over at Kristy, seeming to notice her for the first time. "What's your part in all this?"

"I'm in the choir, and I volunteer at the church," she responded in a soft voice, nervous and demure. "I am engaged to this man, and I'm here for support."

Chuck smiled then paused. He called Carol B on the intercom again to see if she had reached Ken. She told him there was no response. It looked like our meeting was winding down without input from our ally.

"How do you feel about the church now?" Chuck asked. "Has this made your faith in Christ waiver any?" He polled us one by one. We each responded with confidence that our faith was unshaken.

Chuck went on to say that an experience like this generally makes a person bitter, wanting to leave the Lord and anything to do with church.

We acknowledged what he said and but didn't change our answers. For my part, I was clear that this situation came about because of the choices of a few individuals – not because of any failings of the Lord. I only wanted to set the course straight again. At the time, we didn't understand the weight of our response or the sensitivity towards other Christian ministries and denominations.

Chuck closed our meeting in prayer, and we left his office. Elaine, Kristy and I walked out to the parking lot and huddled. After talking briefly talked about what had happened in the meeting, we all felt a bit let down. At least the great Chuck Smith was in the know now and he would be in contact with Ken eventually. We would all have to wait until then.

One Pastor Replies

After our meeting with Chuck, we discovered we sent out our letters to the ministers with the wrong return address. At the start, we didn't know what kind of responses we would get from them, if any at all. Now it looked hopeless.

It turned out that we did get one response. That letter came from Vernon G., a third-generation minister who was the head pastor of a church in San Marcos, California. He offered his full support of Brant.

I later found out this was the same man who was the father of Marjoe G., a child prodigy in the service of God. Marjoe's name was contrived by his parents as an amalgam of "Mary & Joseph." However, he was not as revered by his parents as his name would suggest. They alternately exulted him and exploited him as a child.

In the late 1940s through early '50s, Marjoe acquired some claim within the Pentecostal circle. At the age of three, apparently Marjoe saw a vision from God when he was taking a bath. His parents disciplined him for his claims until he denied what he had seen. They did this by dunking his head underwater in the bathtub rather than beating him because they did not want to leave any marks his body. Later, the three-year-old Marjoe stood by his claims.

Soon after that, the parents had a change of heart. They groomed their son to be a child Evangelist. Marjoe quickly became known as the "world's youngest ordained minister" at the age of four. He rose to stardom after a crew from Paramount Studios filmed Marjoe performing a wedding ceremony. The documentary was a sensation, and Marjoe's career as a Pentecostal preacher was sealed.

Even as a small child, Marjoe was able to preach the Gospel from memory and perform faith healings. His parents traveled with him throughout the United States, holding revival meetings wherever they went. They taught him to use dramatic gestures and movements to win over the congregation and loosen their wallets. He promised to heal the sick with holy objects that members of the congregation could buy at revival meetings.

By the time he was sixteen, Marjoe was disillusioned with his parents and his faith. His father apparently abandoned the family with Marjoe's earnings, more than a million dollars. This was a low point for Marjoe and his mother, and he quit preaching.

The break didn't last long, though, and in time he went back to the ministry. It was the only way he knew to make a decent living. He would work for half the year and raise enough money from donations to live on, traveling the rest of the time.

Marjoe felt guilty about his dual life, and he decided that if he went into show business, he could make an honest living as an actor or singer. This decision led to a connection with a documentary crew who wanted to follow him around with a camera during his sermons. Marjoe agreed, and the resulting film "Marjoe" won the Academy Award for Best Documentary in 1972.

I saw this movie in the theater with my friend Sue when I was in high school. It featured revealing backstage interviews with Marjoe and other ministers, showing how he deceived people on his tours. When I saw this movie, I did not realize at the time that it was a prelude of what was going to take place in my own life over the next several years.

Even though Marjoe was estranged from his father, eventually they reconnected. By then, Vernon had a church of his own in Escondido. Like Billy Adams, Pastor Vernon came from the Foursquare background under the ministry of Aimee Semple McPherson. But then he had seen the error of his ways – fleecing the flock of God in his younger days – and preached with sincerity. Vernon apparently had some regrets about the way he raised his son. He had been a young zealous father, grooming his son into a child Evangelist while making a profitable living off of his star power. But there are some things money can't buy.

By the time the Shekinah outreach services came to Vernon's church, he was already an admirer of Brant's ministry, feeling Brant was genuine. Maybe Brant's showmanship reminded Vernon of his own son Marjoe. It seemed Vernon's way of making up for his past was to promote Shekinah ministry.

The response Elaine and I got from the pastor was a scathing letter defending Brant's ministry. I don't know his motive, but I can't help thinking he knew about what often goes on behind the scenes of a ministry like Shekinah. Vernon defended Brant's flamboyant style and unilateral leadership decisions. He said nothing of Brant's unloving actions toward those who tried hardest to support him.

I think Vernon's letter was intended to discredit us, rebuke us, and mitigate any more damage to ministries of this nature. He sent a copy to Brant and closed with a condescending promise to pray for us. Elaine and I had little hope that anything about Shekinah was going to change. The ability to turn Shekinah around had been taken out of our hands. It was time to move on.

CHAPTER 18:

MARRIAGE AND FAMILY

Kristy and I had remained in touch with Mike., the previous minister of Shekinah Christian Center. He had started a small Calvary Chapel in San Pedro, and he invited us to come. Besides the Calvary Chapel, Mike and his wife Judy were also working and living at a youth hostel in San Pedro. Kristy and I did visit them a few times, and we also babysat their two children. It was great to have this connection to the earlier days of Shekinah and seeing them gave us hope.

Since Mike was involved with the ministry, we told him a little about what I had been planning to do to help Brant. Mike's response was that the Baker family had a lot of problems to work out. Mike was concerned for Brant, even though he himself had been fired from that ministry.

Kristy and I were clear that we wanted to get married, but it would have to wait until a later date. I was thinking of going to school and not really clear on what direction I was going to take.

After I had lived for a few months with Kristy and her folks, things took a sudden turn that practically threw us together. Kristy's mom decided to take in foster children, and she needed the extra bedroom. She was already licensed; she wanted to help the children and needed the money. She insisted that Kristy and I share the same bedroom. It left us both feeling awkward.

My grandfather's antique couch was in one corner of the bedroom, and Kristy decided to sleep on that. We did manage to avoid sexual contact, and up to this point we rarely even held hands. We wanted to avoid sexual temptation and preserve our virginity. We laughed about our situation, wondering if anyone would believe us.

Kristy and I were both feeling kind of lost since we left the Brant Baker Ministry, trying to figure out what we were going to do next. We wanted goals and direction, someone to guide us on our spiritual journey and in life. We talked to Mike and Judy about our situation to get their perspective.

What Mike suggested surprised us both. He suggested that, since we were living under the same roof at Kristy's house, we should not to wait to get married. We should just go ahead and do it now and enjoy the benefits of marriage.

Mike's words stunned me. I thought he would tell me I was living in sin and needed to move out. Instead he gave me encouragement to move into the next phase of life. Up to this point, all of my sexual and romantic experiences involved tremendous guilt and shame. Now here was a man of the cloth encouraging me to embrace the totality of my love for Kristy and become her husband. A tremendous weight was lifted from my heart.

Kristy and I looked at each other, and instantly we had the same epiphany. We realized we had no reason not to get married now. All the obstacles vanished before us and suddenly we knew it was meant to be. Immediately we started to make plans to be joined in holy matrimony. It was the brightest spot in our lives up to that point. Nothing compared with the joy we felt, as if the floodgates of happiness had finally opened for us both.

Our Two Weddings

We set the date for April 19. We planned to have a private ceremony at the San Pedro Youth Hostel where Mike and Judy lived and worked. Then we were going to have a public ceremony in June. Mike would perform the ceremony.

We had very little money, and I could only give Kristy an inexpensive costume ring to wear temporarily. We picked it out together at Ports O' Call Village in San Pedro, a charming waterside tourist trap with shops and seafood dining. The trip there gave us a chance to be alone and offered a break in the whirlwind of events around planning our wedding.

Slowly but surely, the details came together. We got our blood tests and marriage license at Long Beach City Hall. Soon the wedding party was decided on. Elaine offered to be my "best man," and Judy was Kristy's bridesmaid. Kristy's girlfriend Betty found a pretty wedding dress for Kristy to wear and dropped it off.

Kristy and I discussed the issue of children, and we both agreed that we weren't yet ready to bring a child into the world. This made it essential to practice birth control. I was embarrassed when I first bought prophylactics at a drug store to use on our wedding night. I use the word "prophylactic" because that was the word used in the Christian sex book I was reading. I barely knew how to pronounce the word, and I did not realize that "condom" and "prophylactic" were the same thing.

When I went to the drug store, I asked the pharmacist where the prophylactics were. He pointed to them behind the counter, and I was confused because I saw the word "condom" on the package. He asked what size I needed. I didn't know, so I asked for the regular size. He gave me a box and I asked him how to use them. He looked at me puzzled.

I hid my embarrassment. "They must come with instructions," I said. He just smiled. Then I asked for a tube of lubricant. He put the products in a brown paper bag for me. I paid him and left, wondering if I could ever go into that store again.

More details came into focus as we got nearer to our wedding date. We planned to drive away in my 1966 Mustang, but it broke down the day before our wedding. Mike loaned us his camper van to use. It didn't have quite the same panache as an American muscle car, but it beat walking. Elaine picked us up in her car on the big day to take us to Mike and Judy's for the ceremony.

The night before or ceremony, Kristy and I had a startling spiritual experience. Kristy was asleep on the couch in my room, and I was sleeping in the bed. I had a nightmare that some kind of an alien creature was attacking me, and I felt myself choking. I remember calling, "Jesus!"

"Jud," she called in a hushed voice. I woke up. "Don't you see that?" she said.

"See what?" I was groggy, still waking up.

She saw a transparent figure standing over my bed. He had long white hair and a beard, and he wore a long white robe with a hood. He was leaning over me, rubbing my chest, comforting me.

"You didn't see it?" She explained what she saw. At first, she thought it was Jesus but then realized it was some other spirit, perhaps a priest. She said she could see him very clearly. I felt a comforting presence but saw nothing. We took this apparition as some kind of sign.

The following morning while getting ready for our ceremony, Kristy's folks gave us a brown paper shopping bag that held a bottle of apple cider vinegar, a douche bag and a greeting card. The receipt was still in in the bag. This, along with a pair of wine glasses, was their wedding gift to us.

Kristy looked at the contents of the bag and blushed. I laughed and didn't really know how to take it, while her parents just smiled. Her father gave us some last-minute advice about marriage, saying, "Things don't always work out the way you want them to."

"How strange," I thought but thanked him. I was sure they meant well, despite the embarrassingly personal nature of the gift. Kristy was dumbstruck. A moment later Elaine came to the door to pick us up, and we all heaved a sigh of relief.

Elaine did not tell us at first, but she could not bear the idea that Kristy and I did not have wedding bands. All through our engagement she wanted to surprise us with a gift, so she went on a hunt to find a pair of gold bands she could afford. After looking several places, she was getting frustrated, wondering if she would ever find a matched set in her price range. She checked one last jewelry shop, blurting out our story to the jeweler as she browsed through the glass cases.

The jeweler was impressed by Elaine's narrative. "Wait here," he told her, and he went into the back room. A moment later he brought out a pair of plain gold bands that another couple had just returned to the shop. A couple had decided to get rings that were a little more ornate, leaving this pair for the jeweler to re-sell.

The jeweler practically gave the rings to Elaine, offering her a generous discount. Elaine was thrilled and bought them on the spot. She thanked him over and over as he wrapped them up.

When Elaine came by our home to pick us up, she told us the story and gave the rings to Kristy and me as a wedding gift. We were blown away, both by Elaine's thoughtfulness and the jeweler's generosity. It all came together so easily. We saw this as an important sign.

We had a short ceremony, with Elaine serving as a witness and my "best man." Judy stood next to Kristy as her maid of honor, holding a bouquet of flowers. Mike performed the ceremony as their kids watched from the living room.

Kristy and I exchanged vows and wedding rings. That's when I kissed Kristy for the first time. She was stunned, wriggling in my embrace. She started to push me away but surrendered to the moment. We both laughed.

After the ceremony, we signed our marriage license with the help of our witnesses. We all chatted excitedly, then Mike gave me the keys to his van. We went outside, and I carried Kristy to the door of the van. She tossed her bouquet into the air, and Judy caught it.

With what little money we had, we managed to plan a short honeymoon for a couple of days. We decided to drive toward San Clemente Beach. When we got there, we had discovered it was taken over by a rough crowd of bikers – not the best company for a newlywed Christian couple. We decided to head back to Costa Mesa for a couple of days where we could find a decent hotel room in our price range. We checked into the Vagabond Hotel.

Both Kristy and I were nervous about our wedding night. We'd had so little physical contact with each other before, and now we were facing the prospect of enjoying the most intimate kind of touch. But if things didn't go well, it could be a devastating start to our marriage.

We decided to relax and have a romantic time before we went out to dinner that evening. We started by reading a couple Christian books on marriage and sex. One book came with diagrams of the anatomy and flow chart, showing various sexual positions. The best advice we got from the books was to take it slow.

Here we were, two virgins before the Father, Son and Holy Ghost, giggling like young teenagers as we tried to figure out the charts. Now we had a license not just for foreplay but to go all the way. It was safe for Kristy not to get pregnant at this time. Just in case, I had those condoms I'd bought at the drug store a couple of weeks earlier.

My first attempt at making love to a woman would not get an Academy Award in romantic drama – maybe more of a comedy. We started to undress each other slowly, and we both felt lightheaded. I almost felt like passing out and had to sit down on the bed for a moment.

We took a bubble bath together to help relax, and we caressed each other. From there we got into the bed, continuing our foreplay. But every time I tried to use the condom; things would go flat. After several attempts, we decided to try again later, maybe after we got back from dinner.

At dinner we went over what had happened so far during our wedding day, laughing at our first attempts to make love. We talked about all the things we'd done and seen that day, and we were excited for the life ahead of us. We finished our meal then went back to our hotel and took a short nap.

One thing led to another, and we started to make love. Again, when I went to put on a condom, my member would go flat. Kristy just tore off the condom and away we went. It was rough, but we made a home run, officially consummating our marriage.

The following morning, I called my mother to let her know I eloped with Kristy. I told her we would be having a public ceremony in a couple months. She laughed, saying she thought Kristy and I were up to something. She was happy for us.

I told her I was no longer a virgin. She paused a beat. "Actually, all my children were immaculate conceptions." She laughed, and I blushed.

My mom told me she loved me and that she would call my father and let him know about our wedding. We hung up the phone.

That day, we went to a public wedding at Calvary Chapel in Costa mesa. The wedding was between my old music group my friends Ralph, an old roommate, and Meg, my friend since high school. Many of our former Shekinah associates would be there. We expected that it was going to be an awkward event since it had only been a few weeks since Elaine and I sent out the letters to the ministry.

When we returned back to Kristy's folks, we were both exhausted and not feeling well. Kristy's friend Betty gave us a surprise wedding shower with a number of her friends and some family members. Since this was a private affair it felt uncomfortable to celebrate it so publicly, but Kristy appreciated the effort from her friend.

The following week I returned to my job program, brushing up on some basic professional skills. Once I finished the course, I could take a test issued by Los Angeles County and get a job at a hospital as a medical biller. I was eyeing the UCLA Medical Center in Torrance.

Kristy considered taking some classes at the local community college, then she decided to enroll at a local beauty college. Eventually got her manicure license.

As Kristy and I worked to get into the rhythm in our new life together, we were planning our public wedding. At first it appeared her parents would choose a location for the ceremony with Kristy's input, and her folks were going to a venue and cover the cost for us. But Kristy's parents kept putting it off. Out of frustration, Kristy and I took the matter into our own hands.

The location was a park in Costa Mesa close to my middle sister's house. We set the date for June. The event would be far more formal than our simple secret ceremony, and it required a lot of planning. Because of our budget, we would have to count on the support and creativity of our friends and family. We hoped that others would be more reliable than Kristy's folks had been, as their sluggish response was a source of angst for us.

In fact, we wondered how many people we knew from the Shekinah ministry would respond to our wedding invitation. We knew some of them would be alienated because of the letters we sent out about Brant. Even for something as personal as our wedding day, Brant's influence still cast a shadow over us. It turned out that Kristy and I were shunned by some from the ministry, but others were glad to see us, and they brought with them a lot of love and joy.

Our wedding invitations were done like a short book with an old-fashioned picture of us on the front cover. Besides the wedding details, there was a short bio about each of us on the inside. My father provided the invitations as a wedding gift since he worked for a printing company. He also paid for postage, which was considerable because of the size of the invitations. It all turned out beautifully, and many of our guests commented on our creative invitations.

Others pitched in and helped us minimize the cost of the wedding. My mother provided the flowers and decorations to go with our chosen theme. A friend of ours from the ministry made a three-layer cake. It featured a delicate hand-blown glass centerpiece in a heart shape with doves and a cross in the middle. The food was potluck, and a number of our friends and family brought extravagant dishes for the reception.

Even our wedding attire came to us as gifts. Kristy's gown was a gift from a friend who had it made for her own wedding but never used it. I wore a white double-breasted jacket that Brant had given to me when I worked for him. We both felt chic and elegant.

A few friends from the ministry orchestra came with their instruments and provided the music. My friends Meg, Kathy and Inez were each scheduled to sing a solo backed by the orchestra. To complete the band, the musicians pushed an upright piano from my sister's house into the park.

They later told me that the sight of an upright piano rolling down the sidewalk made quite a stir in the neighborhood, and cars slowed down to rubberneck as they drove by. The crew could barely control the unwieldy thing, and it careened ahead of them more than once. It was the stuff of silent movies, something out of the Keystone Cops or Charlie Chaplin. Of all the antics that day, I'm sorry I missed this one.

The weather was beautiful – Southern California sunshine, and not too hot. Everywhere there was a feeling of joy, and laughter filled the park as we came together to celebrate.

Kristy's bridesmaids were her friend Betty and my middle sister. My old friend Brad was my best man, and not Elaine., although this time she did attend.

My parents and all my siblings showed up, with one exception. My older brother was living in Oregon then, and the trek was too far for him to attend. Many high school friends and lots of my relatives also came, some of them I had not seen in years. Kristy's folks and relatives also attended. We even had a number of onlookers who were passing through the park.

The moment arrived, and one by one, the wedding party walked down the aisle. First came the groomsmen and bridesmaids. I followed solemnly, taking in the weight of the moment and the beauty of the scene. Even after all we had been through, here we were, enjoying life's most coveted reward. My heart swelled as I turned to watch my bride approach.

There was a slight commotion behind the seated congregation, a tussle of elbows and a flurry from the skirt of Kristy's gown. Kristy and her father made it to the altar, in spite of him. Her dad hung back, thinking it was the wrong music cue for them, and she had to pull him down the aisle. Maybe he just wasn't ready to give away his little girl. Yet it seemed that no matter what the antics that day, everything always seemed to work out.

My beautiful bride stood next to me, and Mike reaffirmed our vows. Kristy the angel, was now my wife before God and the world. Even though we had shared our vows before, now I felt blessed and complete, and I knew I would never be alone again.

A moment later, the whole thing was done, and everyone was throwing rice on us. One of our ministry friends took our formal wedding pictures as we posed and mugged for the camera. Everyone enjoyed the food, an ample feast prepared by so many loving hands. Then Kristy and I sliced into the three-tiered cake, my hand on hers, wearing the rings that Elaine and the jeweler had gifted to us on that fateful day. Clearly it was all meant to be.

One Last Olive Branch

Kristy and I were just exhausted when everything was put away and it was all over. Then we got the flu. Truly we shared everything now.

In the weeks that followed, we sent out thank you cards with a letter. I was just learning how to use a word processor from my job training, and I used it to type up the letter.

I was just finishing up my training with CETA when we got married. Soon afterwards, I took the clerical test for the Los Angeles County, and I passed. It wasn't long before I got the job I had been eyeing, working as a medical biller for the UCLA Medical Center in Torrance. The work was routine, maybe a bit dull, but at least it provided a steady income.

Having a steady paycheck was more important than ever. Kristy was several months pregnant by now. Our initial fear of bringing a baby into the world gradually went away as our life together found its own natural stride. One thing led to another, and soon Kristy was carrying our first child.

Even before the wedding, Kristy and I realized we needed to attend church somewhere, especially now that she was expecting. We started to look for another congregation to join. We started to go to a Foursquare Church near Long Beach.

The pastor was Rich Buhler, and he had founded a radio ministry called "Talk from the Heart" on KBRT. It later became well known in the Southern California area.

Pastor Buhler was a jolly, heavy set guy who had a large young family of nine or ten children. He was kind enough to hear our story, listening patiently as we talked about the experience we had just come from. He knew a little about Brant and Billy Adams from those in the Foursquare Church who had attended one of Brant's outreach services. Though he said little to us about Brant, it was clear he was familiar with Brant's flamboyant style.

Pastor Buhler offered to send Kristy and me to a Basic Youth Conflicts seminar, thinking it would help us and give us some answers and closure with our recent experiences at Shekinah. Though we were married and starting a growing family, we were still quite young by any standard. We agreed to go.

We went to a seminar led by Bill Gothard, as Buhler suggested. That's where Kristy and I ran into Jim M, a former minister at Shekinah Christian Center. It was great to see a familiar face, and we took it as a good omen that we encountered Jim M there.

During a break, Jim M, Kristy and I discussed the contents of the seminar. We talked about religion's psychological effect on people and how attending church impacts our spiritual life. We agreed on the ways the teachings could be applied to our own lives, and how the information from the seminar could help Brant as well if he were exposed to it.

It was then I decided to attempt to contact Brant one more time. I was hoping we could make some kind of amends, but I was not going to ask to return to the ministry. I was influenced and encouraged by the seminar, and I wanted to clear up any hard feelings between Brant and us. Kristy and I wrote him a letter that we wanted to give him in person.

The ministry had left the Fox West Coast Theater several months before. They could no longer afford the rent, and the congregation was dwindling in size. When Kristy and I went to see Brant, the Saturday services were now being conducted at the Long Beach High School.

We parked outside the auditorium and saw our friend David W., who was in the orchestra. He said he would give our message and the letter directly to Brant.

David W was one of our inside sources of information about what was being said to the choir. A rumor had already circulated about Elaine and me after we delivered our letter to the ministry. In Jo Ellen's typical fashion, she and Brant shifted the blame off themselves and concocted a story that I'd had a breakdown – just like all the others who had been pushed out of the ministry. They said that Brant, Ken G. and I met over lunch and cleared things up, and I told them I was sorry for what I'd done. Supposedly soon afterwards I had a meltdown about what I had done to Brant, and they all came to see me in the hospital. Poor pitiful me.

Hearing this outrageous lie set me back on my heels. This fresh slight made it hard for me to go ahead with the meeting I'd hoped for. Still, I calmed myself and made the choice to put the past behind me. I hoped that Brant could do the same, especially since he still clung to the role of spiritual leader, dwindling though it was.

Prior to attempting to see Brant, I told Elaine what I was planning to do. I gave her a draft of the letter that I was going to give to him. She was concerned I was letting him off the hook, and she said it sounded like I was the one who needed to change. She gave me some solid tips on rewording the substance of my message. I made the changes she suggested before I attended the Saturday service to deliver the letter.

Kristy and I were waiting nervously in the car, and I was preparing what to say to Brant if he saw us. I was rehearsing myself for the awkwardness of a meeting with him, especially after hearing the lies he and his mother circulated about me. I decided I was just going to embrace him and bless him, and then leave.

David W came back to the car, squinting into the sun and stooping to look through my window. He said Brant did not want to see me since I hurt him so badly. Still I could come back to the ministry if I wanted to.

I was stung and relieved at the same time. This fresh cut confirmed that Brant had not changed his position, only ignored any constructive criticism. He did not want to deal with the problem, even though his dying congregation screamed that he must change. He and Jo Ellen fabricated a story that I was in a mental hospital and that we supposedly had talked things over. Now he refused to talk to me. In Typical Brant fashion, he wouldn't face me. He couldn't. I don't know why I thought it would be different when I tried to reconcile with him.

Kristy and I figured I'd done my part, and that's all that God cared about. I did follow up with another letter to Brant, Kevin and Jo Ellen. I told them I released any hard feelings toward them and blessed them. This was for my own health and peace of mind so that my conscience was clear.

Of course, it hurt when I did not get any response even to this, but his lack of response was clearly predictable. I realized it was over and had to live with the consequences.

Kristy and I were now focused on adjusting to married life with a baby on the way. There were better, happier places to invest my attention.

Experiencing the birth classes together and rehearsing all the Lamaze technique was new to us. When we first started our classes, we were amazed to see a large room of pregnant women. There must have been around a hundred women, all due about the same time as ours.

By November, our fist daughter was born. The moment finally came, and we went to the hospital after a couple false alarms. I remember it so clearly – we were watching "The Incredible Hulk" TV series when Kristy told me her water broke. At first, I wasn't sure if I should believe her. Soon it was very clear that it was time to go.

Witnessing the birth of my daughter was amazing. I watched in the mirror as I stood behind Kristy. I remember thinking, "This is it. It's really happening." I was in awe of the miracle of birth, and I was deeply moved to hear her first cry. Life had renewed itself.

The House Is Not Empty

During the pregnancy we were living next door to Kristy's folks. We thought it would be convenient to have them as neighbors, both for emotional support and to have a couple extra pairs of hands with our newborn child. We even painted a nursery room to get ready. After two months before Kristy gave birth, the owner died and had to move since the family wanted the property.

Kristy's childhood friend, Brenda, had approached us with a proposition. Her parents' house was directly across the street from us, and it was sitting empty. Her mother had passed away a few months earlier. They needed someone to occupy the house while they made long range plans. Brenda decided with her older sister for Kristy and me to move into her mother's old home.

The house had the same floor plan as all the other houses on that street. One of the rooms was being used for storage and so was the garage, and we did not have access to them. It didn't matter much to us, though. We were thankful to get a place.

When we brought our daughter home, we soon found out that the house was haunted. Several things started to happen. There were strange occurrences taking place that we couldn't explain.

The first things we noticed were sounds coming from the next room. Soon Kristy would hear dishes in the kitchen rattle in the cupboard while she was standing just a few feet away.

Other odd things happened too. For instance, there was a potted tree in the living room. Kristy saw it shake all by itself. The next day, the leaves fell off the tree and it died.

One-night Kristy and I felt something crawl into our bed, but neither one of us saw anything – it was incredibly spooky. Also, the back room where Brenda's parent's things were stored had a strange presence in there, and it felt very cold. The most unsettling thing was that we had the baby bassinet in our room, and Kristy felt a presence over the bassinet when our daughter was napping in it.

Each of these things by itself was spooky enough. When taken together, they told a dark tale of misery and a life unfinished. We discovered that Brenda's mother had committed suicide in the house by shooting herself. Part of her still remained, a residue of her spirit left in the house. In our rush to have our own place, we didn't even consider that the place was haunted. That item is not usually on a checklist of questions to ask when searching for a home.

We told Mike. about it, and he agreed to come over and pray with us. He brought his Bible and some anointing oil. We showed him the various parts of the house where the events were happening. He read some scripture and anointed them with oil.

Finally, we prayed in the kitchen area, and Mike rebuked the spirit in the name of Jesus. Immediately the lights from the garage went on and off, and we heard a crash out there. We all looked at each other and went to see what had happened, but nothing seemed out of place. We prayed again for the spirit to leave. We strained our ears but did not hear anything more. After that, we didn't have any further trouble.

We Move Downtown

We lived in the house less than two months when Brenda's oldest sister decided to sell it. The issues with the ghost were too much for the family, and the equity in the home was a factor too. It meant Kristy and I had to move once again.

We didn't have a car at this point, and we took the city bus everywhere. My Mustang had broken down and it was too expensive to fix, so we junked it. This made it hard for us to look for a new place to live, and it limited our options to rentals along the bus line.

We ended up moving into a fourplex in downtown Long Beach. It was easy for me to catch a bus into Torrance to go to work. The place was an older one-bedroom apartment with a bit of charm, and it was convenient for shopping. We made our home there for the time being.

Kristy and I would take long walks around downtown with our baby happily sleeping in the stroller. Every night we'd look at all the older homes and stores in the neighborhood.

The downtown area was in the process of being gentrified, and there were lots of old buildings being torn down to make way for a mall. We hated to see some of them go, but at the same time we were excited by the energy of the urban renewal going on around us. One time we ran into Claudia N downtown and she saw our baby. She was kind and we engaged in small talk though we did not talk about the ministry at all.

We started to go back to the Neighborhood Foursquare Church. It was easy to get to Rich Buhler's church by bus, and it was nice to see Pastor Adams and his wife again. We never really talked about the Shekinah ministry – it was a dead subject for us. While attending on Sunday mornings, I sang a few times as a soloist.

During this time, Kelly and Lilly moved back from Atlanta, Georgia. Lilly was pregnant with their second child, and Kelly stopped by to visit us. It was great to see Kelly after a few years but also a little strange under the circumstances. He was starting over again himself, undecided about what his next step was. When he learned how much we were struggling financially, he gave us some money as an offering. He felt inspired to do so, and we were in no position to turn him down. We appreciated it very much.

Kristy and I began thinking of moving out of the area. My brother Barry had just moved to the small town of Ashland, Oregon, and he told us it would be a good place to raise a family. Compared to Southern California, the cost of living was low, and it offered a more wholesome atmosphere. He also said he had a business opportunity that might work for us. He was vague about the details, and we left it at that.

The adventure of moving sounded exciting to Kristy and me. We saw it as a chance to get out of the area and make a fresh start. We brooded about it for some time, but one day turned into another, and the problem of moving became harder to embrace as time went on.

Soon, though, something happened that really gave us a push. There was a fire in our fourplex in the apartment right next door to us. This was no small kitchen fire – it was deliberately set, and someone died.

Kristy and I always heard arguing in that apartment and other signs of chaos. That night, the young lady who lived there took an overdose of drugs, and her boyfriend started the fire and left her lifeless body.

It all happened late at night while we were sleeping. Our apartment started getting hot. Our baby woke us up, coughing in her crib. Kristy got up to tend to her, and I went to the back porch to see what was going on. I saw smoke coming from the apartment next door.

I called the fire department right away. The landlord lived only a couple blocks from us, so I called him to let the fire department in before they broke the door down. I also pounded on the door downstairs from the apartment that was on fire to wake them and evacuate the apartment. I knew they had a baby as well. They heard me, and the family got out in time.

Once the fire was over, we collected ourselves and gave thanks that we were all alive and unharmed. After a few days, though, we were still shaken by the danger we had just faced and the trauma of death so close to home. This feeling was intensified when we saw part of the charcoal remains of the body in the bedroom on the mattress where the fire had started.

There was little structural damage, other than the hole burned in the floor. Mostly there was a lot of smoke damage and the smell left from the burning flesh. It was an ugly scene; a haunting wakeup call about the urban bedlam surrounding us.

A couple weeks after the fire, my older sister Meredith and her husband told us they planned to go to Hawaii for a couple weeks. They asked us to watch their home in Riverside and feed their horses while they were gone. I had some vacation time saved up for a couple weeks, so an extended trip about an hour out of town seemed like just the break we needed. We said yes.

During those two weeks, Kristy and I went to the Calvary Chapel in Riverside and saw Randy. and his wife Marla, former elders of Shekinah. It was encouraging to see Randy and Marla and remembered a few years earlier when we were all living in the Shekinah house together.

We ended up going out to lunch with them after church. They knew about the letter we sent out and that we had left Brant's ministry. They told us that when they first left the ministry, it was one of the hardest things they had to do. For them it was like going through a divorce – painful and ultimate. Somehow, knowing that they understood our difficulty made it more bearable. We parted with sweet sorrow, not knowing when we would see them again.

Leaving Long Beach

After we got back to our home in Long Beach, we finally made the decision to move to Ashland, Oregon. We did not know really what to expect, other than the fact that it was a small town. Compared to the city conditions we were living in, that was a good thing.

Regardless of the business opportunity my brother was offering, we made the decision to move based on faith. At the time, I did not realize what a good entry level job I had as a medical biller. I found out later it could have led to something greater if I stayed with it.

But we wanted to move, and I was not patient enough to work out the problems we were having in Long Beach. The seedy apartment building where we lived was typical of our neighborhood. The construction around us meant constant noise, and the streets were dirty. There was also a high crime factor that drove us out. It simply seemed like it was time for a complete change.

I knew I would miss the people from work, and I was touched when they gave me a going away party. We were making plans to move to Ashland because we felt that was where God wanted us to go. That must be our priority.

As the time drew near, Kristy called her friends one by one to say goodbye, feeling sad. She talked to Sister Edith from the ministry, and she gave us a blessing.

Sister Edith also told Kristy that she herself was from Oregon, and the Northwest was God's country – rich in natural beauty and a kindly climate. With an endorsement like that, we could only be encouraged.

My father gave me some money to help cover the expenses and rent a truck. I also cashed in my retirement account, deciding instead to use the little money I had from the City to buy us a car when we got to Oregon. The car would help in a number of ways, especially when it came time for me to look for work.

We started packing, leaving only a few things out until we were finally ready to go. The biggest factor was our baby. She needed lots of clean clothes, diapers, toys, bottles, a pacifier – a whole set of luggage all on her own. It's amazing how fast things accumulate when you have a child.

My father, mother and my nephew Steve came to help us load the truck the day before we left. It would be several years before I'd see them again. I choked back a few tears when we finally said goodbye. My parents both gave a special hug to their granddaughter, a mix of pride and disbelief clouding their eyes.

We spent the night with Kristy's grandfather, and left early the next morning under clear skies.

When moving day arrived, we both confessed to mixed feelings about our adventure. There was so much that remained uncertain. It was a new beginning for Kristy and me, a fresh chapter as a young married couple and new family. We still had so many lessons to learn. Another chapter in our journey was starting, closing the door behind us as we left the ministry, friends and relations. It truly was like a divorce, just the way Randy and Marla explained it to us.

As the road climbed up the mountains and we drove across the California border into Oregon, the impact of moving hit Kristy hard. She suddenly realized we really were leaving our family and friends hundreds of miles away, and she started to cry. Craggy peaks and black evergreens towered over us, seeming to cut us off from the only world we'd known. I comforted her as best I could. With one hand on the wheel and one arm around my weeping wife, I navigated the winding mountain road through the wilderness. It was a truly poignant moment.

Despite the uncertainty and the pain of parting with people we loved, our overriding feeling was excitement. We were finally taking our future into our own hands, and we were making our way to God's country where new opportunities awaited us.

CHAPTER 19:

GOD'S COUNTRY

Arriving in Ashland, Oregon was like taking a step back in time. The town had a population of only 10,000 at the time, and life seemed to move at a slower pace than any other place we had seen.

The center of town looked like a page from Charles Dickens' "A Christmas Carol", complete with Victorian lamp posts, gingerbread houses, and a fountain in the center of the village. The town was nestled against the base of the towering Siskiyou Mountains and situated near the floor of the green Rogue River Valley. The mighty Cascade Range rose to the east, snow-capped until early summer.

Besides all this natural beauty and inherent charm, Ashland offered us a dash of culture. It was home to a small college, which I later attended. There was also a Shakespearean theater with a regular season, attracting thousands of tourists during each year. Eventually I was involved with this theater as our family grew.

A California Visit

It was the winter of 1983 when we decided to scrape some money together and visit Southern California. Our family had another girl, Jamie, and Kristy pregnant with our third. It was exciting to go back after a few years to visit our family and friends. We stayed at my oldest sister's house with Meredith and her family while we went around to visit. We met up with some of our Shekinah Fellowship friends that were part of the music group I was in. Some were already having young families as well and in new careers that appeared to be happy and working out for them. They all went to Calvary Chapel in Costa Mesa and another went to an Assembly of God church.

We drove into Long Beach to go visit where we lived in the last apartment before we moved after the fire. We went by the location of the West Coast Fox Theater were the ministry was before they moved to a high school location. To our amazement some of the buildings were being torn down around it. The porn theaters, coffee shop, gift shop and the apartment in the back was gone. We parked the car and walked along the sidewalk with the strollers to look around the property.

Kristy and I got to visit with our friend Elaine. We were glad to see her after several years. She was still in the same job as a respiratory therapist while she was deeply involved in production work in TV and theater.

We talked about the changes in our lives and the directions we were taking. I mentioned that the Fox theater was still there but some of the buildings were gone. She shook her head and said, "It is only a matter of time. Someday we will read in the newspaper about the whole Baker family being dead."

She was entertained by our girls as she watched them play and interceded just before one of them knocked her Tiffany floor lamp over. She laughed and said, "You've got your hands full."

Once we visited California, we could clearly see our connection to Shekinah was truly over. Now, back in Ashland, it was time to reflect on the future and my career. It was a happy and sad moment.

Brant & Kevin's Last Breath

In 1985, my sophomore year of college, one day out of the blue, Kristy got a phone call from our friend Linda H. in Long Beach. Linda was the last volunteer secretary of the Shekinah ministry. She called Kristy to tell us the news – Brant was dying.

I was still in contact with Claudia off and on, and I called her to get some more detail. She and Eric already had left the ministry by then. Eric was in medical school at the time studying to be a doctor. She told me Brant had moved to Florida to get help for his medical condition. I asked if he had AIDS, and Claudia told me no. She said Eric had told her that Brant had complications from pneumonia.

Still not knowing much about AIDS myself, I knew enough to understand that HIV weakens the body to let the AIDS virus take over. Pneumonia was one of the symptoms. I felt she was still protecting Brant and could not accept the fact that he had contracted AIDS. Claudia said she would let me know if she found out anything more.

Shortly after the phone call to Claudia, Linda sent me a cassette recording of Brant. It came in a package from the Maude Amie Foundation. The ministry had changed its name again, this time after Brant's grandmother. The recording was his last message to his followers.

The message was a summary of his previous messages on following Jesus, giving your all, and on the forgiveness and mercy of God. Brant's voice sounded very weak, and Kristy and I were saddened to hear this. Within that week, Kristy got another phone call from Linda, this time telling us that Brant had passed away. The date was November 26, 1985.

That month, I called Linda myself to get further details about what happened to the ministry and Brant's illness. Linda was cool but polite. I found out that the Fox West Coast Theater in Long Beach had been condemned and was scheduled to be demolished. I thought this was incredibly symbolic. Once the ministry's books were closed, any leftover funds would go to Mother Teresa's foundation in India.

A week or two later, I received a letter in the mail from Claudia. There was no note, just a blank piece of paper with clip to an obituary from the Long Beach newspaper. It was Brant's.

My mind was numb. My heart sank. This is it. So sad. It's final. No large healing ministry to travel the world and no second coming of Jesus. What happened?

Perhaps Brant had been a product of his time as much as he was someone who helped shape the world around him. Just as his words fed the spiritual needs of a generation, his deeds belied his own troubled soul. His charisma led us by the thousands to the high places. His ego betrayed us, even as he betrayed himself. Yet Brant was not the only evangelist to fall from grace.

In 1987, another Baker family member passed away. Kevin Baker also died of AIDS like his brother Brant. Kevin had been more sexually reckless than Brant, especially when it came to his sexual activity with men.

Joe. was with Kevin in the hospital up until his death, along with JoEllen Baker and Pastor Adams. Joe showed compassion toward Kevin in his last hours and prayed with him. Kevin respected Joe for putting his gay lifestyle aside. Joe left his leadership position at the Metropolitan Community Church after a change in conviction. He returned to his Calvary Chapel roots and was working towards a pastoral degree in counseling and in another heterosexual relationship again.

I was told Kevin felt sorry about the many things he'd done, and he repented of his sins. I was angry and sad for him – angry that he got away with things as long as he did, sad that he lost his life so young. In some ways I felt envious that he was Brant's spoiled younger brother, escaping responsibilities because his mother was always bailing him out.

I don't know how much Kevin struggled with his sexual identity or railed against being gay in a Christian environment. I fought my own inner war, resisting my sexual temptations and straining to hold onto my morals as a Christian. I fought to uphold my responsibilities while I was in school, married, supporting a young family, and in the military. Everyone has his cross to bear.

It seemed that in some ways, Kevin and I were the same. We simply chose to respond to our urges differently. He died so young, what seemed to me at the time to be taking the easy way out. He got to be with his brother and grandmother on the other side.

I felt sad that he suffered from the virus, sad that he yearned to be in the spotlight while living in the shadow of his brother, the charismatic healing evangelist. Most of all I felt sad that so many of us at Shekinah Fellowship had worked together, shared good times and friendship, and our fellowship was taken away by Brant's selfishness and caprice. So many of us had been spurned without ceremony, cast out, never mentioned again, until finally there was no one left in the congregation.

Reflections

I shared the lives of all those people like a family working as a team for a bigger cause to serve others. Living in Ashland was a different group of people, passionate about their country and jobs, unlike the Brant B. ministry of the past. This was different.

Time had passed, and I had a variety of experiences I never could have imagined as a teenager living in Orange County. Reflecting on this was a recovery process, dealing with what I thought and viewed back then in my late teens.

It was not until several years after my involvement with the Shekinah ministry that I learned others were secretly dealing with their own sexual issues. Some went to counseling to get direction and came to their own personal conclusions.

Christian resources in the early 70's was slim when it came to deal with sexual or moral issues, especially when it came to LGBT issues from a Christian perspective. The mainstream evangelical Christian culture did not talk openly about gay issues at the time. Anyone would be secretly shunned if they mentioned the gay subject. We were all left alone to search for our own answers, find self-acceptance and closure, then move on. Few made it through the gauntlet unscathed.

Given the unsettling backgrounds that many of the youth of the ministry came from, we were impressionable. We followed the evangelical zeal of our youth to the point of obsession. The bulk of us were still in our late teens. We just wanted love and acceptance, and we could only get it from our Christian environment.

Many of us were seduced by the power we derived from spiritual leadership positions. We perceived our mission as a prestigious healing miracle ministry on a grandiose scale. It made us feel special as we got an adrenaline rush from all the highs and lows, doing our best to perform in the name of Christ.

What we didn't understand is that this kind of leadership is a responsibility that takes years of spiritual development, strength of character, depth of education, and plenty of life experience to develop. Some paid the price by taking their youth or health for granted. They either ended up becoming victims, or they died early.

I was caught up in the vision and thankful to be in a position of learning and training. However, the privilege came with a price. I learned what I thought was spirituality through my limited perception at the time. I lacked the maturity to fully understand my situation, and the positive role models around me were limited.

At the time, I did not question what my involvement with Shekinah was really doing to me. I didn't know enough to question the integrity of the leaders around me, even though as I witnessed their behavior, it did not feel right inside me. I was too naive at the time to realize we were just too young to handle the kind of responsibilities we were given. We were forced to make decisions to keep the ministry operating without knowing what the pressure was doing to us individually.

Elaine Comes Out

In 1991, I already had graduated, and our family moved to Washington state. My National Guard unit was called to active to support Desert Storm. We were temporary stationed at Fort Ord in the bay area of California. On a weekend leave I made a trip to Southern California, and I stayed with Kristy's grandparents. My old friend Elaine came to pick me up at their home, and Elaine and I spent a morning together. Our plan was to swing by Long Beach and take a nostalgic tour of the different buildings where Shekinah Fellowship had once met. Then we were going to have lunch and part ways.

On the way to Long Beach, Elaine was her upbeat, talkative self but I noticed a slight change had come over her. She pulled out a cigarette and started to light it. I was surprised. I had never seen her smoke before. Elaine asked if it was okay. I said it was, and she rolled down the window a little. She made a comment about trying to quit but blamed the stress of her life – her work, plus television and theater projects.

"I know it's bad," she offered, "what with my being a respiratory ther-apist and all. It comes with the territory sometimes."

I had a flash of the class Elaine and I had taken with Lucille Ball many years earlier. Lucy made a comment then about her own smoking, blandly remarking that it was going to kill her someday – then she took a puff.

There was something else weighing in the air as we made our way around Long Beach. I felt she was leading up to something important that she had to say. We drove without talking for several blocks, then she blurted it out: "I'm a lesbian."

There was a tense moment as she waited for me to respond. She glanced over to me, silent as I digested her confession.

"I kind of suspected it," I told her. She cocked her head, trying to keep one eye on the road while detecting my response. "I don't think any less of you."

Elaine put out her cigarette, apparently glad that was over, and we were okay. But the topic wasn't closed for me.

"I still struggle with homosexual feelings at times," I confided. She gave a slight nod but that was all. The other shoe had dropped, I felt, and no more needed to be said. But we were far from done with the topic.

As we drove, I told her about my family and made a verbal sketch of my home life. She talked about some of the important people in her life. She said she was a feminist, and she brought up some of the issues women were facing at the time.

Then Elaine told me about her transition in life – about her move to Hollywood and coming out as a lesbian. Telling her family wasn't easy, she said, and I could only imagine what that conversation must have been like. I never trusted my parents enough to divulge my homosexual feelings. In a way, I felt in awe of her courage.

At the same time, I never fully understood how she could reconcile her attraction to the same sex and her devotion to the Lord. I couldn't bring myself to pry. I figured she would share with me as much as was comfortable for her.

The relationship she was in was a bit complicated. The straight community was not always understanding, and the gay community was often subject to unfiltered gossip. In fact, Elaine told me she heard rumors from one of her lesbian friends, Nancy W, about Brant himself. When Elaine told Nancy W she'd been involved in Brant's ministry, her friend responded that she knew who Brant was and what he was doing. Nancy W was in a leadership position at the Metropolitan Community Church (MCC) and she referred to him by name, described him and his activities in the ministry. Elaine even researched it. Yes – it was Brant, all right.

It seems Brant had come out and was fully embracing the gay lifestyle. Brant was regularly going to gay bars, he attended the MCC, and he was even a noted speaker there. It seems the epiphany he'd had that night at his mother's condo in Palm Springs had finally taken hold.

Elaine went on to tell me that once she took care of Brant's father, Bob, as a patient while she was at work. He didn't recognize her because her nose and mouth were covered, and she was wearing scrubs. At first, she wondered if he was the same person she knew from Shekinah. She went over to his bed and looked at his chart. Sure enough, his name was Bob Baker. and his spouse was Jo Ellen Baker. Seeing him scared her. She was afraid he might recognize her and startle him, given the dramatic way she had departed from the ministry.

Elaine told me that Bob Baker had an advanced case of emphysema, and he looked really bad. She tried to keep herself from shaking as she administered his treatment. It seems her fear came to nothing. When she returned the next day, Bob was not there. She didn't know if he was discharged or if he died. Apparently, it was only a matter of time, his illness was so severe.

Elaine and I made our nostalgic tour of the different buildings where the ministry had met in Long Beach, sharing a few memories about each location. The last place we went was the site of the old Fox West Coast Theater. After it was condemned, the building was razed and all traces of it were removed. In its place, now was a four-star hotel over ten stories high.

Elaine and I strolled around the impressive lobby. Flashes went through my mind of various services and events we held there, and all the emotions of them came flooding back – the joys and the sorrows. I vividly remembered when Kristy came down the stairs to look for me. She was wearing her white choir dress and a flower in her hair. It was an angelic moment, and she touched my heart.

Then it hit me. I looked up at the high lobby ceiling five floors above, and I realized that's where the theater offices once were. I remembered that board meeting over ten years ago when a group of us were going to talk to the board about the direction of the ministry.

Jo Ellen, Kevin, Eric, Claudia and rest were all present, along with other key members of the ministry. They each had a chance to share their comments, but I was stopped cold. I remembered the flash and the vision I'd had – the one where Jo Ellen was sitting there, and the room began to shake. In my vision, the chandelier came crashing down onto the long conference table, and the walls fell down around all of the Board members. It was the end of the ministry.

Standing there in the lobby I realized that it really did happen. My vision was real, and the ministry came crashing down. Even the building was no longer here. Now Brant, Kevin and their father were dead. I looked back at Elaine and discovered she was watching me. She must have read my mind, by the look on her face. I believe she too felt validated.

Outside the hotel there was a small courtyard with a water fountain and a statue of Venus mounted above it. The statue had once adorned the top of the Fox Theater. There was a plaque next to the statue, commemorating the historic theater that once graced the spot. I stood on the fountain next to Venus, and Elaine took a picture of me as though I conquered something.

Elaine and I had lunch and reminisced some more, but we spoke as much about the present and future. Though our visit wound close, our friendship has sustained, and we have stayed in touch through the years.

EPILOGUE

The Ministry In Context

Since leaving the ministry in Long Beach in the late 1970's, other large evangelical ministries have taken over the scene. Other personalities have taken the spotlight in healing ministries such as Benny Hinn, who emulated the Kathryn Kuhlman format later promoted by the large Christian television networks.

Mega churches have sprung up like so many Walmart stores dominating the marketplace, overshadowing the small neighborhood churches in close-knit communities. We have seen the rise and fall of some grandiose television evangelists through the years. Other movements in the Christian faith such as the Dominion theology demonstrate the Christian plot to take over the political power for world domination. The Emerging Church movement is a mixture of evangelical and liberal theology.

For years I tried to find the same high and rush I experienced during Brant's sermons and services. It was similar to a rock star or entertainer, riding the wave again that created that magic moment.

The Brant B. ministry of Shekinah Fellowship was not on a grand scale like the mega churches of today, but the feeling and the desire were the same. Through time, all the pieces came together to create a truly unique and powerful experience.

The Brant that I knew and loved became a different person as the ministry was evolving. He was trying to balance a double life, caught between the evangelicals of the healing ministry and his self-discovery struggle as a gay man. He was looking for acceptance among his gay Christian supporters.

Those who grew to know him and became involved in his life saw him in a different light than I did, because I shared the same burden of spiritual and sexual conflicts. In the end, Brant had his path to follow, and I had mine.

Had I stayed; I don't know what would have happened to me. But it was time for me to move forward on a different course to learn other life lessons for the sake of my soul.

In a strange way, I felt Brant's spirit was encouraging me to write my experiences about him and the ministry – to help shed some light and illuminate his greater transgressions to learn from these experiences. It's been my task to make sure that the history is given, and a record is made from an insider's perspective of the events. My task is to help others who were involved in that ministry and help those who have experienced something similar.

In the early years after Kristy and I left Shekinah Fellowship, I had a series of dreams about Brant and the ministry. Often the dreams would take place in the Foursquare Church or the Fox Theater in Brant's dressing room or in the great hall. I would have short conversations with Brant, and sometimes pray for people in the healing lines. Other times I found Brant sick in his dressing room. He would tell me to put on his suit and tie and go out to preach his sermon. Even though I felt embarrassed, I thought in some way he was reaching out to me.

In other dreams, Brant told me he was angry with me at first but then he saw things from my point of view. I believe these dreams were flushing out memories from my subconscious mind, bringing about the healing of old hurts and wounds.

Now Brant, Kevin, Joe Ellen & Bob Baker are dead. I believe they are with the Lord. Joe Ellen's and Bob's two sons had both died of the same mysterious incurable disease. The flock had scattered to the winds, and youth was spent, wasted by a thousand cuts.

I felt sad for Brant, I had to forgive him to heal. I did forgive him according to Mathew 6:14 and Mark 11:25-26. I had forgiven them all.

APPENDIX

List of Characters

Ann S	spouse to Jeff
Alan	school friend
Ben	bus driver and ministry friend
Betty	ministry friend
Bill	ministry elder
Bob L	ministry friend played in orchestra
Bob Baker	Brant's father
Bob W	ministry elder
Brad	school friend
Bruce	stepfather
Brant Baker	head minister of ministry
Bill Laskey	friend to ministry and Brant
Brigid	ministry friend and choir director
Carol	spouse to Jim R
Carol B	ministry friend
Chad	gay flower shop employer
Charlene C	spouse to John C elder

Cindy	high school friend
Claudia W & N	Brant's assistant
Chuck Smith	Pastor of Calvary Chapel Costa Mesa, Ca
Danny	Kyle's brother
Danny R	deacon and ministry friend
David K	ministry friend, musician leader
David W	ministry friend and played in orchestra
Debbie	spouse to Danny
Dennis	organ player
Dino Kartsonakis	piano player to Kathryn Kuhlman ministry
Diane	ministry friend and secretary
Eddie Laughton	great uncle and actor
Earl	uncle
Eric N	spouse to Claudia and Brant's assistant
Eric Freiwald	uncle and TV writer
Elaine	ministry friend
Frances Hoyt, Mc Gowan	mother
Frances Loughton	great aunt, stage actress
Frank	childhood friend
Georgette A	Spouse to Steve A and friend
Ginger	high school friend
Greg	choir director
Greg L	early ministry elder
Geri	spouse to Dennis
George Seaton	great uncle & Hollywood celebrity
Hal K Dawson	great uncle and Hollywood actor
Jan Crouch	spouse to Paul Crouch TBN
Jack	deacon, ministry friend
Jim Bakker	worked with TBN & founder of PTL with spouse Tammy
Jim M	pastor or Shekinah Christian Center
Jim R	ministry friend, deacon
Judson Hoyt	protagonist

John Hoyt	father
Jenny	aunt, spouse to uncle Earl
Joel	ministry friend and roommate
John	babyface John, roommate, deacon
John C	ministry elder
Joe	ministry elder, piano player
Jeff	ministry friend and elder
Joellen Baker	Brant's mother
Judy	spouse to Mike
Kathy B	ministry friend, secretary,
Kathryn Kuhlman	minister evangelist
Ken G	minister of Vineyard
Kevin Baker	Brant's younger brother
Kyle	ministry member Brant's friend
Kelly G	ministry elder
Kathryn Kuhlman	evangelist
Kristy	choir member, ministry friend, spouse to Jud
Lilly G	ministry friend wife to Kelly G
Lisa G	ministry friend, choir member & Kelly G sister
Linda	spouse to Joe
Linda H	ministry secretary
Lonnie Frisbee	hippie evangelist
Loraine	Foursquare Church friend
Lydia	ministry friend and singer
Madge	ministry and singing partner
Marla	spouse to Randy
Madam Sheikh	friend to ministry
Melissa	lifetime friend
Meg	high school and ministry friend
Meredith	older sister
Mike	pastor of Shekinah Christian Center
Mrs. Adams	spouse to pastor Adams
Michael	cousin

Pam	ministry friend
Paul Crouch	TBN founder
Pastor Adams	foursquare pastor
Pastor Sanders	North Hollywood Assembly of God pastor
Peggy	high school friend
Phyllis Seaton	great aunt, Hollywood celebrity, mayor of Beverly Hills
Ralph	ministry friend, roommate
Randy S	deacon and drummer
Randy	ministry elder, musician
Rich Buhler	pastor and radio host
Robbie	ministry elder
Rocky	ministry friend, deacon, in singing group
Romaine	pastor of Calvary Chapel Costa Mesa
Ruth	Chad's business partner
Scott	high school friend and deacon
Stacey	spouse to Bill
Steve	ministry elder
Sue E	high school friend
Sue O	school friend
Sister Edith	minister and ministry partner with Kathryn Kuhlman
Steve A	ministry friend and singing group
Terry B	Foursquare elder and choir director
Terry H	ministry friend, deacon and orchestra player
Teddi	ministry friend, spouse to Steve
Terri	spouse to Jack and friend
Tim	cousin
Trudi	Claudia W & N mother

Resources

Joe Dallas: books, seminars, counseling services:

Joedallas.com

Joel Comiskey: books, coaching, conferences:

joelcomiskeygroup.com

New Life: workshops, life recovery, counselors, groups, articles/Tips:

newlife.com

Anne Paulk: books, conferences, network of
interdenominational Christian ministries:

restoredhopenetwork.org

George Carneal: Book (From queer To Christ) and LGBT resources:

georgecarneal.com

LA County Lesbian, Bisexual & Queer Women's Health Collaborative:
https://www.uclahealth.org/womenshealth/lbqwhc

About the Author

Judson grew up in Orange County, California. After high school, he moved to Long Beach, California to enter the ministry. Later, he moved to Ashland, Oregon with his wife and one daughter at the time. In Ashland, he attended Southern Oregon University and earned a BS in Business Administration/Accounting. After moving to Washington and two more daughters later, he further earned a Masters in Elementary Education at the University of Phoenix. His further roles in life are and have been: Author, Actor, Bodybuilder, Christian, Director, Entrepreneur, Father, Grandpa, Husband, Minister, Patriot, Teacher, 24 years US Army & Air Force Veteran.

For inquiries about the author, this book and other memoir books in this series, please visit: judsonhoyt.com or email jud@judsonhoyt.com

The author reserves the right to prosecute, to the fullest extent of the law, those who send harassing, defamatory or menacing messages.